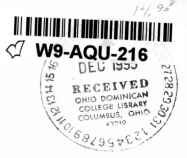

Yeats and the Beginning
of the Irish Renaissance

Irish Studies

W. B. Yeats in 1896, from a portrait by J. B. Yeats.
Used by permission of Michael B. Yeats, Anne Yeats,
and A. P. Watt Ltd.

Yeats and the Beginning of the Irish Renaissance

✿ PHILLIP L. MARCUS

SECOND EDITION

Syracuse University Press   1987

The appropriate parties have kindly renewed the permissions to quote published
and unpublished materials granted for the original edition. Additional permission for quotations from George Russell has been granted by A. M. Heath and
Company, Limited, Blackie and Son Limited, and Mr. Colin Smythe.

The paper used in this publication meets the minimum requirements of American
National Standard for Information Sciences—Permanence of Paper for Printed
Library Materials, ANSI Z39.48-1984. ∞™

Library of Congress Cataloging-in-Publication Data

Marcus, Phillip L., 1941–
   Yeats and the beginning of the Irish renaissance.

   (Irish studies)
   "Yeat's best book lists": p.
   Includes bibliographies and index.
     1. Yeats, W. B. (William Butler), 1865–1939—
Criticism and interpretation. 2. English literature—
Irish authors—History and criticism. 3. English
literature—19th century—History and criticism.
4. Ireland—Intellectual life. 5. Ireland in literature.
6. Mythology, Celtic, in literature. I. Title.
II. Series: Irish studies (Syracuse University. Press)
PR5907.M27 1987   821'.8   86-22969
ISBN 0-8156-2398-4 (pbk. : alk. paper)

To John V. Kelleher

Contents

Portraits

Abbreviations

In references to books by W. B. Yeats, the following abbreviations have been used:

Au   *The Autobiography of William Butler Yeats*. New York: The Macmillan Company, 1953.

BV   *A Book of Irish Verse*. London: Methuen and Co., 1895.

EI   *Essays and Introductions*. New York: The Macmillan Company, 1961.

Explor   *Explorations*. New York: The Macmillan Company, 1962.

Letters   *The Letters of W. B. Yeats*, edited by Allan Wade. New York: The Macmillan Company, 1955.

LNI   *Letters to the New Island*, edited by Horace Reynolds. Cambridge, Mass.: Harvard University Press, 1934.

VP   *The Variorum Edition of the Poems of W. B. Yeats*, edited by Peter Allt and Russell K. Alspach. New York: The Macmillan Company, 1957.

VPlays   *The Variorum Edition of the Plays of W. B. Yeats*, edited by Russell K. Alspach and Catharine C. Alspach. New York: The Macmillan Company, 1966.

Preface to the New Edition

Twenty years ago, when I began the research for this book, serious study of modern Irish literature in English was still in its infancy. Yeats, of course, had already been the subject of many studies, but much of his published work remained unedited or uncollected, while a great deal of the abundant manuscript material was still in the possession of the Yeats family and uncatalogued. With the less well-known figures, the situation was far worse: there was virtually no tradition of scholarship dealing with them, often not even a checklist of their publications. Facts, even mere dates, were often hard to come by. The best general study of the early years of the movement was still E. A. Boyd's *Ireland's Literary Renaissance*, first published half a century before.

Blowing the dust from forgotten volumes in Widener Library, I felt myself at the time something of a pioneer, but in reality I was only part of the burgeoning of interest in Irish culture that has developed over the past two decades. In retrospect, the Yeats Centenary in 1965 and the fiftieth anniversary of the Easter Rising perhaps constitute a watershed. Since then, Yeats has benefited from a rigorous scholarly attention to his texts, including collections of his fugitive journalism, the variorum edition of *The Secret Rose*, and most recently the first volume of the *Collected Letters*. Much manuscript material has been edited and published, including such significant early texts as *The Speckled Bird* and the draft versions of *The Shadowy Waters*; and the manuscript material formerly in the private collection of Senator Michael B. Yeats is now readily accessible. With other writers, the situation in regard to primary materials has also improved, though less dramatically. Critical studies of Yeats have become ever more specialized and sophisticated; and, thanks in part to the Bucknell and Twayne series and the establishment of several valuable journals, critical work on many of the other early figures is available. A survey of scholarly and critical studies up through the 1970s can be found in the MLA's *Anglo-Irish Literature: A Review of Research* and its five-year supplement (both edited by Richard Finneran). Nothing published since the appearance of my own book has invalidated its central arguments, and their exposition in the individual chapters remains useful and basically accurate. The volume still deserves its place, I think, as the standard account of Yeats's seminal role in the development of modern Irish literature.

Still, I have learned much from the more recent work of others and from my own further researches. There was a second printing of *Yeats and the Beginning of the Irish Renaissance* in 1979, and at that time I was able to make some corrections and other slight changes. (The corrected text has been used in this edition.) There are of course more changes that could be made. On page 75, for instance, the second of the "two folklore Anthologies" seems to me now clearly to have been *Irish Fairy Tales*, published in Fisher Unwin's Children's Library in 1892. Portions of the "lost" Gaelic Athletic Association organ *The Gael* have been recovered, and its contents masterfully reconstructed and analyzed, by John Kelly (see *YBIR*, pp. 134–35). Willilam H. O'Donnell has shown that Yeats was at work on *The Speckled Bird* as late as 1902–1903 (*YBIR*, p. 58). Some unpublished notes (now in the Berg

Collection) about folklorist Alfred Nutt show that although Yeats never developed a real interest in William Larminie, he did at least lament his early death as a "great loss" to the modern Irish intellectual movement (*YBIR*, pp. 216–17). And the publication of some of Maud Gonne's correspondence confirms that it was she who translated de Jubainville for Yeats (*YBIR*, pp. 249–50). Much new detail could be added. It is fascinating to find John Todhunter joining the Golden Dawn, probably under Yeats's influence; and Lionel Johnson's delightful explanation of his claims to Irish nationality—"My people lived in Ireland for about two centuries, and became as usual Hibernis Hiberniores: I have endless swarms of Irish relatives; and I am connected with Yeats, which ought to be enough of itself to make me Irish"—demands quotation. Manuscript evidence reveals that Yeats once thought of including "Michael Clancy, the Great Dhoul, and Death" in *The Secret Rose* (*YBIR*, pp. 57–58); and that Lady Gregory, probably working closely with Yeats, even attempted a "Kiltartan" version of "The Binding of the Hair" (*YBIR*, pp. 205–206).[1]

If I were writing the book now I would have foundations available for much fuller discussion of folklore; of *The Speckled Bird* (which anticipated Joyce's *Portrait* so closely, in so many ways, that its publication before 1904 would have made it very difficult for Joyce to write *his* novel); and especially of John Butler Yeats, whose central importance has been demonstrated in the splendid studies of William M. Murphy and Douglas N. Archibald. While much has been done, much more work is needed in most areas: the second volume of the *Collected Letters*, editions of the manuscripts of the bulk of the early poems and of *The Countess Cathleen*, and further scholarly attention to all the minor figures. The results would offer still more potential for enrichment of my volume.

Because Chapter 5, "Old Irish Myth and Modern Irish Literature," deals with *ongoing* interest in the early legends, it is intrinsically open-ended and subject to modification by later developments. In the early years of the movement Yeats was fond of stressing the attractiveness of the legends as a virtually untapped resource; by the time of the publication of *Finnegans Wake* in 1939 they had been given such widespread attention that one might have thought their potential exhausted, yet Irish writers have continued to turn to them. At the time the first edition of this study appeared, Thomas Kinsella has just brought out his deservedly admired "good story" version of *The Táin*. As recently as 1983, Seamus Heaney published *Sweeney Astray*, based on the Irish *Buile Suibhne*. Like Kinsella and so many others, Heaney altered the form of the source: "I occasionally abbreviated the linking narrative and in places have used free verse to render the more heightened prose passages. O'Keeffe has been my guide to the interpretation of the line-by-line meaning, though I have now and again invested the poems with a more subjective tone than they possess in Irish." He also spelled into it some peculiarly personal associations and modern implications:

Insofar as Sweeney is also a figure of the artist, displaced, guilty, assuaging himself by his utterance, it is possible to read the work as an aspect of the quarrel between free creative imagination and the constraints of religious, political, and domestic obligation. It is equally possible, in a more opportunistic spirit, to dwell upon Sweeney's easy sense of cultural affinity with both western Scotland and southern Ireland as exemplary for all men and women in contemporary Ulster.[2]

Even more recently, the most famous of all the early Irish epic heroes nearly made it onto the pop record charts. In 1985 the Irish punk-folk group the Pogues did a song called "The Sick Bed of Cuchulain," in which the wasting sickness of the title figure became a metaphor for the delirium tremens of a twentieth-century Irish boozehound. In place of Fergus, Conall, Lugaid Réoderg, and Eithne Inguba,

[xiv]

McCormack and Richard Tauber are singing by the bed,
There's a glass of punch below your feet and an angel at your head
There's devils on each side of you with bottles in their hands
You need one more drop of poison and you'll dream of foreign lands.

With the current popularity of fantasy literature and movies, it will surely not be long till Hollywood gets into the act.

The tension I have traced between the urge towards fidelity to the received text and the impulse to transform has a history almost as long as the stories themselves. Two scribal notes at the end of the Book of Leinster version of the *Táin* epitomize the problem:

[in Irish] A blessing on every one who shall faithfully memorise the Táin as it is written here and shall not add any other form to it.

[in Latin] But I who have written [i.e., copied] this story, or rather this fable, give no credence to the various incidents related in it. For some things in it are the deceptions of demons, others poetic figments; some are probable, others improbable; while still others are intended for the delectation of foolish men.[3]

Yeats well knew that there was ample precedent in the early evolution of the tales for his own practice of transforming the inherited versions and using them as vehicles for personal expression: they had been "made by no one man, but by the nation itself through a slow process of modification and adaption, to express its loves and its hates, its likes and its dislikes."[4] Yet, as a complementary emphasis to the stress in the original edition upon Yeats's use of traditional materials as correlatives for his own vision and feelings, I would now call attention more forcefully to the opposite phenomenon, that "emotions which seem vague or extravagant when expressed under the influence of modern literature, cease to be vague and extravagant when associated with ancient legend and mythology."[5] Embodiments of the universal and archetypal, they offered not only a way of transcending parochialism but also a source of positive values absent in modern life, a way of reapproaching the unfallen world.

These observations bring me to what I consider the most important new material, material so important that I am incorporating an examination of it here. In 1979 I published an essay entitled "Artificers of the Great Moment" that traced in Yeats's work during the early years of the theater movement an aesthetic based on a paradoxical inversion of the commonplace that art imitates life.[6] Since then I have seen with increasing clarity that this aesthetic in rudimentary form shaped Yeats's thought almost from the beginning of his career, and developed throughout the early Renaissance period. Because that process of development touched upon not only the use of Irish legends but also every other major topic examined in the first edition of this book, tracing the process at some length will enable me to weave this new material into the fabric of the whole.

In 1885 and 1886, when Yeats, under the spell of John O'Leary, was reading widely in Irish literature and history, he encountered two significant models for the role of Irish writer. One was provided by the *filid*, the bardic tradition, stretching from the mists of prehistory down to the eighteenth century. The early Irish bard was a figure of *power*. Possessing visionary and magical gifts, esoteric knowledge on one hand, an almost incredible metrical sophistication and a mastery both of technique and of a long literary tradition on the other, he held a high and prominent place in Irish society, his verse serving important public functions, his satire thought capable even of physical harm to its unfortunate targets. As Yeats summarized in a review, "The bards were the most powerful influence in the land, and all manner of superstitious reverence environed them round. No gift they demanded might be refused them. One king being asked for his eye by a bard in quest of an excuse for rousing the people against him plucked it out and gave it. . . . A poem and an incantation were almost the same. A satire could fill a whole country-side with famine."[7] Although presumably not himself aspiring to the more perverse and destructive powers possessed by these figures, Yeats was nevertheless impressed.

The other model he encountered was provided by the writers of Young Ireland. The Young Ireland movement represented a new beginning rather than a continuation of the earlier tradition, which survived only vestigially, in old manuscripts and in the memories of Irish-speaking peasants. The language of the Young Irelanders was English. They lacked the esoteric associations and technical virtuosity of their predecessors, but they had a similarly central and powerful role in Irish society: by means of song they had, as O'Leary echoed one of them, "brought a soul into Eire."[8] Yeats, in sorting out the implications for his own identity as a *national* poet, was obviously attracted by certain aspects of both models. Art *mattered*, could preserve a culture, even generate rebellions. This was not inconsistent, at least by the bardic model, with the pursuit of occult wisdom and with the quest for consummate artistry to which Yeats's early cosmopolitanism had already exposed him in other literatures. But the bards had devoted much verse to celebrations of minor military victories and fulsome panegyrics of patrons, and Young Ireland was virtually synonymous with swiftly written ballads in which propaganda for the national cause and immediate influence of public opinion were primary. Yeats, though a Nationalist himself, was by no means sure that he wanted to devote the greater part of his literary energies to overtly political work or that his own literary strengths lay in that area. (Even his recently discovered "The Protestants' Leap," an 1887 ballad that consciously emulated the Young Ireland mode and was published in *The Gael*, proved politically so confusing and ambiguous that John O'Leary's sister thought it written from the *anti*-national side [Kelly, pp. 115–33].) Early Irish legendary literature and the folk tradition attracted him strongly.

Was there a way in which he could combine the powerful social role and influence of both models, the mastery of the craft and esoteric wisdom of the bards, the language and modern Nationalist goals of the Young Irelanders, and subject matter that was national but not necessarily of any *obvious* and *immediate* political relevance? He found his answer in part in the work of Ferguson and O'Grady, two political Unionists who yet shared his interest in the Celtic past.

Ferguson died in 1886. In the following passages from one of Yeats's two celebratory articles about him, the young poet's own concerns emerge very clearly:

Sir Samuel Ferguson's special claim to our attention is that he went back to the Irish cycle [of legends], finding it, in truth, a fountain that, in the passage of the centuries, was overgrown with weeds and grass, so that the very way to it was forgotten of the poets; but now that his feet have worn the pathway, many others will follow, and bring thence living waters for the healing of our nation, helping us to live the larger life of the Spirit, and lifting our souls away from their selfish joys and sorrows to be the companions of those who lived greatly among the woods and hills when the world was young. . . . Well then, perhaps, some one will say, if [Deirdre's lament] has come from so far off, what good can it do us moderns, with our complex life? Assuredly it will not help you to make a fortune, or even live respectably that little life of yours. Great poetry does not teach us anything—it changes us. Man is like a musical instrument of many strings, of which only a few are sounded by the narrow interests of his daily life; and the others, for want of use, are continually becoming tuneless and forgotten. Heroic poetry is a phantom finger swept over all the strings, arousing from man's whole nature a song of answering harmony. It is the poetry of action, for such alone can arouse the whole nature of man. It touches all the strings—those of wonder and pity, of fear and joy. It ignores morals, for its business is not in any way to make us rules for life, but to make character. It is not, as a great English writer has said, 'a criticism of life,' but rather a fire in the spirit, burning away what is mean and deepening what is shallow.[9]

Ferguson's poems on Irish legends, far from being escapist or merely antiquarian, could have a profound influence on modern Ireland, not only developing in individuals what Yeats would later term "Unity of Being" but also bringing from the past "living waters for the healing of our nation." This last phrase *sounds* at least vaguely political, and Yeats may even have courted the ambiguity, but the primary thrust of his thought here went in quite a different direction. The passage explicitly rejects practical and meanly utilitarian concerns, and even Arnoldian moral ones, in favor of "the spirit." A passage Yeats wrote near the end of the century, in an 1898 defense of the use of legendary materials in modern literature, returns to the same subject and helps gloss the earlier passage:

I believe that all men will more and more reject the opinion that poetry is 'a criticism of life,' and be more and more convinced that it is a revelation of a hidden life, and that they may even come to think 'painting, poetry, and music' 'the only means of conversing with eternity left to man on earth.'[10]

Using the old legends, the artist brings an ideal image of life to bear upon his own time and changes his world by making it more like the ideal one.

In his essay on Yeats and *The Gael*, John Kelly has observed a process repeated throughout Yeats's career: "working by the light of an apparently straightforward idea, or cluster of ideas, he is time and again brought up against unforeseen complications that arise from an attempt to impose ready-made formulas on the refractory intricacies of experience and the restless energies of his own creativity. In the end, creativity and felt experience win—the theory is revised to accommodate their inconvenient demands—and the story of their victories is the story of Yeats's artistic ripening" (p. 135). True enough, and *Yeats and the Beginning of the Irish Renaissance* would certainly provide supporting examples. Yet I think the other side of the coin is worth emphasizing also. I have been impressed with how early and how often during this formative period Yeats discovered large general principles that (with whatever metamorphoses) guided him till 1939. This first published of his essays contains just such a discovery.

What Yeats was doing in the 1886 piece was reading Ferguson in the light of Shelley's *A Defense of Poetry* (with its memorable conclusion, "Poets are the unacknowledged legislators of the world") and perhaps of Arthur O'Shaughnessy's "Ode" (1874):

> With wonderful deathless ditties
> We build up the world's great cities,
>   And out of a fabulous story
>   We fashion an Empire's glory:
> One man with a dream at pleasure,
>   Shall go forth and conquer a crown;
> And three with a new song's measure
>   Can trample a kingdom down.
>
> We, in the ages lying
>   In the buried past of the earth
> Built Nineveh with our sighing,
>   And Babel itself in our mirth;
> And o'erthrew them with prophesying
>   To the old of the new world's worth;
> For each age is a dream that is dying,
>   Or one that is coming to birth.
>
> A breath of our inspiration
> Is the life of each generation. . . .[11]

A welcomely national expression of similar ideas was available to Yeats in O'Grady (himself the author of a little book on Shelley), who had traced the glories of Greece to its bards, to whom "we must remotely attribute all the enormous influence which Greece has exercised on the world. But for them, the Greece that we know would not have been. . . . It was

[xx]

they . . . who supplied the types, and the fire, ideality, and creative impulses. The great age of Hellas was not an accident, but an emergence into light, and a bursting as it were into flower of that which was generated and nursed in earlier obscurer centuries. Those rude elder forgotten bards were the root of all that floral magnificence of the Periclean and subsequent ages." Similarly he had stressed the importance of the "bardic history" of Ireland, arguing that "legends represent the imagination of the country; they are that kind of history which a nation desires to possess."[12] John Kelly is surely correct in seeing echoes of O'Grady in Yeats's 1887 essay on the bardic hero Fionn Mac Cumhaill:

Under all these old legends there is, without doubt, much fact, though, I confess, I care but little whether there be or not. A nation's history is not in what it does, this invader or that other; the elements or destiny decides all that; but what a nation imagines that is its history, there is its heart; than its legends, a nation owns nothing more precious. Without her possible mythical siege of Troy, perhaps, Greece would never have had her real Thermopylæ.[13]

In Yeats's 1890 discussion of the power of the bards he suggested that that power "was responsible, it may be, for one curious thing in ancient Celtic history: its self-consciousness. The warriors were not simply warriors, the kings simply kings, the smiths simply smiths: they all seem striving to bring something out of the world of thoughts into the world of deeds—a something that always eluded them." The Fiana, living in a materialistic age, "wanted to revive the kind of life lived in old days" (pp. 182–83). Again, the bards lead men to emulate a lost "better" world.

Yeats would find reinforcement and clarification of the aesthetic underlying these thoughts in the most brilliant of all its formulations, a work by an Irish contemporary very different from O'Grady: Oscar Wilde's *The Decay of Lying*. Arguing the paradox that "Life imitates Art," Wilde described the mechanism of influence with an image that stayed in Yeats's mind for decades:

The Greeks . . . set in the bride's chamber the statue of Hermes or of Apollo, that she might bear children as lovely as the works of art that she looked at in her rapture or her pain. They knew that Life gains from Art not merely spirituality, depth of thought and feeling, soul-turmoil or soul-peace, but that she can form herself on the very lines and colours of art, and can reproduce the dignity of Pheidias as well as the grace of Praxiteles.

The idea that the artist could bring his world "spirituality, depth of thought and feeling" was a virtual echo of Yeats's phrase from the Ferguson article—"a fire in the spirit, burning away what is mean and deepening what is shallow." Elsewhere in Wilde's essay, "spirituality" is given as philosophical context a Platonism that for Wilde was in all probability metaphorical but which Yeats's immersion in occultism ensured that he would treat more literally. Art, according to Wilde, "is a veil, rather than a mirror. . . . She makes and unmakes man worlds. . . . Hers are the 'forms more real than living man,' and hers the great archetypes of which things that have existence are but unfinished copies."[14] It was precisely because art embodies the archetypal that it could be a "revelation of a hidden life" and enable us still to converse with eternity. Finally, the artist affecting the child through the mother (an image Wilde may have found in Pater's essay on Winckelmann[15]) suggested a slow, *indirect* form of influence, but also a deep and organic one—appropriate for describing the distinction Yeats would come to make between the influence of immediately intelligible but superficial and inferior "popular" literature such as that of the Young Irelanders and the difficult, esoteric work he himself so often produced.

Blake also seemed to provide support, as witnessed by Yeats's later use of him in the 1898 controversy with John Eglinton over the legendary materials. It was Blake who had

[xxii]

referred to "Poetry, Painting, and Music,—the three powers in man of conversing with Paradise which the flood did not sweep away." The art capable of doing this was not in the ordinary sense an imitation of life. "Why are copies of nature incorrect," Blake had asked rhetorically, "while copies of imagination are correct?" Imagination was the faculty by which the "hidden life" sought by Yeats was revealed: "The world of imagination is the world of eternity. . . . There exist in that eternal world the eternal realities of everything which we see reflected in this vegetable glass [i.e., mirror] of nature." The natural world was the fallen world, the world of Plato's imperfect copies, but the visionary artist could help regain Paradise through his art. Blake himself had claimed that "the nature of my work is Visionary or Imagination. It is an endeavour to restore what the Ancients called the golden age." Yeats attempted to connect such thoughts more closely to his own national interests when he identified Blake as an Irishman in the edition of his work that he began preparing shortly after he first encountered Wilde's essay.[16]

This aesthetic for national art, this model for the poet's role, Yeats fully articulated only after the turn of the century, but in emergent form it underlies his critical and creative work and even his organizational activities during the 1890s. Thus in October 1891 he attempted to revive moribund Young Ireland Societies and to open reading rooms in the small towns in connection with them. The reading-room libraries were to contain "before all else . . . the books that feed the imagination. . . . Imagination, and not learning, is the centre of life, and from the direction it takes spring thought and conduct."[17] This stress on imagination undoubtedly reflects not only Blake, but also O'Grady's perception that the imagined history of a country represents its heart, its deepest desires, and thus is crucially important in shaping its development. Yeats almost at once formulated a plan to ensure the availability of appropriate books by starting a new "Library of

Ireland," inspired by the one so successfully developed by Young Ireland in the 1840s but intended to feature work generally more imaginative and higher in quality than the books in the earlier series. After the bitter struggle in which he lost control of the series to Gavan Duffy, Yeats in 1894 vigorously attacked the first volumes: "Believing, as I do, that literature is almost the most profound influence that ever comes into a nation, I recognise with deep regret, and not a little anger, that the 'New Irish Library' is so far the most serious difficulty in the way of our movement, and that it drives from us those very educated classes we desire to enlist, and supplies our opponents with what looks like evidence of our lack of any fine education, of any admirable precision and balance of mind, of the very qualities which make literature possible."[18]

The Dowden controversy of the following year, in which that learned cosmopolitan leveled just such criticisms at the current national literary movement, led Yeats to offer his own *precise* and *balanced* survey of "Irish National Literature" in a series of four articles in the *Bookman*. In the first of them he criticized the Young Irelanders as primarily "orators" rather than "poets or romance-writers, priests of those Immortal Moods which are the true builders of nations, the secret transformers of the world, and need a subtle, appropriate language or a minute, manifold knowledge for their revelation." The passage incorporates another echo of Blake ("minutely appropriate words"); and the Ellis-Yeats edition had included also an exploration of the concept of the Moods, which correspond to the "archetypes" in Wilde's essay.[19] "Secret transformers of the world" obviously paraphrases Shelley's *Defense*. In order to forge the necessary vehicles, the modern Irish writers would need not the slipshod "rhetoric" of the writers of *The Nation* but rather a sophisticated artistry comparable to that of the bardic tradition.[20] In the third essay, AE was especially praised for having "a subtle rhythm, precision of phrase, an emotional relation to form and colour, and a perfect understanding that the business of poetry is not to enforce an opinion or expound an action, but to bring us into communion with the moods and passions which are the creative powers behind the universe; that though the poet may need to master many opinions, they are but the body and symbols for his art, the formula of evocation for making the invisible visible." In quoting one of AE's own allusions to Blake—"every word which really inspires is spoken as if the golden age had never passed away"—and adding the observation that "surely criticism, even criticism of life, is of the fall and the fatal tree," Yeats was repeating the rejection of Arnold and the assertion of the power of heroic literature to help us recapture the prelapsarian past in the early article on Ferguson. Consequently, at the end of this 1895 piece he noted with approval that "even A.E. has begun to dig for new symbols in the stories of Fin and Oisin."21

By 1897 Yeats claimed about the "spiritual group," in which he included AE, Nora Hopper, and Lionel Johnson, that although unlike many of their predecessors not almost exclusively Nationalistic, they were nevertheless "speaking with . . . the truest voice of the Celt." Terming them "spiritual" because all believed that "a beauty, not a worldly beauty, lives in worldly things," he went on to predict that "this new school cannot fail to influence Irish thought very strongly, for it is full of the dreams that we dream in our most exalted moments. Few who have not read deeply in the history of literary movements, know how strong is the influence of the highest kind of poetry, for it does not directly influence many minds, but it influences the finest minds and through them many minds. This new school, and the ever increasing knowledge of the old poetry in Gaelic, must in time make many strong and delicate minds spend themselves in the service of Ireland that would else have spent themselves in alien causes, and Ireland may become again a spiritual influence in the world."22

It was in such a context that he said of his own contemporary volume *The Secret Rose* that it was "an honest attempt towards that aristocratic esoteric Irish literature, which has been my chief ambition. We have a literature for the people but nothing yet for the few."[23]

The previous year, AE had proposed to Yeats a collaborative book of essays (to contain a contribution by O'Grady among others) on "the renewal in Ireland of the heroic figures of our own dawn"—a proposal eventually realized in the 1898 controversy about the legendary materials.[24] In one of AE's own contributions he argued that Irish culture was in a period comparable "to Greece before the first perfect statue had fixed an ideal of beauty which mothers dreamed of to mould their yet unborn children" and that modern Ireland thus needed "the creation of heroic figures, types, whether legendary or taken from history, and enlarged to epic proportions by our writers, who would use them in common, as Cuculain, Fionn, Ossian, and Oscar, were used by the generations of poets who have left us the bardic history of Ireland. . . . [F]rom iteration and persistent dwelling on a few heroes their imaginative images found echoes in life, and other heroes arose continuing their tradition of chivalry. That such types are of the highest importance and have the most ennobling influence on a country, cannot be denied."[25] Although AE, too, had read his O'Grady, and presumably also his Wilde, he and Yeats were at this time working very closely together, and this passage almost seems like critical ventriloquism.

In Yeats's propagandist writings on behalf of the new movement he very seldom discussed his own creative work, but in that work he was in fact exploring the same questions. There is, for instance, an obvious nexus between the "Irish National Literature" series and his prose story "The Wisdom of the King," which was first published in September 1895, the same month as the third of the articles. The "wisdom" the king pours at the feet of his beloved includes a reference to "the great Moods, which are alone immortal, and the creators of mortal things; and how every Mood is a being that wears, to mortal eyes, the shape of Fintain, who dwells, disguised as a salmon, in the floods; or of the Dagda, whose cauldron is never empty; or of Lir, whose children wail upon the waters; or of Angus, whose kisses were changed into birds; or of Len, the goldsmith, from whose furnace rainbows break."[26] Here the Irish legendary material and the Moods coalesce. The story as a whole has interesting implications in regard to Yeats's own literary quest. The protagonist is not a poet, but his differentness and his possession of occult knowledge link him to a popular Romantic image of the poet that Yeats did identify with. The king has a "bird" father and a human mother, alerting us that the story anticipates Yeats's famous lyric "Leda and the Swan" in its concern with the relationship of wisdom and power. In the Ferguson piece, Yeats had denied that the business of heroic poetry was to "make us rules for life," comparing its effect to "a fire in the spirit, burning away what is mean and deepening what is shallow." When the king in the story attempts to bring his wisdom into the world, the effects are disastrous: on the practical plane, the people who listen to him function *less* well than before; and some "remembered words and sentences that became like a fire in their hearts, and made all kindly joys and traffic between man and man as nothing, and went different ways, but all into vague regret." The fire that purifies must thereby also disturb. At the end of the story the king has realized that "wisdom the gods have made, and no man shall live by its light." Here the optimism of the programmatic writings finds its antinomy in the possibility that wisdom and power may be ontologically irreconcilable; the dark ending may be the correlative of a Yeatsian fear that his own poetic mission might fail, Irish culture remain unmetamorphosed.

Such fears would have brought with them a concomitant sense that he would need all his resourcefulness if his own creative work was going to succeed in the difficult task of mediating between the two ontological realms. "The Valley of the Black Pig," published 1896, offers a fascinating example of that resourcefulness. While much of his poetry of this period turns totally away from the "patriotic" tradition, this lyric actually grows out of that tradition; but in it Young Ireland verse has undergone a sort of "spiritual" sublimation process. The imagery of armed conflict dear to the earlier movement is there, and Yeats himself related in a note that the country people from whom he heard the legend upon which the poem is based saw in the battle a coming military struggle between Ireland and England. But in the poem the Nationalistic level has been subsumed within larger, archetypal patterns. Reading the "black pig" legend in the light of Frazer and Rhys, Yeats intended to suggest that "the battle is a mythological battle." In the notes he piled up numerous parallels from other cultures and times and concluded that "all these battles are one. . . . Once a symbolism has possessed the imagination of large numbers of men, it becomes . . . an embodiment of disembodied powers, and repeats itself in dreams and visions, age after age." The Moods, again, pervade the legends, and again the key faculty of imagination is crucial to the process. Similarly, the conventional, energetic but mechanical ballad rhythms characteristic of the poets of *The Nation* have yielded to "wavering, meditative, organic rhythms" that would liberate the mind from the pressure of the will and make the reader receptive to communication by symbol and archetype. Yeats was here showing the way towards the realization of the hope he had expressed in one of the "Irish National Literature" articles: "some day, in the maturity of our traditions, to fashion out of the world about us, and the things that our fathers have told us, a new ritual for the builders of peoples, the imperishable moods."[27]

The power of art to shape life was itself the *subject* of at least one of Yeats's lyrics of the nineties, "Aedh thinks of those who have Spoken Evil of his Beloved," published first (under the rubric "Aodh to Dectora / Three Songs") in 1898 and included in *The Wind Among the Reeds* the following year:

> Half close your eyelids, loosen your hair,
> And dream about the great and their pride;
> They have spoken against you everywhere,
> But weigh this song with the great and their pride;
> I made it out of a mouthful of air,
> Their children's children shall say they have lied. (1899 version)

In Yeats's story "The Binding of the Hair" a famous ancient Irish bard named Aodh promises to sing for his beloved, Queen Dectira, after an imminent battle. During the encounter he is killed and beheaded, but his severed head carries out his promise, singing for her another of the lyrics that Yeats would include in *The Wind Among the Reeds*, where it was titled "Aedh gives his Beloved certain Rhymes." Although as Allen R. Grossman has noted, Aodh or Aedh was linked in Yeats's imagination with death, the context in "Aedh thinks of those who have Spoken Evil of his Beloved" seems clearly positive.[28] Yeats speaks here *as* Irish bard, and claims that his powerful song will eventually give the lie to the beloved's detractors. It will do this by that long-term process of influence imaged for Yeats by the Greek children formed after the statues in the bridal chambers of their mothers. Many years later Yeats echoed this lyric in "To a Shade," where Hugh Lane (also a victim of slander) had offered works of art that, had they not been rejected by the people of Dublin, "Had given their children's children loftier thought, / Sweeter emotion. . . ."

It is significant that we find Yeats celebrating this power on the eve of the theater movement. That movement itself was as first conceived clearly an effort to win back some of the more "popular" Irish audience, from which Yeats had felt increasingly alienated since the controversy over the New Irish Library. But he had not forgotten the lessons he had so painfully learned, and they were reinforced for him by the opposition to *The Countess Cathleen* in 1899. Thus in 1900 he was careful to maintain that his own work and that of his contemporaries "must for a long time to come be the chief influence in shaping the opinions and the emotions of the leisured classes in Ireland, in so far as they are concerned with Irish things, and the more sincere it is, the more lofty it is, the more beautiful it is, the more will the general life of Ireland be sweetened by its influence, through its influence over a few governing minds. It will always be too separate from the general life of Ireland to influence it directly."[29] (The words "lofty" and "sweetened" anticipate "To a Shade.") By 1903 Yeats's principles were once again put to the test; the source of the challenge was attacks on the controversial John Synge, whose play *The Shadow of the Glen* was destined to stir up intense hostility among the extreme Nationalists. Synge was in fact attacked for *lacking* idealism, for presenting too sordid a vision of Irish life, but the very integrity and power of the artist seemed to be at stake, and Yeats was moved to defend them in his contemporary play *The King's Threshold*. He chose as his protagonist a medieval Irish bard. Harold Bloom has claimed that "Shelley is the ultimate model for Seanchan, and *A Defense of Poetry* the deepest quarry" for his convictions. George Bornstein has noted the echoes of *The Decay of Lying*, including Seanchan's lines "I said the poets hung / Images of the life that was in Eden / About the childbed of the world, that it, / Looking upon those images, might bear / Triumphant children. . . . "[30] Such a passage looks backwards to 1886, when Yeats had praised Ferguson for restoring access to the fountain of the Irish legends, from which other modern writers could bring "living waters for the healing of our nation, helping us to live the larger life of the Spirit, and lifting our souls away from their selfish joys and sorrows to be the companions of those who lived greatly among the woods and hills when the world was young"; and ahead to 1938, when at the end

[xxx]

of his life he would embody a similar vision in "The Statues" and *The Death of Cuchulain*.

The King's Threshold and the other texts have been little heeded, however. Seamus Deane is perhaps the most recent of those who, since the early days of the theater movement, have attacked Yeats on grounds the reverse of those alleged about Synge, for presenting distorted, *overglamorous* pictures of the Irish peasantry and aristocracy.[31] Such criticism is often correct about his inaccuracy, but misses the point. Yeats cared almost as little about sociological precision in describing these classes as he did about the possible historicity of the Firbolg and the Fomorians: "What a nation imagines that is its history, there is its heart." He knew perfectly well that he was making myths, that his aristocrats and peasants were ideal types only very seldom actually to be found even in Connacht. This was political sophistication, not naiveté: he was trying to shape a *future* reality.

In *Wheels and Butterflies* (1934) he tells of how "in the eighties of the last century Standish O'Grady, his mind full of Homer [whose images of the siege of Troy perhaps inspired Thermopylæ], retold the story of Cuchulain that he might bring back an heroic ideal." Yeats himself carried on the effort, but had to interrupt it when "the mood of Ireland changed" early in the twentieth century. The split in the Irish Party following the death of Parnell had been a stimulus to the figures of the early Renaissance period: "When Parnell was dragged down, his shattered party gave itself up to nine years' vituperation, and Irish imagination fled the sordid scene. . . . Repelled by what had seemed the sole reality, we had turned to romantic dreaming, to the nobility of tradition." Then came the "Cork Realists" and Joyce, who, instead of "turning their backs upon the actual Ireland of their day . . . attacked everything that had made it possible" and virtually eliminated the audience for literature of the other sort. Joyce may even have taken Yeats's own aesthetic as one of the objects of his satire, for in *Ulysses* Dublin citizen Bloom visits the statues of goddesses in the Museum only to ascertain whether they are "anatomically correct" and Mulligan—who in the opening pages quotes Wilde and dresses the part— jestingly predicts during the episode in the maternity hospital that in the future "plastercast reproductions of the classical statues such as Venus and Apollo . . . would enable ladies who were in a particular condition to pass the intervening months in a most enjoyable manner"; but the novel does reincarnate an ancient Greek hero, and in his next book Joyce not only moved totally to the archetypal plane but also chose Fionn as one of the chief avatars of his universal protagonist.[32] By the late 1930s, too, Yeats felt he could discern the return to favor of schools of thought that "in all ancient countries sustained heroic art" and resumed his efforts to bring back "the heroic ideal." The consequences of such efforts, he now knew, could sometimes be tragic: a play might send men out to be shot by the English. But "The Statues" depicts art shaping life in modern Ireland as well as in Classical Greece, the idealized images of Cú Chulainn that inspired Pearse corresponding to the Pheidian statues that had given Athenian "women dreams and dreams their looking-glass." The poem ends, as *The King's Threshold* originally had, with an evocation of "the great race that is to come." The final lyric of *The Death of Cuchulain* is frank about the "unrealistic" nature of the play's legendary hero and the author's nonmimetic intent in evoking him:

> No body like his body
> Has modern woman borne,
> But an old man looking back on life
> Imagines it in scorn.[33]

At the end of his career, as at the beginning, Yeats recognized that putting the demands of art before those of politics need not preclude a politically potent art, and this final image

[xxxii]

of the artist emphasizes the same power that had attracted him over half a century before.

PHILLIP L. MARCUS

Ithaca, New York
June 1986

NOTES

1. The letter in which Yeats referred to the "two folklore Anthologies" has now been published: see *The Collected Letters of W. B. Yeats, Volume One, 1865–1895*, ed. John Kelly, assoc. ed. Eric Domville (Oxford: Clarendon Press, 1986), pp. 425–26; I follow the *Collected Letters* text in capitalizing "Anthologies" here. See also *Yeats and the Beginning of the Irish Renaissance* (hereafter *YBIR*), pp. 148–51. Kelly's essay is "Aesthete among the Athletes: Yeats's Contributions to *The Gael*," *Yeats: An Annual*, ed. Richard J. Finneran, 2 (1984), 75–143; *The Speckled Bird*, ed. William H. O'Donnell (Toronto: McClelland and Stewart, 1976), pp. xxxi, li; Samuel Levenson, *Maud Gonne* (New York: Reader's Digest Press, 1976), p. 392; Ellic Howe, *The Magicians of the Golden Dawn* (London: Routledge & Kegan Paul, 1972), p. 51; Karl Beckson, "Yeats and the Rhymers' Club," *Yeats Studies*, No. 1 (1971), 23n; *The Secret Rose, Stories by W. B. Yeats: A Variorum Edition*, ed. Phillip L. Marcus, Warwick Gould, and Michael J. Sidnell (Ithaca: Cornell University Press, 1981), pp. 256–59.

2. Seamus Heaney, "Introduction," in *Sweeney Astray* (1983; rpt. New York: Farrar Straus Giroux, 1985), n. p.

3. *Táin Bó Cúalnge*, ed. Cecile O'Rahilly (Dublin: Dublin Institute for Advanced Studies, 1967), p. 272.

4. "Nationality and Literature," *United Ireland*, May 27, 1893, p. 2.

5. See *YBIR*, p. 254 (where the second "vague or extravagant" should read "vague and extravagant").

6. "Artificers of the Great Moment: An Essay on Yeats and National Literature," *CLQ* 15 (1979), 71–92.

7. "Bardic Ireland," *Scots Observer*, January 4, 1890, p. 182. It is interesting to note that in the ultimate source for Yeats's play *The King's Threshold* the bards were savagely satirized for their arrogance and excessive demands, but Yeats's version adopts their point of view and eliminates the satire; see "The Proceedings of the Great Bardic Institution," ed. Owen Connellan, in *Transactions of the Ossianic Society* 5 (1860), xv–132. Connellan's intro-

ductory essay "The Bards of Ireland" was probably, along with O'Grady and O'Curry, one of Yeats's earliest sources of information about the bardic tradition. Although in early Irish society a distinction was made between the *fili* and the (lower-ranking) bard, this distinction was not preserved by Yeats, and I have followed his practice in using "bard" as a general term.

8. "What Irishmen Should Know," quoted by Kelly, "Aesthete among the Athletes," p. 80.

9. "The Poetry of Sir Samuel Ferguson," *Irish Fireside*, October 9, 1886, p. 220.

10. *Literary Ideals in Ireland* (London: T. Fisher Unwin, and Dublin: at the *Daily Express* Office, 1899), p. 36; this article was first published in 1898.

11. In May 1887, Yeats praised Katharine Tynan's *Irish Fireside* article on O'Shaughnessy: *Collected Letters* I, 12. See also "Artificers of the Great Moment," pp. 73–74 for a 1900 reference, and *The Speckled Bird*, p. 53, for an allusion in the 1902 "final version."

12. Standish O'Grady, *History of Ireland: Critical and Philosophical*, Vol. I (London: Sampson Low, and Dublin: E. Ponsonby, 1881), p. 58; *History of Ireland: The Heroic Period* (London: Sampson Low, Searle, Marston & Rivington, and Dublin: E. Ponsonby, 1878), p. 22.

13. "Aesthete among the Athletes," pp. 82, 91. See also Kelly's essay "Choosing and Inventing: Yeats and Ireland," in *Across a Roaring Hill*, ed. Gerald Dawe and Edna Longley (Belfast, Ireland and Dover, N.H.: Blackstaff Press, 1985), pp. 6–8.

14. *The Decay of Lying*, in *The Critic as Artist: Critical Writings of Oscar Wilde*, ed. Richard Ellmann (New York: Vintage, 1970), pp. 306, 307–308. See also Yeats, *Autobiographies* (London: Macmillan, 1966), p. 135; and Ellmann, *Eminent Domain* (New York: Oxford, 1967), pp. 9–27. Wilde read the proofs of the periodical version of his essay to Yeats on Christmas Day, 1888. In 1891, Yeats praised *Intentions* (which included Wilde's essay) as "a wonderful book" and said that it "hides within its immense paradox some of the most subtle literary criticism we are likely to see for many a long day" (*Collected Letters* I, 252; "Oscar Wilde's Last Book," *United Ireland*, September 26, 1891). Yeats's 1898 reference to the renewal of belief liberating the arts from their age and from life and leaving them free to lose themselves in beauty and in "old faiths, myths, dreams" (*Literary Ideals*, p. 36; Yeats's quotation marks) may echo Wilde's description of Renaissance drama: "Old myth and legend and dream took shape and substance. History was entirely re-written, and there was hardly one of the dramatists who did not recognize that the object of Art is not simple truth but complex beauty" (*The Decay of Lying*, p. 302).

15. Walter Pater, *The Renaissance*, ed. Donald L. Hill (Berkeley: University of California Press, 1980), p. 166, quoting Winckelmann himself.

16. *The Works of William Blake*, ed. Edwin John Ellis and William Butler Yeats, 3 vols. (London: Bernard Quaritch, 1893), II, 384, 392, 394, 393 (in this quotation, modern eds. read "Imaginative" for "Imagination"); I, 2–4. See also *YBIR*, p. 24.

17. "The Young Ireland League," *United Ireland*, October 3, 1891, p. 5.

18. *Collected Letters*, I, 397–98.

19. *Blake*, II, 383; I, 238–45. Yeats's poem "The Moods" was first published in 1893, and in the same year was linked with traditional Irish material through its use as an epigraph for *The Celtic Twilight*.

20. "Irish National Literature. From Callanan to Carleton," *Bookman*, July 1895, pp. 105–107. It may be significant that Lionel Johnson had emphasized the Irish bardic "passion for perfection" and contrasted it with Young Ireland work in his 1894 lecture "Poetry and Patriotism in Ireland"; see *YBIR*, pp. 169–71.

21. "Irish National Literature. III.—Contemporary Irish Poets," *Bookman*, September 1895, pp. 169–70. The Blake passage is one of those cited earlier, from *Blake*, II, 393; Yeats himself quoted it in "The New Irish Library," *Bookman*, June 1896, p. 83.

22. "Three Irish Poets," *Irish Homestead*, December 1897, pp. 7–8.

23. *The Letters of W. B. Yeats*, ed. Allan Wade (New York: Macmillan, 1955), p. 286.

24. See *YBIR*, pp. 126–28; and *Some Passages from the Letters of Æ to W. B. Yeats* (Dublin: Cuala Press, 1936), pp. 1–6.

25. *Literary Ideals*, pp. 84–86; also *YBIR*, pp. 194–95.

26. This and subsequent references are to *The Secret Rose*, ed. Marcus, Gould, and Sidnell, pp. 25–33.

27. *The Variorum Edition of the Poems of W. B. Yeats*, ed. Peter Allt and Russell K. Alspach (1957; rpt. New York: Macmillan, 1973), pp. 161, 808–11; *Essays and Introductions* (New York: Macmillan, 1961), p. 163; "Irish National Literature. Contemporary Prose Writers," *Bookman*, August 1895, p. 140.

28. *The Secret Rose*, ed. Marcus, Gould, and Sidnell, pp. 177–81; Allen R. Grossman, *Poetic Knowledge in the Early Yeats* (Charlottesville: University Press of Virginia, 1969), pp. 109–14.

29. See "Artificers of the Great Moment," pp. 74–75.

30. See "Artificers of the Great Moment," pp. 75–78.

31. Seamus Deane, *Celtic Revivals* (London: Faber and Faber, 1985), pp. 28–37. Yeats might seem to have criticized Young Ireland work on such grounds (*YBIR*, p. 9), but his real objection was not that the Young Irelanders were not realists but that the ideals *they* envisioned were not the *true* ones, did not reflect the divine world; significantly, they had made comparatively very little use of the early legendary materials.

32. James Joyce, *Ulysses*, the Corrected Text (New York: Vintage, 1986), 8.920–32, 14.1251–56. There are also allusions in "Scylla and Charybdis" to "the Platonic dialogues Wilde wrote" (9.1069). In addition to linking Wilde (along with Yeats and AE, among others) to the "Platonic" pole in the pattern of opposites that informs the structure of the episode, the allusions may indirectly signal a challenge. From that episode on, the growingly self-referential narrative mode of *Ulysses* suggests that the paradox of life imitating art, which still involves a mimetic process, was ultimately no more acceptable to Joyce than the realist aesthetic of holding "the mirror up to nature" (15.3820). The statues in the Museum, apparently put on display in 1885 (the year of Yeats's fateful meeting with O'Leary) were removed in 1927 and replaced with replicas of Celtic crosses; see Cyril Pearl, *Dublin in Bloomtime* (New York: Viking Press, 1969), p. 31, where there is a photograph.

33. For a fuller discussion of the passages from *Wheels and Butterflies* and of the play, see *The Death of Cuchulain: Manuscript Materials*, ed. Phillip L. Marcus (Ithaca: Cornell University Press, 1982), pp. 3–16.

Preface

This book treats the literary activities of W. B. Yeats during the period between 1885, when his first published poetry appeared, and 1899, the year of the formal debut of the Irish Literary Theatre. In giving a fuller, more detailed picture than any now available of Yeats's role in the beginning of the Irish Literary Renaissance, I hope also to cast some new light upon the development of that movement.

As a young writer in a country where literature itself was suspect and continually subject to strong pressure for immediate political utility, Yeats found it particularly important to formulate literary ideals that would justify his own practice of the art. These ideals were exemplified by and to a considerable extent worked out in his creative writings, not only the poetry and plays but also the less well known body of prose fiction. Yeats was not content, however, merely to satisfy his own creative impulses: he wanted to spread his ideals to others and to initiate a literary *movement*. Consequently he propagandized diligently, engaged in impassioned controversy with opponents of his position, and tried to exert a direct influence upon other contemporary Irish writers. In both specific and intangible ways his influence was great, as can be seen in the history of his interaction with his co-workers and of the role he played in the emergence of a body of creative literature in English based upon early Irish myth and legend. The effect was lasting and was felt during the theater movement and the later years of the Renaissance.

Fortunately for the literary historian, Yeats has left abundant documentation of the period being examined: contemporary records, including his creative work, his early letters, and his masses of articles and reviews; and later recollections, in various essays and especially in his autobiographical writings. I have drawn very heavily upon the earlier group, though of course wherever possible I have checked one statement against another and against external evidence. The later materials are used with greater hesitation, for Yeats's mind was given to metamorphosing, and there are many points at which his own retrospective accounts of his beliefs and activities during the eighties and nineties differ considerably from contemporary accounts. Consequently I have referred to the autobiographies and other later writings primarily where they support points for which there is documentary evidence in the early records.

The surviving materials of other writers of these years are predictably fragmentary and scattered, though Alan Denson has recently improved this situation in regard to AE by collecting his letters and tracking down his voluminous periodical publications. I have quoted extensively from primary sources, partly because so many of them are not readily available and partly because my study, being particularly concerned with the rhetoric of literary programs and propaganda, requires close familiarity with the texture as well as the content of those sources.

Among the many volumes of Yeats criticism that deal with his early career, the most helpful to me have been Richard Ellmann's two excellent studies, *Yeats: The Man and the Masks* and *The Identity of Yeats*. The fullest and in many ways still the best general critical account of the period is E. A. Boyd's *Ireland's Literary Renaissance*, first published over fifty years ago, in 1916, when Yeats's development was only half complete and the Renaissance was still in progress. A number of other books dealing with subjects related to mine have appeared since I began this study, and while I have been able to make little specific use of them, I would like to record a general debt especially to William Irwin Thompson's *The Imagination of an Insurrection*, Richard J. Loftus' *Nationalism in Modern Anglo-Irish Poetry*, and *The World of W. B. Yeats*, edited by Robin Skelton and Ann Saddlemyer.

A number of individuals have aided me in various ways. Foremost among these is Professor John V. Kelleher of Harvard University, who in the truest spirit of humane scholarship was always willing to share his great knowledge of Ireland and its literature; whatever value this study may have it owes primarily to him. Mr. John L. Sweeney made many helpful criticisms of the manuscript in an earlier form. Professor Curtis Bradford of Grinnell College kindly made available to me his transcription of Yeats's unfinished novel "The Speckled Bird." Professor Roger Rosenblatt of Harvard provided me with some useful materials and many fruitful discussions. Philip Weinstein of Harvard and my Cornell colleagues Douglas N. Archibald, Frank McConnell, and Winthrop Wetherbee have all contributed to my general understanding of literature. The staff of Cornell University Press improved my work in many ways. I would like also to express my gratitude to the Woodrow Wilson National Fellowship Foundation for a Dissertation Fellowship which made possible my initial work on the subject and to Cornell University for grants from the Clark Fund and the Humanities Faculty Research Grants Fund which helped finance the project in its later stages.

A portion of Chapter 5 has been published in the *Irish University Review* and is reprinted with the permission of the editor, Mr. Maurice Harmon.

Permission to quote unpublished materials was generously granted by Mr. M. B. Yeats, Miss Anne Yeats, Mr. Austin

Clarke, Mr. Diarmuid Russell, Mr. Alan Denson, and the Harvard College Library. Mr. Yeats also personally provided valuable information concerning the various works by John Butler Yeats used as illustrations in this volume.

For permission to quote from copyrighted materials, acknowledgment is gratefully made to the following:

To the Dolmen Press and Mr. Austin Clarke for quotations of Austin Clarke from *Later Poems*.

To John Baker Publishers, Limited, for quotations from *The Complete Poems of Lionel Johnson*.

To Mr. Diarmuid Russell for quotations of George Russell from *The Divine Vision and Other Poems* and *The Internationalist*.

To Mr. Russell, Abelard-Schuman, Ltd., and Mr. Alan Denson for quotations from *Letters from AE,* edited by A. Denson; copyright Diarmuid Russell, 1961; copyright this edition Alan Denson, 1961. Published by Abelard-Schuman, Limited, London, New York, Toronto.

To the Society of Authors and Miss Pamela Hinkson for quotations of Katharine Tynan Hinkson from *Shamrocks, Ballads and Lyrics,* and *The Century Guild Hobby Horse*.

To the Harvard University Press for quotations from William Butler Yeats, *Letters to the New Island,* Horace Reynolds, editor, Harvard University Press, Cambridge, Mass.; copyright 1934 by the President and Fellows of Harvard College, 1962 by Horace Mason Reynolds. Quoted also by permission of the Clarendon Press, Oxford, which is publishing a new edition of the volume in 1970.

To Mr. M. B. Yeats, Miss Anne Yeats, and the Macmillan Company for quotations from *The Variorum Edition of the Poems of W. B. Yeats,* edited by Peter Allt and Russell K. Alspach, copyright 1903, 1906, 1907, 1912, 1916, 1918, 1919,

PHILLIP L. MARCUS

Ithaca, N.Y.
June 1970

1. Yeats's Ideals for Irish Literature

In 1885, Yeats met the Irish patriot John O'Leary, who had recently returned to Ireland after many years of imprisonment and forced exile. Up to this time Yeats's verse had been in the manner of Spenser and Shelley. O'Leary's idealism, his great sacrifice, and his charismatic personality made him a compelling figure, and under the influence of his assertion that "there is no great literature without nationality, no great nationality without literature," [1] Yeats decided to become an *Irish* writer. He then had to define for himself precisely what the distinguishing characteristics of Irish literature might be, what qualities might give it an identity distinct from that of English literature and all others.

One answer was already at hand. During the 1840's the writers of the "Young Ireland" school had created a national image for Ireland and fostered the idea of a distinctive essence of Irishness, an "Irish note." This idea was embodied in the motto of their organ, *The Nation:* "Racy of the Soil." Any literary work "racy of the soil" was distinctively Irish. In later years both Ernest Renan's *The Poetry of the Celtic Races* (1857) and Matthew Arnold's *On the Study of Celtic*

1. *LNI*, pp. 75–76, 103. See also "I Became an Author," *The Listener*, August 4, 1938, p. 218; and *VP*, pp. 841, 843–844, 845.

[1]

Literature (1866–1867) devoted much attention to the "Celtic genius."

Unfortunately, so intangible a concept proved very hard to isolate. Lionel Johnson epitomized the difficulty in establishing a substantial area of agreement:

> After all, who is to decide what is, absolutely and definitely, the Celtic and Irish note? Many a time I have shown my English friends Irish poems, which Irish critics have declared to be un-Irish; and the English verdict has constantly been: "How un-English! how Celtic! what a strange, remote far-away beauty in the music and in the colour!" [2]

The definition made by Katharine Tynan when Yeats was first confronting the problem illustrates how unsatisfactory attempts at formulizing could be:

> By the Irish note I mean that distinctive quality in Celtic poetry the charm of which is so much easier to feel than to explain. . . . Some of the parts which go to make up its whole are a simplicity which is *naive*—a freshness, an archness, a light touching of the cords as with fairy-finger tips; a shade of underlying melancholy as delicately evanescent as a breath upon glass, which yet gives its undertone and its shadow to all; fatalism side by side with buoyant hopefulness; laughter with tears; love with hatred; a rainbow of all colours where none conflict; a gamut of all notes which join to make perfect harmony.[3]

Furthermore, while Arnold's delineation of the "Celtic note" gained wide acceptance, it permitted such broad interpretation that the Irish transformed features he considered defects into virtues.[4]

2. "Poetry and Patriotism in Ireland," in *Post Liminium: Essays and Critical Papers,* ed. Thomas Whittemore (London: Elkin Mathews, 1911), pp. 172–173.

3. "The Poetry of William Allingham," *Irish Fireside,* October 30, 1886, pp. 261–262.

4. See John V. Kelleher, "Matthew Arnold and the Celtic Revival," in *Perspectives of Criticism,* ed. Harry Levin (Cambridge, Mass.: Harvard University Press, 1950), pp. 197–222.

[2]

Thus, the idea of a "real voice of Ireland" [5] was too nebulous an index to the character of *Irish* literature. In the absence of fixed guidelines, two particular questions arose: (1) To what extent must the national literature be politically Nationalistic? (2) What were the boundaries of Irish national literature; to what extent could it incorporate not obviously "Irish" elements and influences without losing its identity and becoming "cosmopolitan"? Yeats's basic problem was thus twofold, and he had to formulate solutions for both aspects.

The alternatives Yeats faced in dealing with the first question can be seen in historical perspective. The concept of an Irish national literature was, as already suggested, largely a product of the Young Ireland movement of the 1840's. This group sprang up during a period of intense agitation for repeal of the Union, and its leaders—the most famous of whom were Thomas Davis and Charles Gavan Duffy—were ardently pro-Repeal. Consequently, most of the literature they fostered through the media of *The Nation* and the "Library of Ireland" (a series of books for popular consumption) was written with a Nationalistic political slant: it was propaganda intended directly to influence contemporary public opinion. The famous anthology *The Spirit of the Nation,* reprinted dozens of times during the century, contained much verse in this vein:

> How thrive we by the Union?
> Look round our native land;
> In ruined trade and wealth decayed
> See slavery's surest brand;
> Our glory as a nation gone,
> Our substance drained away;
> A wretched province trampled on,
> Is all we've left to-day.
> Then curse with me the Union,
> That juggle foul and base—
> The baneful root that bore such fruit
> Of ruin and disgrace.

5. W. B. Yeats, "Three Irish Poets," *A Celtic Christmas* (Christmas number of *The Irish Homestead*), December, 1897, p. 7.

And shall it last, this Union,
To grind and waste us so?
O'er hill and lea, from sea to sea,
All Ireland thunders, No!
Eight million necks are stiff to bow—
We know our might as men;
We conquered once before, and now
We'll conquer once again,
And rend the cursed Union,
And fling it to the wind—
And Ireland's laws in Ireland's cause
Alone our hearts shall bind!

["The Nation," by John O'Hagan].

At its origins, then, the ideal of a national literature in Ireland
was closely identified with political Nationalism.

In contrast, Samuel Ferguson, William Allingham, and
Aubrey de Vere, the three most important poets of the next
generation, were not connected with the Nationalist movement and wrote little political verse. Ferguson, it is true, had
for a time sympathized with the Young Irelanders and had
written a famous elegy on the death of Thomas Davis, but he
was never a party man; and with the failure of the movement he
returned to the conservative, pro-Unionist position of his youth,
though he had friends among men of all political factions.[6]
Most of his poetry is nonpolitical: adaptations of Irish myths
and history, and songs such as "Pastheen Finn" and "Molly
Asthore." His only excursions into immediately political verse
during those years were a poem on the hanging of several men
for agrarian outrages and two on the Phoenix Park murders
of 1882;[7] while highly critical of the acts of violence, he did
not publish the poems, indicating that he had no intention of

6. See Charles Gavan Duffy, *Four Years of Irish History: 1845–1849*
(New York, London, and Paris: Cassell, Petter and Co., 1882), pp. 578–
579; and Lady Mary Ferguson, *Sir Samuel Ferguson in the Ireland of
His Day* (Edinburgh and London: W. Blackwood and Sons, 1896), I,
237–267.

7. Printed in Lady Ferguson's *Sir Samuel Ferguson*, I, 258–266.

[4]

attempting to influence public opinion, and the fact that the latter two are dramatic monologues in the manner of Browning suggests that his main concern in writing them was with criminal psychology. Ferguson evidently believed that a non-Nationalist could write national poetry, bearing the "true Celtic note," for he stated, "We will have to make a literature for this country whatever be the fate of this or that policy. It must be lofty, moral, and distinctively Irish. The poets will save the people." [8] A Unionist writer could be national if he loved Ireland and gave it fitting expression in his work. There is a hint in Ferguson's last sentence of a conception that was to become very important for Yeats and find its culminating statement in "The Statues": that life sometimes imitates art, and that artists, by embodying desired ideals in their work, actually determine the nature of their society. Ferguson's success according to the standards he himself set was attested to by Yeats, who in late 1886 termed him the "most Celtic" of Irish writers,[9] and shortly afterward by Alfred Percival Graves, who chose him rather than Davis or Tom Moore as the "national poet of Ireland." [10]

Allingham, like Ferguson, seldom wrote political poetry, preferring subjects drawn from the life of his native Ballyshannon. The major exception is his novel-in-verse, *Lawrence Bloomfield in Ireland* (1864), and it is a perfect example of a work intended to be national without being militantly Nationalistic. In his preface Allingham says that the poem is "neither of an orange nor of a green complexion," and adds,

> We're one at heart, if you be Ireland's friend,
> Though leagues asunder our opinions tend.
> There are but two great parties in the end.

8. Quoted in *Songs and Ballads of Young Ireland,* ed. Martin MacDermott (London: Downey and Co., 1896), p. 164.

9. "The Poetry of Sir Samuel Ferguson," *Dublin University Review,* November, 1886, p. 940.

10. "Has Ireland a National Poet?" *The Reflector,* April 14, 1888, pp. 380–383.

The poem itself, concerned with land agitation and bad land-lords, advocates a limited transfer of land to hard-working peasants and offers the picture of a model landlord in Bloom-field. Its strongest point, however, is not economic theories, but rather its detailed descriptions of nearly every aspect of Irish life, from landlords' tables to peasants' hovels and Rib-bon Lodges, where members plotted agrarian crimes. Yeats several times expressed the opinion that Allingham's work in general should have been *more* "national." [11] It definitely stood apart from the Young Ireland tradition of literary pro-pagandizing for the Nationalist movement.

Aubrey de Vere was linked as closely with English as with Irish tradition, but nevertheless he wrote many poems on Irish subjects, primarily chronicles of various periods of Irish history and modern versions of old legends. Although de Vere shared Ferguson's and Allingham's concern about hard con-ditions in the country, he refused to countenance agitation for independence and was very critical of what he termed Irish "jacobinism." [12] Consequently, he too was little read by those who cared for Irish poetry—an audience conditioned almost entirely by Young Ireland tastes. As Yeats put it,

The alliance of politics and literature that marked the " '48 move-ment" resulted in so great a popularity for the poets and prose writers who taught the doctrine of nationality that we are accus-tomed ever since to think of those years as our one period of literary activity. The writers who came after, lacking the great wind of politics to fill their sails, have lived and wrought almost forgotten of the nation.[13]

These same conditions still prevailed at the beginning of the "Renaissance": even in 1895, Yeats could say, "The most

11. *LNI*, pp. 172–173; *Au*, p. 286; "Irish Literature. A Poet We Have Neglected," *United Ireland*, December 12, 1891, p. 5.

12. Wilfred Ward, *Aubrey de Vere: A Memoir*, 2nd ed. (London: Longmans and Co., 1904), pp. 282–283.

13. "Dr. Todhunter's Irish Poems," *United Ireland*, January 23, 1892, p. 5.

that read Irish national literature read from patriotism and political enthusiasm." [14] Thus, in determining the extent to which national literature had to be Nationalistic, he was confronted on the one hand with the Nationalistic Young Ireland literature and its great popularity, and on the other with the virtual oblivion into which the "merely" national work of men like Ferguson, Allingham, and de Vere had fallen.

For a writer like Yeats, Nationalist in sympathies but not interested in writing about current events, there was a potential dilemma here, but it did not become serious at once. It is true that in his early *Irish* poetry there are no Nationalistic poems. "The Two Titans: A Political Poem" (March, 1886) deals with the conflict between England and Ireland, but if the subject is typical of Young Ireland, the treatment is not: there are no apparent references to current incidents or even to famous historical events. In fact, the use of the subtitle suggests apprehension that the political aspect of the poem might otherwise be entirely overlooked. The poem, while perhaps national, is not obviously Nationalistic. Some remarks Yeats made at this time about Ferguson, however, show how he had at least temporarily satisfied his mind on the question. In trying to refute the charge that Ferguson had been an apostate from the Nationalist cause, he argued that Ferguson's later suppression of some of his patriotic poems was not sufficient evidence, that the Nationalists could still claim him, for "Irish singers who are genuinely Irish in thought, subject and style must, whether they will or no, nourish the forces that make for the political liberties of Ireland." [15] In other words, national literature could not be other than Nationalistic as well, whether or not it was directly concerned with Nationalist politics. Yeats did not explain how, but the connection may be surmised: any truly national literature

14. "Irish National Literature, IV.—A List of the Best Irish Books," *The Bookman*, October, 1895, p. 21.

15. "The Poetry of Sir Samuel Ferguson," *Dublin University Review*, November, 1886, p. 937.

would develop the sensibilities of Irishmen, strengthen their love for and loyalty to their country, and ultimately lead them to desire its unfettered development. This position was already outside of the immediate Young Ireland tradition, but he could still reconcile the two.

The reconciliation, however, was short-lived. In the years 1886–1892, Yeats became one of the most prominent Irish writers. His poetry, with the exception of the hastily done poem on the death of Parnell, continued to avoid overt patriotism, but by the end of that period the conception of art shared by the majority of the Nationalists had begun to conflict with his own artistic beliefs. This conflict was precipitated by Yeats's vigorous efforts to organize Irish literary societies in Dublin and London and to arrange for the publication and distribution of a series of inexpensive editions of good Irish books. Some of those with whom he became involved in connection with these projects shared his own interests in literature, but there were also "many who at that time found it hard to refuse if anybody offered for sale a pepper-pot shaped to suggest a round tower with a wolf-dog at its foot, who would have felt it inappropriate to publish an Irish book that had not harp and shamrock and green cover, so completely did their minds move amid Young Ireland images and metaphors" (*Au*, 123). This group wanted Yeats to produce and sanction poetry in the vein of *The Spirit of the Nation,* and they were not satisfied with—perhaps could not even comprehend—the explanation that in the long run truly national poetry would of necessity be Nationalistic as well. Disputes about the merits of the Young Ireland writers so often interrupted organizational meetings that the appearance of one of the societies was delayed for months (*Au*, 125), and the agitation of this faction threatened the harmony that Yeats had established between his political allegiance and his artistic principles.

In introducing Yeats to Young Ireland literature, O'Leary, even though he had been converted to political Nationalism by it, did not claim that it was good *poetry*.[16] Thus, Yeats was confronted from the first with proof that devoted patriotism need not prohibit intelligent criticism of the country's patriotic literature; and since then he had observed for himself that the quality of Young Ireland work was not generally as high as that of the nonpolitical poets. Now during the nineties he began openly to attack the former.

One point he criticized was its incredibly weak content. As political propaganda, it had to present ideas in simple, easily intelligible form. Consequently, even at its best it offered no richness and complexity of thought, no startling perceptions; it seemed schoolboyish.[17] Entirely lacking in psychological penetration, it paid no attention to "the spiritual part of life." [18] At its worst it presented the distorted, artificial picture of an Ireland populated entirely by noble heroes, stalwart peasants, and virtuous maidens, enchained by bloodthirsty English oppressors but full of a latent power ready at any time to burst forth.[19] Yeats admitted Davis' personal sincerity, but believed that he often fell into insincerity in his poetry because, desiring so intensely to see Irishmen as perfect, he already half believed that they were and produced such exaggerations as

Lead him to fight for native land,
His is no courage cold and wary,
The troops live not on earth would stand
The headlong charge of Tipperary.[20]

One reason Yeats thought James Clarence Mangan the best of the group rather than Davis was that Mangan had only become actively interested in politics very late in his short life and

16. "Mr. John O'Leary," *The Bookman*, February, 1897, p. 147; *Au*, pp. 58, 129; *EI*, p. 510; *VPlays*, p. 957.

17. *Au*, p. 300; *EI*, pp. 312–314.   18. "Three Irish Poets," p. 7.

19. See "An Irish Patriot," *The Bookman*, May, 1896, p. 50; *Au*, pp. 125, 300, 317; *VP*, p. 834; *EI*, pp. 312–314, 316.

20. "Introduction" to *BV*, pp. xiv–xv. The lines Yeats quotes are from Davis' poem "The Men of Tipperary."

consequently had been able to produce a number of poems in which sincerity was not sacrificed to politics. And with the exception of the "Lament for Eoghan Ruadh O'Neill," the poems by Davis that Yeats found praiseworthy were as close to being nonpolitical as Young Ireland verse could be: "The Marriage," "A Plea for Love," "Mary Bhan Astór." [21]

Yeats was also highly critical of Young Ireland style. He believed that one cause of its weaknesses was the Young Irelanders' conviction that almost anyone could be a writer; he quoted a letter from Davis to a friend urging him to write a national play: "Have you ever tried dramatic writing? Do you know Taylor's 'Philip Van Artevelde,' and Griffith's 'Gissippus'? I think them the two best serious dramas written in English since Shakespeare's time. A drama equal to either of them on an Irish subject would be useful and popular to an extent you can hardly suppose." [22] Propagandistic motives hurt style as well as content, for no great artistic care was required to please "the dull ears of the common man" (*BV*, xiv–xv). Even when writing with a purely artistic purpose, the Young Irelanders often "failed to shake off habits of carelessness and commonness acquired in thinking of the widest rather than the best audience." [23] Yeats's favorite epithet for their poetry was "rhetorical," [24] a term he used to connote bombast and noisy argumentativeness such as these lines from J. D. Fraser's "The Gathering of the Nation":

> Denial met our just demands,
> And hatred met our love;

21. See *Letters,* p. 204 (1892); *BV,* pp. xiv–xv and the selections from Davis in the text; "Professor Dowden and Irish Literature," *Daily Express* (Dublin), January 26, 1895; "Irish National Literature: from Callanan to Carleton," *The Bookman,* July, 1895, p. 105.

22. "Young Ireland," *The Bookman,* January, 1897, p. 120.

23. "An Irish Patriot," *The Bookman,* May, 1896, p. 50.

24. See, for example, "The Evangel of Folklore," *The Bookman,* June, 1894, p. 86; "Irish National Literature. IV.—A List of the Best Irish Books," *The Bookman,* October, 1895, p. 21; *Au,* p. 120; *Early Poems and Stories* (London: Macmillan, 1925), p. v.

[10]

Till now, by heaven! for grasp of hands
We'll give them clash of battle-brands,
And gauntlet 'stead of glove.
And may the Saxon stamp his heel
Upon the coward's front
Who sheathes his own unbroken steel
Until for mercy tyrants kneel,
Who forced us to the brunt!

Even Mangan, "whenever he had no fine ancient song to inspire him, . . . fell into rhetoric." [25] The diction of this poetry was trite and stereotyped; key words such as "gore," "wrath," "wrongs," "just," "true," "brave," "chains," "fight," "slave," "swords," "liberty," occurred again and again. The language, "carried beyond life perpetually" by propaganda and exaggeration, was "worn and cold" (*EI*, 312–314).

Rhyme and rhythm were just as unsatisfactory. *The Spirit of the Nation* contained such slipshod rhymes as "director" —"victor," "impossible"—"will," "choose them"—"bosom," "wide ill"—"idle," "freedom"—"need them." Yeats mocked the "jigging doggerel" of a Denis Florence MacCarthy poem:

Come, Liberty, come! we are ripe for thy coming;
Come, freshen the hearts where thy rival has trod;
Come, richest and rarest! come, purest and fairest,
Come, daughter of science! come, gift of the god! [26]

He traced the use of "conventional," "mechanical" ballad rhythms to the Young Irelanders' desire to please the masses, who "had forgotten Gaelic poetry and had not learned the subtleties of English poetry." [27] Mangan, too, was often guilty of these faults, but in his best poetry he attained metrical effects far superior to anything ever produced by Davis and his fellows, as illustrated by every stanza of his rendering of

25. *BV*, p. xvi. For an example, see his "A Highway for Freedom," in *The Spirit of the Nation*.
26. "Some Irish National Books," *The Bookman*, August, 1894, p. 151.
27. *Ideals in Ireland*, ed. Lady Augusta Gregory (London: Unicorn Press, 1901), p. 87; *BV*, pp. xiv–xv.

O'Hussey's "Ode to the Maguire," a poem often praised by
Yeats: [28]

Though he were even a wolf, ranging the round green woods,
Though he were even a pleasant salmon in the unchainable sea,
Though he were a wild mountain eagle, he could scarce bear, he
This sharp, sore sleet, these howling floods.

Significantly, only Mangan had, at least in his "translations"
from the Irish, what might be called a native style; Davis and
the rest sprinkled their poems with Gaelic phrases but emulated English modes, and not those of the great Romantics
or of Tennyson, but rather of writers like Macaulay and
Scott.[29]

Such objections reveal the gap between Yeats and his opponents, who continued to maintain, as Martin MacDermott,
a surviving member of the original Young Ireland group, put
it in an 1896 anthology of Nationalistic verse, "Patriotism
. . . can *make* poetry." [30] Yeats's own ideal, clarified and
strengthened for him by this opposition, was always to place the
concerns of art before those of politics. The artist *could* be
active politically (he himself became involved with the revolutionary Irish Republican Brotherhood in 1896), but "he
should, no matter how strong be his political interests, endeavour to become a master of his craft, and be ever careful to
keep rhetoric, or the tendency to think of his audience rather
than of the perfect and the True, out of his writing." [31] In
1903 he reiterated this ideal in relation to his own patriotic
play *Cathleen ni Houlihan:*

28. See "Young Ireland," *The Bookman,* January, 1897, p. 120; "Professor Dowden and Irish Literature," *Daily Express* (Dublin), January
26, 1895; *Au,* p. 240; *VP,* p. 851.

29. See "Irish National Literature: from Callanan to Carleton," *The
Bookman,* July, 1895, pp. 105–106; and C. H. Rolleston, *Portrait of an
Irishman* (London: Methuen and Co., 1939), p. 16.

30. *Songs and Ballads of Young Ireland,* p. xvii.

31. "The Silenced Sister," *United Ireland,* December 23, 1893, p. 5.

A community that is opinion-ridden, even when those opinions are in themselves noble, is likely to put its creative minds into some sort of a prison. If creative minds preoccupy themselves with incidents from the political history of Ireland, so much the better, but we must not force them to select those incidents. If, in the sincere working out of their plot, they alight on a moral that is obviously and directly serviceable to the Nationalist cause, so much the better, but we must not force that moral upon them. I am a Nationalist. . . . But if some external necessity had forced me to write nothing but drama with an obviously patriotic intention, instead of letting my work shape itself under the casual impulses of dream and daily thoughts, I would have lost, in a short time, the power to write movingly on any theme. I could have aroused opinion, but I could not have touched the heart [*Explor*, 115–116].

His later work provides many more examples, most interesting perhaps being the poetic celebration of his allegiance to this ideal in "The Grey Rock" of 1913. In that poem he addresses his old fellow Rhymers, relating to them a parable the moral of which they can appreciate along with Yeats because of their own devotion to the demands of art. Like him, they "never made a poorer song" that they "might have a heavier purse, / Nor gave loud service to a cause" in order to have a "troop of friends." The vehicle for the parable is a fabled incident associated with the Battle of Clontarf in 1014.[32] Dunlaing O'Hartigan, loved by the goddess Aoibheall, had received from her the gift of invisibility but cast it off to be equal with his friend Murchadh, and both were killed in the battle. What might in other Yeatsian contexts be a positive act, an example of heroic recklessness, is here a betrayal of principle: Aoibheall is a sort of Irish muse, the grey rock her Parnassus, and Dunlaing, claiming "his country's need was most," has been untrue to her. Applying the parable to himself and looking back upon the quarrels of the last two decades, Yeats justly boasted: "*I have kept my faith, though faith was tried, / To that rock-*

32. Yeats's source for the story was probably Lady Gregory's *Gods and Fighting Men* (London: John Murray, 1904), pp. 87–88.

born, rock-wandering foot." He was to keep the faith for the rest of his life.

Yeats's response to the question of the extent to which Irish literature could be influenced by or incorporate not obviously Irish elements without losing its identity and becoming cosmopolitan, leads back once again to the early influence of John O'Leary and his principle that a great literature *must* be a national literature. Yeats adopted this principle and preached it. His early criticism repeatedly stressed that "no man who deserts his own literature for another's can hope for the highest rank. The cradles of the greatest writers are rocked among the scenes they are to celebrate." [33] He warned that "whenever an Irish writer has strayed away from Irish themes and Irish feeling, in almost all cases he has done no more than make alms for oblivion" (*LNI*, 103). It was customary at this time for Irishmen to include among their native writers men whose only connection with Ireland was birth there, if their names could add lustre to Irish literature: Sterne and Sheridan are prominent examples. Yeats would have none of this: although it might lessen the prestige of Irish literature, he preferred to include only those writers "who have written under Irish influence and of Irish subjects."

Once a country has given "perfect expression to itself in literature," has "carried to maturity its literary tradition," then its writers bear its influence "no matter what they write of"; [34] but Irish tradition was obviously not yet mature enough for the "Celtic note" to make itself heard regardless of its surroundings. In Ireland, which he contrasted in this respect with Scotland, national feeling had not yet been "elaborated and expounded by men of genius with minds as full of Irish

33. "The Irish Intellectual Capital: Where Is It? The Publication of Irish Books," *United Ireland*, May 14, 1892, p. 2.
34. "Irish National Literature: From Callanan to Carleton," *The Bookman*, July, 1895, p. 105.

[14]

history, scenery, and character as the minds of Burns and Scott were full of Scottish history, scenery, and character." [35] The maturation of an Irish tradition was by no means assured, owing to the constant threat of "denationalization" by England. Yeats stated his general agreement with Douglas Hyde's famous speech on the necessity for de-Anglicizing Ireland, and one of the central goals of the Irish Literary Society in London, which he helped to found, was to counter the trend away from indigenous culture.[36]

"Cosmopolitanism" is used as a derogatory term throughout his criticism of these years. Thus, in commenting upon an assertion by Justin McCarthy that Irishmen were exercising little influence upon contemporary literature because of their absorption with journalism and politics, Yeats concurred, but added that McCarthy

did not mention all the things that absorb us. Cosmopolitanism is one of the worst. We are not content to dig our own potato patch in peace. We peer over the wall at our neighbour's instead of making our own garden green and beautiful. And yet it is a good garden, and there have been great transactions within it, from the death of Cuchulain to the flight of Michael Dwyer from the burning cabin [LNI, 106–107].

The work of Allingham, though its technical competence attracted Yeats, seemed to him only incompletely Irish: "Allingham was the poet of Ballyshannon, though not of Ireland." But "if he was no national poet, he was at any rate, no thin-blooded cosmopolitan, but loved the hills about him and the land under his feet." That Allingham had originally published a number of his poems in broadside form indicated "his genuine wish to be considered an Irish poet, and not a mere cosmopolitan choosing his themes from Ireland, as he

35. "Irish National Literature. IV.—A List of the Best Irish Books," *The Bookman*, October, 1895, p. 21.
36. "The Irish Intellectual Capital: Where Is It? The Publication of Irish Books," *United Ireland*, May 14, 1892, p. 1.

might choose them in another way from Kamskchatka." [37]

"Creative work has always a fatherland" (*LNI*, 74) because

to the greater poets everything they see has its relation to the national life, and through that to the universal and divine life: nothing is an isolated artistic moment; there is a unity everywhere; . . . But to this universalism, this seeing of unity everywhere, you can only attain through what is near you, your nation, or, if you be no traveller, your village and the cobwebs on your walls. You can no more have the greater poetry without a nation than religion without symbols. One can only reach out to the universe with a gloved hand—that glove is one's nation, the only thing one knows even a little of [*LNI*, 174].

He later gave a second reason in one of his autobiographies; in the nineties, disturbed by contemporary fragmentation of society, he wished to start a movement back toward unity: but he could not endure an "international art" that picked its "stories and symbols where it pleased." He believed that all races have had "their first unity from a mythology, that marries them to rock and hill"; he would therefore have to create a new *Prometheus Unbound* in which Patrick or Columbkil, Oisin or Fionn would be substituted for Prometheus, Cro Patrick or Ben Bulben for Caucasus (*Au*, 119).

But in arguing for national literature, Yeats never fell into the error, so common among his countrymen, of insularity. This was partly because in his own scale of values the national, important as it was, yet served a greater end, "the universal and divine life"; and partly because he had been influenced by his father's tastes and then lived in such close contact with contemporary English literature through Morris, Henley, and the Rhymers (as well as having, once he became friendly with Arthur Symons, a taproot to current French writers). So throughout the period, he argued, "We can learn from English and other literatures without loss of national individuality," [38]

37. "Irish Literature. A Poet We Have Neglected," *United Ireland*, December 12, 1891, p. 5.

38. "Nationality and Literature," *United Ireland*, May 27, 1893.

[16]

and as he was to put it later, "A writer is not less national because he shows the influence of other countries and of the great writers of the world" (*Explor*, 157–158).

These beliefs dictated his answer to the peculiarly Irish problem of whether Irish literature could preserve its nationality when it employed for its expression a "foreign" tongue. He made very clear his belief that English *could* be the language for the national literature. Hyde in his de-Anglicising speech had been rather pessimistic about the possibility of reviving the moribund Irish language as a means of combating pervasive English influence. Yeats saw no cause for discouragement:

Can we not build up a national tradition, a national literature, which shall be none the less Irish in spirit for being English in language? [He then enumerated several good recently published books in English on Irish subjects.] Let us make these books and the books of our older writers known among the people and we will do more to de-Anglicize Ireland than by longing to recall the Gaelic tongue and the snows of yester year. Let us by all means prevent the decay of the tongue where we can, and preserve it always among us as a learned language to be a fountain of nationality in our midst, but do not let us base upon it our hopes of nationhood. When we remember the majesty of Cuchullin and the beauty of sorrowing Deirdre we should not forget that it is that majesty and that beauty which are immortal, and not the perishing tongue that first told of them.[39]

Of course he did have a personal stake in the matter, having no Irish himself, but the entire corpus of his criticism testifies to his disinterested concern for the welfare of his country's literature, and its success in this century would seem to prove his assertion.

Hyde's position, when pushed to its extreme (as it was soon to be by his followers), would rule out *any* contact with

39. "The De-Anglicising of Ireland," *United Ireland*, December 17, 1892, p. 1. Yeats repeated this stand in "Mr. W. B. Yeats," *The Leader*, September 1, 1900, p. 13.

English or other foreign literary traditions. Even Stopford Brooke's 1893 call for good English translations of medieval Irish literary texts was decried by the Gaelic Leaguers as destructive to their principles.[40] Yeats, on the other hand, favored a selective approach. In an 1893 article entitled "Nationality and Literature," he argued that the literature of every country passes through three stages, the epic, the dramatic, and the lyrical, the third being the most complex and cosmopolitan. In most countries literature had already reached the third stage, but in Ireland it had not. Consequently, Irish writers were not to imitate those of other countries and to write for foreign audiences as they had so often done; but neither were they to close their minds to all but the Irish tradition:

Though we must not imitate the writers of any other country, we must study them constantly and learn from them the secret of their greatness. Only by study of the great models can we acquire style, and this, St. Beuf says, is the only thing in literature that is immortal. We must learn, too, from the old nations to make literature almost the most serious thing in our lives if we would understand it properly, and quite the most serious thing if we would write it well. . . . The inspiration of God, which is, indeed, the source of all which is greatest in the world, comes only to him who labours at rhythm and cadence, at form and style, until they have no secret hidden from him. This art we must learn from the old literatures of the world. . . . We must learn from the literature of France and England to be supreme artists and then God will send us a supreme inspiration.[41]

What Yeats wanted, then, was a discriminating use of foreign literatures as an aid in developing the literature of Ireland.

Here was another source of his dissatisfaction with the writings of the Young Irelanders and of Tom Moore as well. They had imitated rather than studied and also had chosen poor models. Subject to the demands of immediate political neces-

40. See T. W. Rolleston, "Twenty-One Years of Irish Art and Thought," in *Souvenir Programme of the Coming of Age of the Irish Literary Society of London, 1892–1913* ([London], n.d.), p. 25.
41. *United Ireland*, May 27, 1893, pp. 1–2.

sity, or simply impatient, they "turned away from the unfolding and developing of an Irish tradition, and borrowed the mature English methods of utterance and used them to sing of Irish wrongs and preach of Irish purposes." Their work was unsatisfactory, "for what was Irish in it looked ungainly in an English garb, and what was English was never perfectly mastered, never wholly absorbed into their being." Moore had "quenched an admirable Celtic lyricism in an artificial glitter learned from the eighteenth century," while Davis and others had borrowed a manner from Scott, Macaulay, and Lockhart, and John Mitchel's work reflected the impact of Carlyle. Unfortunately, they had been the most influential Irish writers of the century, "and their influence was not at all the less because they had not a native style." [42] On the other hand he praised Ferguson, Allingham, and de Vere as "wiser than Young Ireland in the choice of their models, for while drawing not less from purely Irish sources, they turned to the great poets of the world" (BV, xviii). Seeing a contrast between current Irish poetry, which worked with fresh materials but was generally careless of style and form, and English "decadent" verse, where manner had become almost everything, he wanted to combine the virtues of both movements.[43] Thus, he was pleased with Eva Gore-Booth's early poems but felt that she needed, "like all Irish literary people, a proper respect for craftsmanship and that she must get in England" (Letters, 256–257).

Here again Yeats ran into opposition. His opponents over the question of propagandizing in literature were also hostile to the suggestion that Irish writers had anything to learn from the great artists of their political enemy. As Yeats later described the situation,

In those days a patriotic young man would have thought but poorly of himself if he did not believe that The Spirit of the

42. "Irish National Literature: from Callanan to Carleton," *The Bookman*, July, 1895, pp. 105–106.
43. "Hopes and Fears for Irish Literature," *United Ireland*, October 15, 1892, p. 5.

Nation was great lyric poetry, and a much finer kind of poetry than Shelley's *Ode to the West Wind*, or Keats's *Ode on a Grecian Urn*. When two or three of us denied this, we were told that we had effeminate tastes or that we were putting Ireland in a bad light before her enemies. If one said that *The Spirit of the Nation* was but salutary rhetoric, England might overhear us and take up the cry.[44]

When a reviewer of P. J. M'Call's inane verses *Irish Noínins* suggested that Irish writers pay no attention to the opinions of foreign critics, Yeats retorted that while Irish literature should be as national as possible, its writers, deprived of intelligent comment at home, desperately needed international criticism (*Letters*, 238–239).

However weak his French, Yeats had enough familiarity with French literature to see that the study of it could also contribute to the development of Irish writing; but here the opposition was still more vociferous, coming not only from superpatriots but also from religious zealots afraid of immorality and "atheism." Even intelligent new writers like William Larminie thought Yeats inclined "more than is quite safe to the theories of the French schools" and asserted that there are "several instances to be found in which the poetic literature of France has exercised on that of other countries an injurious effect." [45]

Yeats responded that the study of foreign writers could improve the quality of Irish literature without weakening its

44. *Explor*, p. 114 (1903). See also *Au*, pp. 123–124.
45. *Literary Ideals in Ireland* (London: T. Fisher Unwin, and Dublin: at the *Daily Express* Office, 1899), pp. 58, 62. Cf. also *Explor*, pp. 234–235 (1908), where Yeats says that the Irish novelists have "filled the popular mind with images of character, with forms of construction, with a criticism of life, which are so many arguments to prove that some play that has arisen out of a fresh vision is unlike every Irish thing. A real or fancied French influence is pointed out at once and objected to." A still later example of this type of argument can be found in "The Writings of J. M. Synge," *Freeman's Journal*, January 23, 1912, p. 3.

national character. But he also had to deal with the problem of nonnational subject-matter: some work on personal subjects might be included in a volume composed largely of unquestionably Irish poems and perhaps justified as Irish by their style and sensibility, but what about more general material, especially that having associations with other countries? It would give the literature a wider scope and significance, but would it not also decrease its Irishness? Yeats's answer was Yes: excessive concern with, say, the American West or court life in eighteenth-century France would definitely be unacceptable. Such a position, however, was a potential threat to his own work. Unable, like many of his most sensitive contemporaries, to find satisfaction in orthodox Christian faiths, he was strongly attracted to occult philosophies and Oriental systems of belief. As early as 1885 he, Charles Johnston, and others had formed a Dublin Hermetic Society, and throughout his life he was involved in such pursuits. They were no mere pastime but rather lay at the heart of his personal quest for values. He wrote O'Leary, who had criticized such interests,

If I had not made magic my constant study I could not have written a single word of my Blake book, nor would *The Countess Cathleen* have ever come to exist. The mystical life is the centre of all that I do and all that I think and all that I write. It holds to my work the same relation that the philosophy of Godwin held to the work of Shelley and I have always considered myself a voice of what I believe to be a greater renaissance—the revolt of the soul against the intellect—now beginning in the world [*Letters*, 211].

Consequently, to avoid violating his own strictures against literary use of nonnational material he had to find an organic connection between such subjects and Irish tradition.

Such a connection was the subject of his poem "Apologia addressed to Ireland in the coming days," first published in 1892. There he claimed to be as much an Irish poet as "Davis, Mangan, Ferguson," even though

> . . . the red rose bordered hem
> Of her whose history began
> Before God made the angelic clan,
> Trails all about the written page.

When some reviewers misinterpreted the poem as a claim to equal merit, Yeats stated in a letter that he had meant "only community in the treatment of *Irish subjects* after an Irish fashion" (*Letters*, 213; italics added).

In the "Apologia" itself he suggested obliquely the nature of the connection he saw:

> For in the world's first blossoming age
> The light fall of her flying feet
> Made Ireland's heart begin to beat.

From other passages in his work of this period a more concrete argument can be pieced together. As early as 1886 he asserted that the "love of shadowy Hy Brasil is very characteristic of the Celtic race, ever desiring the things that lie beyond the actual; dreamy and fanciful things, unreal if you will, as are all the belongings of the spirit from the point of view of the body, that loves to cry 'dreamer, dreamer,' to its hard task-master the spirit." [46] During the nineties such references became common. In a long note in *The Wind Among the Reeds*, for example, Yeats discussed the traditional symbolic values of the rose, "spiritual love and supreme beauty," and gave examples to justify his placing it poetically upon the Tree of Life. Then he brought in Irish references:

I once stood beside a man in Ireland when he saw it growing there [on the Tree of Life] in a vision. . . . One finds the Rose in the Irish poets, sometimes as a religious symbol, as in the phrase "the rose of Friday," meaning the Rose of austerity, in a Gaelic poem in Dr. Hyde's "Religious Songs of Connacht"; and I think [it] was a symbol of beauty in the Gaelic song, "Roseen Dubh"; and a symbol of Ireland in Mangan's adaptation of "Roseen

46. "The Poetry of R. D. Joyce," *Irish Fireside*, November 27, 1886, p. 331.

Dubh," "My Dark Rosaleen," and in Mr. Aubrey de Vere's "The Little Black Rose." I do not know any evidence to prove whether this symbol came to Ireland with medieval Christianity, or whether it has come down from Celtic times. I have read somewhere that a stone engraved with a Celtic god, who holds what looks like a rose in one hand, has been found somewhere in England. . . . If the Rose was really a symbol of Ireland among the Gaelic poets, and if "Roseen Dubh" is really a political poem, as some think, one may feel pretty certain that the ancient Celts associated the Rose with some principal god or goddess, for such symbols are not suddenly adopted or invented, but come out of mythology [*VP*, 811–812].

Through a subtle web of associations and inferences, the "symbolic rose" tradition in Ireland is pushed back to an antiquity almost as great as that of "her whose history began / Before God made the angelic clan."

To take another instance, Yeats asserted that although the work of contemporary Irish poets, dealing primarily with "a spiritual life," might seem strange and difficult to audiences accustomed to verse of the Young Ireland type, such poets were nevertheless speaking with the "truest voice of the Celt." [47] The dedication of *The Secret Rose*, to co-visionary AE, showed Yeats even more clearly broadening the concept of the "Celtic note" to embrace the mystical and the occult:

My friends in Ireland sometimes ask me when I am going to write a really national poem or romance, and by a national poem or romance I understand them to mean a poem or romance founded upon some moment of famous Irish history, and built up out of the thoughts and feelings which move the greater number of patriotic Irishmen. I on the other hand believe that poetry and romance cannot be made by the most conscientious study of famous moments and of the thoughts and feelings of others, but only by looking into that little, infinite, faltering eternal flame that one calls one's self. . . . So far, however, as this book is visionary it is Irish; for Ireland, which is still predominantly Cel-

47. "Three Irish Poets," *Irish Homestead*, December, 1897, p. 7.

tic, has preserved with some less excellent things a gift of vision, which has died out among more hurried and more successful nations.

This position also played a part in Yeats's attempt to justify his intensive study of Blake, a great poet who had centered his life and work in precisely the same sort of occult studies that he himself was pursuing. In the edition of Blake's work that he prepared with Edwin Ellis, he put forth the theory that Blake was of Irish descent, an origin intentionally obscured by his father:

> But if the old O'Neil origin was hidden, the wild O'Neil blood showed itself strongly in the next generation. William Blake, as we call him, was, before all things, an O'Neil. His descent from a stock who had seldom lacked their attendant banshee, even when hard destiny had brought low their once high estate, and hidden it under the smoke-blackened rafters of some poor cabin, may well have had much to do with his visionary gift. . . . The very manner of Blake's writing has an Irish flavour [i.e., the "Celtic note"], a lofty extravagance of invention and epithet, recalling the *Tain Bo Cuilane* [sic] and other old Irish epics, and his mythology brings to mind the tumultuous vastness of the ancient tales of god and demon that have come to us from the dawn of mystic tradition in what may fairly be called his fatherland.[48]

In the notes to *A Book of Irish Verse* (1895) he went so far as to suggest that in the future Blake's poetry should be included in Irish anthologies.[49]

All these statements point toward the same conclusion: the spiritual, the visionary, and the occult are fit subjects of concern for Irish writers because they are essentially related to

48. *The Works of William Blake* (London: Bernard Quaritch, 1893), I, 2–4. See also *Letters*, p. 125, where Yeats says that it was he who found the "evidence" concerning Blake's birth, and that "Ireland takes a most important place in his mystical system." See also *Letters*, p. 136.

49. *BV*, p. 255. Here Yeats gives as the source of his information "Dr. Carter Blake."

[24]

the true Celtic nature. Under the influence of such books on comparative religion as Frazer's *The Golden Bough* and John Rhys's *Celtic Heathendom*, Yeats argued that Ireland still preserved the ancient natural religion that had once been worldwide and was still discernible in parts of the East but elsewhere had been obscured by the rise of cultures with altered forms of belief: "The common people, wherever civilization has not driven its plough too deep, keep a watch over the roots of all religion and all romance."

This argument is adumbrated in an 1889 article in which Yeats spoke of how "the earliest poet of India and the Irish peasant in his hovel nod to each other across the ages, and are in perfect agreement," both affirming the existence of the spiritual world (*LNI*, 204); and a full statement of it appears in the essay "The Celtic Element in Literature," first published in 1898. He began by summarizing the formulations by Renan and Arnold of the "Celtic note," then proposed to "restate a little" their definitions: Arnold, lacking the benefit of more recent scholarship in the area of folk literature and beliefs, had failed to understand that Irish "natural magic [one of Arnold's touchstones of Celticism] is but the ancient religion of the world, the ancient worship of nature and that troubled ecstasy before her, that certainty of all beautiful places being haunted, which it brought into men's minds" (*EI*, 175–176). There was, then, no clear boundary between the "real voice of Ireland" and the occult tradition and Eastern religions in which the ancient beliefs were also preserved; this meant that the former was perhaps not unique to Ireland (Yeats does not seem to have recognized this potential drawback to the theory), but also that the Irish writer who turned to occultism or Esoteric Buddhism or similar pursuits was not being less national than when he was writing of Irish myth and history.[50]

50. See also *VP*, p. 837 for an important later passage in which Yeats tries to connect Ireland with the East.

Of course Yeats's use of heterodox materials received much criticism. Even a potentially sympathetic critic such as W. P. Ryan wrote in 1894 that for Yeats to become a great poet he would have to "shake himself free from the passing craze of occultism and symbolism." In the same year Arthur Lynch found it "curious that this young man of eminently Irish quality, born in beautiful and breezy Sligo, must needs slay all that has come best to him as his very birthright, and turn the indomitable Irishman into some far off Hindoo, effete through a hundred generations of atony." [51] And the audience reaction at the opening performance of *The Countess Cathleen*, at least as Joyce depicted it in *A Portrait of the Artist as a Young Man*, included the cries "—We want no amateur atheists. / —We want no budding buddhists." No argument could convince such people, but Yeats did convince himself and was thereby able to reconcile several of his current roles: Irish poet, patriot, occult philosopher, and Blake scholar. A poem like "O'Sullivan Rua to the Secret Rose," a Blakean apocalyptic vision which modulates smoothly from the Magi of Christian and occult tradition to an event with both Christian and Irish associations (the death of Conchobor), and from that into a series of incidents from Irish legend, shows that this reconciliation bore tangible fruit.

By broadening the theoretical boundaries of Irish literature and freeing it from the requirement of direct political propagandizing, Yeats's ideals concerning national literature supported and interacted with his other major ideals of this period: experimentally developing new subject-matter for Irish literature, increasing the general level of artistry, and finding more effective modes of expression.

Experimentation was for Yeats only a means, not an end in itself: the stage in which a writer's work or the literature of a country was dominated by experimentation was unsatisfactory but necessary for the emergence of more worthy creations.

51. *Our Poets!* (London: Remington and Co., 1894), p. 58.

Thus, he called Arthur Symons' *London Nights* "too unequal and experimental to be called 'an excellent book, a wonderful book.' " [52]

He used the term similarly in an 1895 article defending contemporary Irish writing and linked it with the quest for new subject-matter: "an experimental literature, a literature preoccupied with hitherto unworked material." [53] The material to which he referred was composed primarily of Irish myth, legend, and folklore. (Here his reverence for the traditional and his experimental efforts coincided perfectly.) Yeats was not the first Irish writer to concern himself with these areas, but he *was* the first to see their full potential as subject-matter for Irish literature. The development of the literary use of the old Irish myths is so complex that I devote a chapter to it later; the folk material represented similar values for Yeats and serves more manageably as an illustration.

Folklore, though of no immediate political relevance, was "Irish of the Irish," and it was often of very high quality, because it rejected the "passing and trivial," "clever and pretty," "vulgar and insincere," and in their place gathered "the simplest and most unforgettable thoughts of the generations." [54] Consequently, it could be of great value to the contemporary Irish writer (*Letters*, 88), not only providing a source of "plots and atmosphere" but also offering a corrective to the pervasive influence of the Young Ireland mode:

Past Irish literary movements were given overmuch to argument and oratory; their poems, with beautiful exceptions, were noisy and rhetorical, and their prose, their stories even, ever too ready to flare out in expostulation. So manifest were these things that

52. "That Subtle Shade," *The Bookman*, August, 1895, p. 144. See also "Miss Fiona Macleod as a Poet," *The Bookman*, December, 1896, p. 93.

53. "Professor Dowden and Irish Literature," *Daily Express* (Dublin), January 26, 1895.

54. *The Celtic Twilight and A Selection of Early Poems* (New York: New American Library, 1962), p. 128 (1901).

many had come to think the Irish nation essentially rhetorical and unpoetical, essentially a nation of public speakers and journalists, for only the careful student could separate the real voice of Ireland, the song which has never been hushed since history began, from all this din and bombast. But now the din and bombast are passing away, or, at any rate, no longer mistaken for serious literature, and life is being sung not for what can be proved or disproved, not for what men can be made do or not do, but for the sake of Beauty "and Time's old daughter Truth." . . . Compare the method of the older writers with the method of the new and lay the difference at the door of the folk-lorist. . . . There is indeed no school for literary Ireland just now like the school of folk-lore.[55]

The "real voice of Ireland" could be heard in folklore because it preserved a tradition predating English, and often even Christian, influence upon Irish life; in it the second century was nearer than the nineteenth.[56] At this time Yeats often shared the revulsion felt by the Pre-Raphaelites and their successors for mechanized, materialistic late Victorian society, and a poem like "The Stolen Child" suggests an element of escapism in his immersion in that "better" realm:

Come away, O human child!
To the waters and the wild
With a faery, hand in hand,
For the world's more full of weeping than you can understand.

But this was minor: the primary attraction of folk tradition was as a storehouse of positive values that could serve as correctives to the modern condition. The spiritual and visionary elements that Yeats came to see as essential components of the true "Celtic note" were denied by the forces of rationalism and materialism in contemporary society but survived in folklore. While modern thought boggled at the possibility of another world beyond the realm of the senses, the Irish country people lived in constant touch with that world. Belief in

55. "The Evangel of Folk-lore," *The Bookman*, June, 1894, p. 86.
56. "Tales from the Twilight," *Scots Observer*, March 1, 1890, p. 408.

spirits was to them as natural as the "process of the seasons." They saw repeatedly "what a king might give his crown and the world its wealth to have seen, and the doubts and speculations, that are in our eyes so great a part of the progress of the world, would be in their eyes, could they understand them, but dust in the hollow of a hand." Quite possibly it was modern "civilized" men and not the far greater multitudes of "primitive and barbaric people" who were the exceptions in the order of nature; perhaps "the seer of visions and hearer of voices" was the "normal and healthy man." [57] Traditional beliefs, unbroken religious faith, and the harshness of their lives had taught the common people "that this world is nothing and that a spiritual world, where all dreams come true, is everything." The poetry arising from this "old wisdom" would turn to religion and to "the law of the hidden world," while that deriving from the "new wisdom" could not forget politics and the law of the visible world. Between the two there could be no lasting peace. [58]

Yeats thought he could already discern a world wide resurgence of the "old wisdom," [59] and he was of course particularly hopeful of seeing it triumph in contemporary Irish literature. During the middle and late nineties his criticism was full of references to the emergence of spiritual concerns among the Irish writers. [60] The first came in an 1894 review of AE's *Homeward: Songs by the Way*:

57. "Irish Fairy Beliefs," *The Speaker,* July 14, 1900, p. 414.

58. *Ideals in Ireland,* pp. 97–98.

59. See, for instance, "Irish National Literature. III.—Contemporary Irish Poets," *The Bookman,* September, 1895, p. 168; "Aglavaine and Selysette," *The Bookman,* September, 1897, p. 155; "Mr. Rhys' Welsh Ballads," *The Bookman,* April, 1898, pp. 14–15; *Literary Ideals in Ireland,* p. 36 and the entire essay "The Autumn of the Flesh"; "The Dominion of Dreams," *The Bookman,* July, 1899, p. 105; and *Ideals in Ireland,* pp. 100–101.

60. His concern with this subject was anticipated in his remarks about AE in "An Irish Visionary," *National Observer,* October 3, 1891 (reprinted in *The Celtic Twilight,* 1893).

A little school of transcendental writers has . . . started up in the last year or two, . . . and made many curious and some beautiful lyrics. . . . About twelve [really nine] years ago seven youths began to study European magic and Oriental mysticism, and . . . agreed to meet at times in a dirty back street and to call their meetings "the Dublin Hermetic Society." They gradually accumulated a set of convictions for themselves, of which a main part was, I think, that the poets were uttering, under the mask of phantasy, the old revelations; . . . they spent their days in battles about the absolute and the alcahest; and I think that none read the newspapers and I am sure that some could not have told you the name of the viceroy. These periodical meetings started a movement, and the movement has begun to make literature.[61]

The allusions to newspapers and viceroys served as an implicit contrast with Young Ireland literature, a literature published mainly in a newspaper, centrally concerned with current events and not at all with matters of the spirit; it was, on the other hand, an obvious implication of the "spiritual" worldview that the artist must not be curbed by any external considerations, political or otherwise:

Everything that can be seen, touched, measured, explained, understood, argued over, is to the imaginative artist nothing more than a means, for he belongs to the invisible life, and delivers its ever new and ever ancient revelation. . . . The only restraint he can obey is the mysterious instinct that has made him an artist, and that teaches him to discover immortal moods in mortal desires.[62]

In 1896, Yeats termed contemporary Irish prose literature "much more subtle, much more spiritual than before," and the following year he revealed still greater optimism, again drawing a contrast with Young Ireland:

The bulk of the poets of modern Ireland has been so exclusively political, or so exclusively national, in a political sense, that it has hardly busied itself, like the poets of Wales and Brittany with

61. "A New Poet," *The Bookman*, August, 1894, pp. 147–148.
62. "Irish National Literature: Contemporary Prose Writers," *The Bookman*, August, 1895, p. 138.

[30]

the spiritual part of life, but now we have several poets who are speaking with what I think is the truest voice of the Celt. I call them spiritual, not because they are religious in the dogmatic sense of the word, but because they touch the deepest and most delicate feelings, and believe that a beauty not a worldly beauty lives in worldly things.[63]

Such assertions appeared frequently in his work up through 1900, when he declared that "most of us who are writing books in Ireland to-day have some kind of a spiritual philosophy." [64]

Of course, folklore played a direct part in only a relatively small portion of this spiritual literature, such as Yeats's "The Valley of the Black Pig":

The dews drop slowly and dreams gather; unknown spears
Suddenly hurtle before my dream-awakened eyes,
And then the clash of fallen horsemen and the cries
Of unknown perishing armies beat about my ears.
We who still labour by the cromlech on the shore,
The grey cairn on the hill, when day sinks drowned in dew,
Being weary of the world's empires, bow down to you,
Master of the still stars and of the flaming door.

The poem had originally been published as one of "Two Poems Concerning Peasant Visionaries" and uses as the vehicle for its vision of imminent apocalypse legends Yeats heard in Sligo of a great battle in that valley in which the enemies of Ireland would be routed.[65] Another example was AE's "The Gates of Dreamland," a poem that had its genesis in a Mayo tale AE heard while traveling for the cooperative movement.[66] But the burden of Yeats's comments is that the positive effects of folklore did not depend entirely upon actual literary use of folk material: the modification of the sensibilities of con-

63. "Three Irish Poets," *Irish Homestead,* December, 1897, p. 7.
64. "The Way of Wisdom," *The Speaker,* April 14, 1900, p. 40.
65. See *VP*, pp. 161, 808–810.
66. See *Letters from AE,* ed. Alan Denson (London, New York, Toronto: Abelard-Schuman, 1961), p. 25, and the detailed discussion in Chapter 4, Part 6, *post.*

temporary Irish writers was perhaps an even more important effect.

In the area of style Yeats's concern arose in part from his perception that the artistic level of Irish literature up to that time had been very rudimentary indeed. In one of his earliest pieces, an 1886 review, he noted "a lack of finish in the style —a besetting sin of the Irish poets," [67] and as the years passed he could generalize with increasing confidence:

We have hitherto been slovens, and even our best writers, if I except Allingham perhaps, have put their best thoughts side by side with the most contemptible commonplaces, and their most musical lines in the midst of the tritest rhythms, and our best prose writers have mingled their own gold dust with every kind of ignoble clay. We have shrunk from the labour that art demands, and have made thereby our best moments of no account.[68]

Moore and the Young Irelanders had been prime offenders, but writers in whom Yeats saw much more merit were also guilty: Ferguson, for example, was often rough and careless in his versification, and William Carleton, not above propaganda and hastily turned out hack-work, had produced a very uneven corpus.[69] Allingham, and to a lesser extent Mangan, had the most consistently competent technique of the earlier writers, and Yeats frequently used them as touchstones in his pronouncements on the need for craftsmanship.

Contact with European literary tradition exposed Yeats to an atmosphere in which artistry was a supreme value, and Sainte-Beuve's *dictum* that only style is immortal came frequently to his mind. He believed that "in this century, he who does not strive to be a perfect craftsman achieves nothing" (*BV*, xxii) and felt that Irish writers could no longer go on in the old, spontaneous, slipshod way, but would have to "add

---

67. "The Poetry of R. D. Joyce," *Irish Fireside,* November 27, 1886, p. 331.

68. "Nationality and Literature," pp. 1–2. See also *LNI*, pp. 129–130.

69. See *Stories from Carleton* (London: Walter Scott, New York and Toronto: W. J. Gage and Co., 1889), p. xv; and "William Carleton," *Scots Observer,* October 19, 1889, pp. 608–609.

art to impulse." Moreover, they needed a "native style," modes of expression that, if not absolutely peculiar to Ireland, would at least be especially suitable for treating the new Irish subjects with which he and others were working. Allingham, de Vere, and Ferguson had begun the search for such a style: they "were all experimenters, trying to find out a literary style that would be polished and yet Irish of the Irish." [70] Their experiments had helped those who came after (including Yeats himself), but there was still much to be done. Yeats traced his own devotion to solving the problem to his early reading of Irish ballad poetry, which he often found moving but knew to be generally very inferior art. He felt that "if somebody could make a style which would not be an English style and yet would be musical and full of colour, many others would catch fire from him, and we would have a really great school of ballad poetry in Ireland." This feeling, coupled with his conviction that the use of subject-matter other than political opinions would make it "easier to get a style," made him "set to work to find a style and things to write about that the ballad-writers might be the better." [71] His concern soon encompassed the whole of current Irish literature, and he pursued the goal diligently.

Perhaps his most extreme conception in this respect was a "native style" in English prose, a peculiarly Irish form of the English language itself.[72] Generally, however, he worked at adapting to Irish needs modes of expression that were not intrinsically the property of any nation. Thus, the method he developed for viably employing the Irish legendary materials had antecedents and parallels in many other literatures.[73] The same was true of the internationally practiced device of literary symbolism. The symbol had particular value, was a virtual

70. "Poems by Miss Tynan," *Evening Herald,* January 2, 1892.

71. *EI,* p. 3. See also *Au,* p. 265: "The difficulties of modern Irish literature, from the loose, romantic, legendary stories of Standish O'Grady to James Joyce and Synge, had been in the formation of a style."

72. See Chapter 4, Part 7, *post.*

73. This subject is discussed in detail in Chapter 5, *post.*

necessity, for those "spiritual" writers whom Yeats saw as so important in shaping the new Irish literature, for it alone had the power to evoke the spiritual world they perceived beyond the ordinary one, to entangle "a part of the Divine Essence." [74] This particular concern called also for poetic rhythms much different from the energetic bombast of Young Ireland, for the "Immortal Moods" are "impatient of rhetoric." [75] He called for "wavering, meditative, organic rhythms" that would liberate the reader's mind from "the pressure of the will" and make him receptive to communication by symbol (*EI*, 163, 159).

Finally, the concern with national drama that culminated in Yeats's role in the founding of the Irish literary theater can be traced back to this period. In one 1889 letter he talked of having *The Countess Cathleen,* which he was writing at the time, acted in Dublin (*Letters,* 114). The next year he expressed the wish that John Todhunter, whose plays were the chief occasions of his early comments on the drama, would try to do an *Irish* play (*LNI*, 106), and before long he was predicting that at the first lull in political excitement Ireland would be "very likely" to have "a fine native drama." [76] Both *The Countess Cathleen* and *The Land of Heart's Desire* were contributions to the development of that drama. In general, however, his essays on national literature during the middle nineties did not mention the theater, and it was only later in the decade that he began to give it significant emphasis. Thus, it was the last mode of expression included in his program of innovative improvement.

74. "Introduction" to W. T. Horton, *A Book of Images* (London: Unicorn Press, 1898), p. 10. See also *Letters,* p. 268; "The New Irish Library," *The Bookman,* June, 1896, p. 83; "The Well at the World's End," *The Bookman,* November, 1896, p. 38; and "Miss Fiona Macleod," *The Sketch,* April 28, 1897, p. 20.

75. "Irish National Literature. Contemporary Prose Writers," *The Bookman,* August, 1895, pp. 138–140.

76. "Plays by an Irish Poet," *United Ireland,* July 11, 1891, p. 5.

2. Contemporary Practice: Yeats's Prose Fiction

The manifestation of Yeats's ideals in his own literary productions could be illustrated with examples chosen from his early poems and the two plays he published during the nineties, and in fact several connections have already been suggested. For extended examination, however, his prose fiction is even more suitable, for it constitutes a body of writing with considerable coherence, exemplifies virtually every facet of the ideals sketched earlier, and is much less well known than his other early work. Furthermore, while it is not of outstanding literary merit, various aspects of it earned the praise of such diverse readers as Edward Garnett, W. E. Henley, Edward Dowden, Lady Wilde, Oscar Wilde, Robert Bridges, George Moore, James Joyce, and AE, which suggests that it perhaps has more worth than is commonly attributed to it today.[1]

With the possible exception of "Michael Clancy . . ." (to

1. Garnett: *Letters,* pp. 65–66; Henley: *Letters,* 187; Dowden: *Letters,* 180; Lady Wilde: *Letters,* 188; Oscar Wilde: *Au,* p. 172; Bridges: Joseph Hone, *W. B. Yeats/1865–1939,* 2nd ed. (London: Macmillan, 1962), p. 136; Moore: Hone, *W. B. Yeats,* p. 135, *Letters,* p. 264; Joyce: Richard Ellmann, *James Joyce* (New York: Oxford University Press, 1959), p. 85, and *Stephen Hero* (London: Jonathan Cape, 1960), p. 183; AE: *Letters from AE,* pp. 18–19.

be discussed later), the story "Dhoya," which Yeats submitted to O'Leary for publication in *The Gael* in December, 1887, is probably his earliest surviving effort at writing fiction. He had done it at the suggestion of his father, but the elder Yeats had had in mind something else entirely—"a story about real people" [2]—and so in early 1888 he began *John Sherman*. Writing this novelette was a challenge, for it meant a radical departure from the type of prose fiction that came most naturally to him. "Dhoya" is, as will be shown, very much in the vein of the group of stories he wrote between 1892 and 1896. *Sherman*, however, deals with "very ordinary persons and events" and is "full of worldly wisdom or what pretends to be such." [3] Understandably he did not at first expect much, hoping merely that the story would be "saleable" (*Letters*, 74), but even at this stage he would not enhance its marketability by compromising his "literary notions of what is good" (*Letters*, 75). The story soon began to go well, but Yeats found it difficult, as he humorously put it, "to keep the characters from turning into eastern symbolic monsters of some sort" (*Letters*, 92). In other words, the impulse expressed in his short stories was impinging upon the prosaicness of *Sherman*.

He completed the first draft by October, 1888, but then he encountered further difficulties. First the concluding section of the story underwent revision, possibly because of suggestions made by Edwin Ellis (*Letters*, 92, 94–95); then in April, 1889, he wrote to Katharine Tynan that "the hero had turned out a bad character" and that consequently he had not tried to get the story published (*Letters*, 123). At this point he was content to see *Sherman* as an "experiment in novel writing" (*Letters*, 123) which had strengthened his writing fluidity and his imagination (*Letters*, 95). More than a year passed before he could inform her that he had "retouched" it and was seeking a publisher.[4] By this time his opinion of its merit had

2. Hone, *W. B. Yeats*, p. 58.

3. *Letters*, pp. 180, 77. See also *Letters*, p. 72: "the style quite sane, and the theme modern."

4. *Letters*, p. 157 (October 6, 1890).

[36]

risen considerably, and he was pleased by Dowden's commendation of it (*Letters*, 174–180).

Yeats himself felt, at least in the early stages of composition, that the construction was "patchy and incoherent." [5] This is not, however, true of the finished story, in which there is a close harmony among setting, structure, and theme. There are five formally divided sections, in which the setting alternates between Ballah (i.e., Sligo) and London. In the first section Sherman decides to leave Ballah, and in the last, after two sojourns in England with a brief trip to Ireland in between, he returns home permanently. Ballah and London represent two ways of life between which Sherman has to choose, and his crossings and recrossings simply dramatize his mental vacillations. His two possible wives, Mary and Margaret, are similarly emblematic. The river in Ballah is even contrasted with the Thames.

In accordance with this construction, plot is primarily important as enactment of choice; there is little dramatic action. This is perhaps what Yeats had in mind when he wrote that reviewers who looked in the book "for the ordinary stuff of novels" would "find nothing" (*Letters*, 174). Twice during the novel's composition he pointed out in letters that character (the ground in which choices are made) was more prominent than plot (*Letters*, 72–73).

In June, 1888, Yeats wrote of his developing story, "There is some good character drawing, I think" (*Letters*, 74), and this claim is generally valid, though one tends to overlook it because Yeats was so seldom centrally concerned with characterization. Of course, as Richard Ellmann has pointed out, Sherman and his friend William Howard can be seen as an early instance of Yeats's use of contrasting *personae* to dramatize opposed elements of his own personality.[6] Yeats himself said of the story in 1891, "There is more of myself in it than in anything I have done" (*Letters*, 165), and even Sherman's eventual

5. *Letters,* p. 74 (June, 1888).
6. *Yeats: The Man and the Masks* (New York: E. P. Dutton, n.d.), pp. 78–79.

hatred for London (which Yeats called the "motif" of the book [7]) can be seen as the young Yeats's own, as a contemporary letter to Katharine Tynan indicates: "When do you come to London? My dislike for the place is certainly not on the decrease. When Blake is done I shall go to Ireland and find my way down to the West and stay there as long as possible." [8] But despite the presence of these personal concerns, the characters are skillful fictional creations.

The most fully rendered figure is Sherman, at one stage of composition a "bad character." How much alteration was required to make him "good" cannot be determined, but in any case the finished product deserves that term. The dominant feature of Sherman's personality is selfishness. Although a grown man, he indulges in a carefree hedonism, refusing to accept any sort of responsibility. His plan is to marry for money to escape the burdens of life; "I wish to be able always to remain a lounger," he admits to Howard.[9] But his personality is complex, and there is a positive side to his desire; it rejects the great bourgeois dream of "getting ahead" in the world. This is represented by his love of Ballah and the quiet provincial way of life. His essential need is to assume adult responsibility without plunging into the fast and vulgar race for mundane success. Thus, going to London is completely wrong for him. There he takes a job with which he has no sympathy in order to begin a career for himself; and he becomes engaged to the wealthy but vulgar Margaret Leland, marriage to whom would enable him to escape financial concerns but force him into a social sphere he dislikes intensely and cut him off completely from the pleasures in which he has always delighted.

At this stage he suddenly discovers that his old friend Mary Carton loves him and that he loves her. When a plan for escaping from the engagement occurs to him, he snatches eagerly at it and successfully carries it out. He then returns to

7. *Letters,* pp. 94–95.   8. *Letters,* p. 166 (March 5, 1891).
9. *John Sherman and Dhoya* (London: T. Fisher Unwin, 1891), p. 12. Subsequent page references to this volume are included in the text.

Ballah and marries Mary. His doing so is no mere relapse into hedonism (though certainly the lure of his old pleasures is instrumental in drawing him back), for in marrying her he is at last assuming responsibility, and he plans to support her by farming (p. 158), the farm representing a significant transformation of the pleasure garden in which he had idled away his time before, and which stood as a symbol of his hedonism. A failure in the worldly sense, Sherman achieves a deeper success, finds and accepts his place in life.

The opposite is true of the High Church clergyman John Howard. He first appears in Ballah, and his detestation of it is elaborately contrasted with Sherman's love for it. Howard is by nature a "man of the world," polished, self-possessed, fit to move in the "finest" circles (p. 126). Marriage to Margaret Leland will give him an entrance into the great world; with her money he might even rise to a bishopric. And yet he will probably be no more happy with her than Sherman would have been: he is too intelligent to remain under the spell of her belladonna-brightened eyes for long. The story is mainly Sherman's, and Yeats does not give Howard's fate full development, but he does clearly suggest it in the scene in which Howard, entering the room on one of his visits to Margaret, suddenly perceives "that her features were quite commonplace" (p. 134). The effect is momentary, but it is surely a portent. Howard will perhaps become a worldly success, but he will not know Sherman's personal happiness and content.

The female characters are naturally more slightly developed, but adequate for Yeats's purposes. The potential spinster Mary Carton's ordinary stance is one of quiet resignation, though in her burning of Sherman's letters there is a hint of the tormented provincial celibate that George Moore would have made of her. The characterization of Margaret Leland is thin but satisfactory, her personality being by nature shallow, and the social comedy arising from Sherman's clever transfer of her "love" from himself to Howard shows that Yeats could be successful in a lighter vein.

While Yeats did manage to keep out the "eastern symbolic

monsters," there are, in addition to the "worldly wisdom" he set out to display, occasional hints of his contemporary preoccupation with less mundane subjects:

It was not merely that saying everything she [Margaret] said nothing, but that continually there came through her wild words the sound of the mysterious flutes and viols of that unconscious nature which dwells so much nearer to woman than to man. How often do we not endow the beautiful and candid with depth and mystery not their own. We do not know that we but hear in their voices those flutes and viols playing to us of the alluring secret of the world [pp. 61–62].

In another passage poetry is defined as "essentially a touch from behind a curtain" (p. 116), and Yeats could not resist making one direct reference to "the mystic Blake" and "the strange and chaotic colours" he "imagined upon the scaled serpent of Eden" (p. 136).

These elements are so unobstrusive that no one could question the national character of *Sherman* on their account. A more challenging objection might be made to the narrow range of society to which he confined himself. But while such common subjects of the Irish novel as the peasantry and the land problem are conspicuously absent, Yeats firmly insisted upon the Irishness of the book; as he wrote to Katharine Tynan:

I have an ambition to be taken as an Irish novelist, not as an English or cosmopolitan one choosing Ireland as a background. I studied my characters in Ireland and described a typical Irish feeling in Sherman's devotion to Ballah. A West of Ireland feeling, I might almost say. . . . I claim for this and other reasons that *Sherman* is as much an Irish novel as anything by Banim or Griffin [*Letters,* 187–188].

Here, then, was another sense in which the story was an experiment, obviously involving the issue of national literature. At the time he was working on *Sherman* he had been reading widely in the Irish novelists for the purpose of prepar-

[40]

ing some anthologies and had detected a decline in nationality in the more recent writers:

The heroines of Carleton or Banim could only have been raised under Irish thatch. One might say the same in less degree of Griffin and Kickham but Kickham is at times, once or twice only, (and merely in his peasant heroines I think) marred by having read Dickens; and Griffin, most facile of all, one feels is Irish on purpose rather than out [of] the necessity of his blood. He could have written like an Englishman had he chosen. But all these writers had a square-built power no later Irishman has approached. Above all Carleton and Banim had it. They saw the whole of everything they looked at, (Carleton and Banim I mean) the brutal with the tender, the coarse with the refined. In Griffin and Kickham the tide began to ebb. . . . It has quite gone out now—our little tide. The writers who make Irish stories sail the sea of common English fiction. It pleases them to hoist Irish colours—and that is well. The Irish manner has gone out of them though. Like common English fiction they want too much to make pleasant tales—and that's not at all well. The old men tried to make one see life plainly but all written down in a kind of fiery shorthand that it might never be forgotten.[10]

Yeats obviously had no pretension of recapturing the power of the earlier writers, but he hoped to regain something of their attitude and approach.

Like *John Sherman*, "Dhoya" is set in the Sligo area and embodies in its title character certain of the author's own feelings.[11] Beyond this, however, the two works have little in common. The time of the action in *Sherman* is contemporary, whereas "Dhoya" takes place in ancient times, before the building of the pyramids. Dhoya has been a captive of the Fomorians, one of the pre-Milesian races according to mythical accounts of the settling of Ireland. In accordance with such a setting, the story is pervaded by a misty, twilight atmosphere not found in *Sherman*. In *Sherman* Yeats had focused upon

10. *Letters*, p. 143 (December, 1889).
11. See Ellmann, *Yeats: The Man and the Masks*, p. 78.

[41]

only a small segment of the social spectrum, but in "Dhoya" there is *no* concern with society as such. In fact, isolation is a central theme of the story, and Dhoya, abandoned by his captors in a strange and desolate region, is the first of those outcasts so common in the later stories. Naturally the whole fabric of "Dhoya" is alien to "worldly wisdom." Instead Yeats gave his spiritual interests a free rein. The love affair between human and immortal is one of those confrontations of the ordinary world with the realm beyond which interested Yeats all his life and again anticipates the *Secret Rose* stories. Other typically Yeatsian motifs are Dhoya's raging at his own shadow and worshipping the moon, and the association of dancing with the immortal world. It is interesting that this story, with so many of the characteristic features of Yeats's prose of the nineties, seems to owe little or nothing to other fiction. O'Grady's *Finn and His Companions,* a work highly praised by Yeats, reminds one in places of his own stories, but it was not published until 1892, more than four years after "Dhoya" had been written.[12]

In September of 1891, Yeats brought "Dhoya" to the attention of W. E. Henley, editor of the *National Observer*. Later in the same year he wrote to O'Leary that the paper had asked him for similar stories, and that he would try to provide them but doubted his ability to make them short enough (*Letters,* 179, 185). Almost a year passed before he mentioned having completed a story, "The Devil's Book," published in *The National Observer,* November 26, 1892 (*Letters,* 221). The next month a second story appeared, "The Twisting of the Rope." Both of these dealt with Owen Roe O'Sullivan, or Red Hanrahan as he is called in *The Secret Rose*. In the dedication to *The Secret Rose,* Yeats said that the individual stories had not been written in accordance with any over-all plan, and even though the continuity between the two stories suggests that he had at least some sort of cumulative effect in

12. See *LNI,* p. 158 for an 1892 reference by Yeats to *Finn and his Companions* and to O'Grady's other stories.

mind from the first, there is evidence that whatever plan he may have had underwent important modifications.

The first two stories were followed by several similar to them in type but not concerned with O'Sullivan. Despite their close resemblance, Yeats may not have planned originally to combine the two groups, for in a November, 1893 interview he referred to the projected volume, already called *The Secret Rose,* as "a collection of weird stories about the middle ages in Ireland": [13] the O'Sullivan stories would seem to be excluded by their eighteenth-century setting. His next reference to a collected volume came in January, 1896, when he announced, "My new book *The Secret Rose* is nearly finished and will be out about June I imagine or perhaps earlier" (*Letters,* 260). By this time eleven stories, including four on O'Sullivan, had appeared in periodicals, and the number of additional stories published during 1896 suggests that several of these had already been written; [14] presumably the two groups had by now fused in Yeats's mind: otherwise he would probably have been referring to a separate volume for the O'Sullivan stories. In spite of Yeats's optimism, the appearance of the collection was delayed for fifteen months, owing in part to very extensive revisions of the page proofs.[15] When finally published, it contained seventeen stories.

The period of composition coincided with Yeats's growing concern with the spiritual, a concern naturally reflected in the stories. In 1895 he had written to Olivia Shakespear, "I am now trying to do some wild Irish stories which shall not be mere phantasies but the signatures—I use a medium's term —of things invisible and ideas" (*Letters,* 255). In his dedica-

13. Katharine Tynan, "An Interview with W. B. Yeats," *The Sketch,* November, 1893, pp. 83–84.

14. This figure does not include "Michael Clancy, the Great Dhoul, and Death," published in December, 1893, but excluded from *The Secret Rose.*

15. See *Letters,* pp. 268, 280, 282; and Curtis Bradford, *Yeats at Work* (Carbondale and Edwardsville, Illinois: Southern Illinois University Press, 1965), pp. 320–321.

tion to the collected volume he asserted that the stories he had brought together had a common theme: "the war of spiritual with natural order." Yeats's progressive devaluation of the concrete world of science and common sense, which reached its culmination in the late nineties, is perhaps reflected in the introduction of the concept of *tension,* rather than mere correspondence, between the two realms. One of the two epigraphs of the book is "As for living, our servants will do that for us"; this famous sentence from *Axël*, spoken as the lovers decide to commit suicide in order to preserve their love from mundane profanation, epitomizes the opposition in its extreme form.[16] In the stories themselves that opposition manifests itself in a variety of ways.

In "The Wisdom of the King" the monarch's other-worldly knowledge, which includes the Yeatsian occult concerns of reincarnation and the Moods, is not merely useless but positively harmful when applied to purely worldly affairs; those to whom he imparts it live "worse" lives than before. Furthermore, it renders *him* completely unfit to remain in the world. In "Out of the Rose" a knight, warned by a Divine Voice that men "would turn from the light of their own hearts, and bow down before external order and fixity," [17] gathers a band of his fellows to oppose the triumph of that order and its values throughout the world. Hanrahan, because he rejects the love of an immortal, is doomed never to find happiness with a mortal woman. "The Rose of Shadow" shows the opposition in its most terrifying form: a girl's ghostly lover destroys the rest of her family so they cannot prevent her from coming to him. In story after story the supernatural intrudes into the sphere of ordinary existence; the widely varied ghostly population includes a severed head that sings, the "washer at

16. The other epigraph, a passage from Leonardo da Vinci concerning Helen of Troy in old age, suggests lost beauty, decrepitude, perhaps a mood of *fin de siècle.*

17. *The Secret Rose* (London: Lawrence and Bullen, 1897), p. 63.

the ford" of Celtic legend, a fairy piper, a *leannan sidhe* (a fairy mistress and muse), the spirit of Dervorgilla, a man turned by enchantment into a heron, a spirit embodied in a hideous old beggar-woman, and another in the form of a beautiful woman with hair full of black lilies. Visions are frequent, and a miracle occurs in "Where There Is Nothing, There Is God."

Because society is in general associated with the realm of natural order, it is not surprising that many of the central characters in these stories are set apart from their kind. The old man in "The Heart of the Spring" and the king in "The Wisdom of the King" are self-exiles, one that he may discover occult mysteries, the other because he has found them. The knight in "Out of the Rose" has become a lone wanderer. In "Where There Is Nothing . . ." the central figure is a beggar-saint who seeks obscurity in order to be closer to his God. The visionary occultist Robartes has withdrawn from the world. According to the prophecy in "Out of the Rose," the "passionate wicked man" might, because of his refusal to think conventionally, escape the taint of worldliness. Costello the Proud is of this type. So is Hanrahan, who is poet, visionary, and self-exile as well: AE wrote to Yeats that he had unveiled "beneath excess and passion a love for spiritual beauty expressing itself pathetically in the life of this wayward outcast." [18] The gleeman in "The Crucifixion of the Outcast" is similar. (The title of this story was originally "A Crucifixion"; Yeats's alteration added emphasis to the "outcast" theme.) All three encounter the violent hostility of ordinary men in incidents recalling the experience of Christ, Himself the archetypal victim of the opposition of the external to the spiritual order: Costello is stoned and falls with his arms flung out "as though he lay upon a rood"; [19] Hanrahan is beaten and driven from a village; the outcast is crucified and left to the wild

18. *Letters from AE,* pp. 18–19.
19. *The Secret Rose,* pp. 12–13.

animals. The beggars who have gathered to watch his fate refuse to protect him, and his last words are "Outcasts, . . . have you also turned against the outcasts?" [20]

In this latter story the Catholic Church is clearly the embodiment of external and material values. The same is true in the Hanrahan stories (he is preached against from the altar), and in "Rosa Alchemica," where pious peasants destroy the Temple of the Alchemical Rose. On the other hand, in "Where There Is Nothing . . ." the image of the Church is positive, and the figure of Saint Patrick in "The Old Men of the Twilight" is noble and impressive. When in "The Curse of the Fires and of the Shadows" Catholic priests are massacred and their church destroyed by Puritans, the priests are promptly avenged by the *sidhe*. And in one case the attitude toward the Church is ambiguous. "The Heart of the Spring" tells of Angus MacForbis, an extremely old man who has spent most of his mature years seeking "the secret of life." He has read in an obscure manuscript that there is a moment between the sun's entrance into the Ram (March 21) and its emergence from the Lion (August 22) that "trembles with the song of the Immortal Powers, and that whosoever finds this moment and listens to the Song shall become like the Immortal Powers themselves." After years of studying occultism and magic, he has at last learned from one of the fairies the exact time when the song can be heard. The story begins on the eve of that moment, and MacForbis is making preparations. He tells Maurteen, his young servant, the meaning of his abstruse researches and then sends him to procure the rushes and flowers necessary for the coming rite. When the lad seeks out his master the next morning—a morning of extreme beauty, in which birds are singing and one can hear "the spring's heart beating"—he finds him dead at his worktable, a staff and

20. *Ibid.*, p. 52. Cf. Yeats's praise, in "A New Poet," *The Bookman,* September, 1892, p. 180, of Edwin Ellis' poems "Outcast" and "Himself" (about Christ as outcast).

wallet by his side. Maurteen, a pious Catholic very frightened of the "pagan" spirits with whom his master dealt, says, "It were better for him . . . to have told his beads and said his prayers like another, and not to have spent his days in seeking among the Immortal Powers for what he could have found in his own deeds and days had he willed. Ah, yes, it were better to have said his prayers and kissed his beads!" Just then on one of the boughs piled against the window a thrush begins to sing.

How one evaluates the treatment of the Church in this story depends upon one's interpretation of what happened to the old man. He had expected some physical journey to follow his discovery and to become young once more. Does the disappointment of these expectations mean that the story is ironic, the old man's hopes false? This would make the youth's moral valid and the thrush's song an ironic contrast to the song the old man had expected to hear. Or is the bird's song indeed that for which he was waiting, and the irony in his having died just before the moment came? Yet another possibility is that the earlier moment at which the birds were singing and the spring's heart could be heard beating was the moment, and the old man's soul, freed into immortality, took the form of the thrush. Elsewhere in Yeats's work the bird is thus associated with the soul, "Sailing to Byzantium" being of course the most famous example.[21] It is noteworthy that in early drafts of that poem an old man of intellectual nature is contrasted with youth in both the Christian form of the infant Jesus and that of the immortal *sidhe*, who have lived for centuries but never age. If this latter interpretation of "The

21. See *LNI*, pp. 169–171, where Yeats in 1888 quotes an Allingham poem about an abbot of Inisfalen whose soul went into the body of a bird; and "The Message of the Folk-lorist" (*The Speaker*, August 19, 1893, p. 189), where he discusses an incident in "The Voyage of Maeldune" involving birds embodying the souls of a saint's relations, and states, "Folk-lore makes the souls of the blessed take upon themselves every evening the shape of white birds."

Heart of the Spring" is valid, then it is not the old man's studies but the orthodox pieties of Maurteen which become ironic.

External information provides a rationale for the contrasting images of Catholicism presented in *The Secret Rose*. In reply to a contemporary reviewer who criticized his treatment of the Church in "The Crucifixion of the Outcast," Yeats attempted to justify his "inconsistency" with the historical argument that there had been a period of decadence in the Irish Church in the late Middle Ages. But he admitted that historical accuracy was not his concern, and his further statement that the negative treatment of the Church in that story had been necessitated by "the symbolism which is the heart of my story" makes it clear that he did not bring Catholicism into the *Secret Rose* stories to evaluate its specific merits and faults, but rather as an instrument for expressing his central theme (*Letters*, 285).

The Rose symbol, so prominent in Yeats's poetry of these years, is another device for expressing that theme, a theme that, as has been suggested, practically demanded symbolism for its full articulation. While the rich associations of the Rose include human passion, it is used in *The Secret Rose* almost exclusively in connection with the spiritual order. In "Out of the Rose" the voice of God issues from "a great Rose of Fire," and the gleeman in "The Crucifixion of the Outcast" hears in his heart "the rustling of the rose-bordered dress" of Eternal Beauty. (Compare the reference to "the red-rose bordered hem / Of her, whose history began / Before God made the angelic clan" in the nearly contemporary "Apologia addressed to Ireland in the coming days.") Hanrahan casts rose petals into the air and sees them turn into spirits, and in "Rosa Alchemica" the petals of the mosaic rose on the ceiling of the temple serve as vehicles for the appearance of The Immortals. The Rose had entered Yeats's fiction in "The Twisting of the Rope," the second story to be published, but only emerged as a central symbol in 1894, with the appearance of "Out of the Rose." In preparing the collected volume, Yeats further increased its prominence: in addition to using it in his title and in the elaborate cover design, and including the poem "To the Secret Rose," he added it to "The Book of the Great Dhoul and Hanrahan the Red," in association with the spirit Cleona, and changed the title of "Those Who Live in the Storm" to "The Rose of Shadow." Appearing from the beginning of the volume to the end, the motif helps bind the stories together and accumulates additional richness of meaning with each repetition.

Yeats decided to arrange his stories in chronological order of the action. The seventeen stories span a period from the earliest times to the period at which Yeats was writing, with most of the important periods in between represented:

1. "The Binding of the Hair"—ancient period
2. "The Wisdom of the King"—ancient period
3. "Where There Is Nothing, There Is God"—late eighth century
4. "The Crucifixion of the Outcast"—approximately eleventh century?
5. "Out of the Rose"—fourteenth century
6. "The Curse of the Fires and of the Shadows"—1642
7. "The Heart of the Spring"—seventeenth century
8. "Of Costello the Proud, of Oona the Daughter of Dermott and of the Bitter Tongue"—reign of Charles II
9-14. The Hanrahan group—begins around the middle of the eighteenth century
15. "The Rose of Shadow"—1765
16. "The Old Men of the Twilight"—eighteenth century
17. "Rosa Alchemica"—contemporary [22]

22. "Where There Is Nothing" is datable by the approximate time of Saint Óengus' residence at Tallaght; an eleventh century date for "The Crucifixion of the Outcast" is suggested by Yeats in a note to the periodical version of the story, *National Observer*, March 24, 1894, p. 481; see also *Aislinge Meic Conglinne/The Vision of Mac Conglinne*, ed. and trans. Kuno Meyer (London: David Nutt, 1892), p. x; Sir Frederick Hamilton's military activities in Sligo, which form part of

Such an arrangement has thematic significance, for it gives historical perspective to the war between spiritual and natural order, illustrates its persistence through the centuries of Irish civilization.

It should be clear from the discussion to this point that, considering its irregular manner of evolution, *The Secret Rose* is a remarkably well-unified collection. The presence of the dominant theme and the recurrence of the Rose symbol help create that unity, as does the repetition of certain types of character and patterns of action. For example, in addition to the many outcasts, exiles, visionaries, and supernatural beings, one character frequently relates to another information the latter cannot comprehend: the fool in "Out of the Rose" is unable to grasp the knight's story of his order and his mission; the old voteen in "The Old Men of the Twilight" is an unsympathetic listener to the ancient pedant's explanation of his state; the king in "The Wisdom of the King" vainly pours out his knowledge for a woman whose mind is on sensual pleasure; and the narrator of "Rosa Alchemica" intentionally draws back from the occult truths of which Robartes has given him a glimpse. Yet another contribution to unity is the consistency of atmosphere and tone. Although Yeats used precise geographical details in his settings, the stories all have a vague, romantic, twilight aura, and an appropriate seriousness is maintained throughout. The conscious nature of this effect is attested to by Yeats's elimination of all humor in transforming his highly comical source for "The Crucifixion of the Outcast."

It is possible to talk about *John Sherman* in terms of characterization and plot, but with the possible exception of the character of Hanrahan, those categories are not really applicable to these stories. Symbol and motif are far more im-

"The Curse of the Fires . . . ," took place in 1642; the suggested date of "Of Costello the Proud . . ." is that of the story's source, Douglas Hyde, *Love Songs of Connacht* (London: T. Fisher Unwin, and Dublin: Gill and Son, 1893), p. 47.

portant, and such excellence as the stories have lies primarily in imaginativeness of conception, strength of effect, and richness of implication.

In revising the stories for volume publication, Yeats made very few important alterations in character and incident. The most radical change was in his portrait of Cleona, or Cleena, Hanrahan's fairy mistress, in "The Book of the Great Dhoul and Hanrahan the Red." In "The Devil's Book," the original version (and the first of the stories to be published), when O'Sullivan rejects her she reacts like a mistreated wife pleading with a bad husband:

"Do not drive me away, Owen: becaze o' ye I left all my own people weepin' for me. Owen, I have always been good to yer family, and did me best to keep the good luck among ye. And ye were the hard family to help and I done it, Owen O'Sullivan."

"Begone from me," he cried, and strode out into the darkness.[23]

In *The Secret Rose,* when Hanrahan starts to leave, Cleena, instead of hurling herself upon the floor in despair as her predecessor may be imagined to have done, strikes back powerfully:

But now she too was angry, and he heard her voice, musical even in anger, and her words staid [sic] long in his ears:

"Owen Hanrahan the Red, you have looked so often upon the dust that when the Rose has blossomed there you think it but a pinch of coloured dust; but now I lay upon you a curse, and you shall see the Rose everywhere, in the noggin, in woman's eye, in drifting phantoms, and seek to come to it in vain; it shall waken a fire in your heart, and in your feet, and in your hands. A sorrow of all sorrows is upon you, Owen Hanrahan the Red." [24]

The whining, pathetic creature of the original version has been transformed into a being of strength and majesty.

Alterations of incident are found in "The Rose of Shadow" (originally "Those Who Live in the Storm"), a story of 1894,

23. "The Devil's Book," *National Observer,* November, 1892, pp. 40–41.

24. *The Secret Rose,* p. 139.

and in "Rosa Alchemica," published first in 1896. In the periodical version of the former story, the roof of the Hearnes' cottage was broken open and the dead lover appeared in the opening amid a mass of flames; then

the rest of the roof rolled up and then fell inward with a crash, and the storm rushed through the house.

* * * * *

The next day the neighbours found the dead in the ruined house, and buried them in the barony of Amharlish, and set over them a tombstone to say they were killed by the great storm of October, 1765.[25]

In *The Secret Rose* this passage has been entirely eliminated, and the story ends with the lover's appearance. The alteration was clearly not for the purpose of obscuring the date of the action, for Yeats placed the story in the appropriate chronological order. And it is clear from an immediately preceding passage (found in both versions) that the father, mother, and brother are going to die, so that Yeats's alteration does not change the incident itself, but rather the way it is presented. Ominousness and implication replace precise detail and the slight irony of the mistaken attribution of the cause of death. As published in *The Savoy*, "Rosa Alchemica" had begun with a paragraph telling of the "death" of Robartes and his associates at the hands of Connemara religious fanatics. For *The Secret Rose* this passage was omitted, and the peasants' attack on the temple and the narrator's flight are dramatized rather than merely related. While this alteration increases the story's vividness, Yeats's central motive was probably a desire to make more prominent the opposition between the orthodox religion and the occult Order of the Alchemical Rose.[26]

25. *The Speaker*, July 21, 1894, p. 75.
26. There were other interesting revisions in "Rosa Alchemica." An important passage on the Moods (*Savoy*, April, 1897, pp. 66–67) was not printed in the *Secret Rose* version. In *The Secret Rose* (pp. 230–231) Robartes burns a rare incense which apparently helps induce the nar-

There are literally hundreds of verbal differences between the periodical versions of the various stories and the *Secret Rose* text, most of them, according to Curtis Bradford, introduced in the page proof stage.[27] The number of revisions *per* story is independent of the date of periodical publication with one exception: "The Devil's Book," the first published, had been highly experimental; Yeats had recognized its faults almost at once and avoided them in subsequent stories. Thus, for example, the unfortunate attempt at peasant brogue was not repeated in the second story, "The Twisting of the Rope." He wanted a peculiarly Irish medium, but saw that he had not the requisite sensitivity to peasant turns of speech. In 1904, when he had Lady Gregory to do the language for him, he achieved his goal in regard to the Hanrahan stories. But "The Devil's Book," which he had already had to revise heavily for *The Secret Rose,* was in the new recasting entirely omitted. Beyond this the revisions reveal no chronological pattern: the late stories "Wisdom" ("The Wisdom of the King"), "The Binding of the Hair," and "Rosa Alchemica" required more alteration than "A Crucifixion" ("The Crucifixion of the Outcast"), while another late story, "Where There Is Nothing . . . ," needed only minor changes.

As Professor Bradford points out, many of these changes were intended to produce a more direct style,[28] and many others were required by Yeats's decision to replace Irish place-names and expressions with English equivalents (for example, "Lugnagall" becomes "the Steep Place of the Strangers," and "poteen," "the Brew of the Little Pot"). Yeats was not trying to make the book less "Irish" by these revisions: his meticulous concern with tieing each story to specific topographical landmarks reveals, if anything, an opposite intention. Probably his goal was rather uniformity of language. But his principle of transliteration is based on the erroneous assumption that one

---

rator's ensuing vision. And Bradford (*Yeats at Work,* p. 324) prints a manuscript passage not used in any printed version.

27. *Yeats at Work,* pp. 320–321.   28. *Ibid.,* p. 321.

is ordinarily aware of the etymological sense of place-names and other such terms, and the result is that his English equivalents call too much attention to themselves and sometimes, as in the case of "the Brew of the Little Pot," are positively ludicrous.

Other motives for revision include modification of sentence rhythm, altered in many places by changes in word order and punctuation, and elaboration of atmosphere. Thus, to a reference in "The Devil's Book" to the "paganism" of the Fianna, Yeats adds a brief list of their deities: "Dana and Angus and the Dagda and Lir and Mannanan [sic], and them that were in the sun, and them that were in the moon." [29] In combination with similar references in several other stories, such a passage contributes to the dominant "Celtic twilight" aura of the book. In fiction as well as poetry Yeats was an indefatigable critic of his own work, and the total effect of his revisions of texture in *The Secret Rose* is a great stylistic improvement.

Unlike traditional Irish fiction, the stories in *The Secret Rose* are not centrally concerned with ordinary human intercourse (for example, the few times the family unit appears it is in the process of being violently broken up: "Of Costello the Proud . . . ," "The Rose of Shadow") or, as Yeats himself granted in his dedication, with "national" subjects such as political problems and major public events. And yet he insisted, as he had done with *Sherman,* upon the Irishness of the collection. In the dedication he asserted, "So far . . . as this book is visionary it is Irish," and in a letter to O'Leary he termed it an attempt at an "aristocratic esoteric Irish literature." [30] He might also have pointed in justification to the close integration of the action with the topography of the country, the wide range of periods in which the stories are set, and especially the extensive use of materials drawn from Irish myth, folklore, and history. For instance, "The Wisdom of the King" combines elements of the legend of King Fergus MacLeide (Fergus Wry-Mouth) with the folk story of the

29. *The Secret Rose*, p. 124.   30. *Letters*, p. 286 (May 30, 1897).

"Horned Women." "The Crucifixion of the Outcast" is based upon a late medieval literary text. In "Where There Is Nothing, There Is God," Yeats superimposed an idea from Madame Blavatsky upon a life of the early Irish saint Óengus "the Culdee" (God-lover). An actual historical incident—a military expedition in Sligo during the seventeenth century—provided the vehicle for the action in "The Curse of the Fires and of the Shadows," which also makes use of fairy lore and of the legendary figure of the ghostly "washer at the ford" whom Yeats found in Ferguson's long poem Congal.[31] For the story of "Proud Costello" Yeats was indebted to the contemporary publication of Hyde's Love Songs of Connacht.[32] Even stray details from Irish sources made their contribution: the folk conception of purgatorial punishment in which spirits were imagined as being spitted upon the points of trees and rocks, a conception Yeats used in "The Curse of the Fires and of the Shadows" and "Those Who Live in the Storm," had been picked up from a book of folklore he had reviewed some years earlier.[33]

Hanrahan's character is based on that of a real person, Owen Roe O'Sullivan (Eoghan Ruadh Ó'Suileabháin), one of the last of the great Irish-language poets, who lived from 1748 to 1784. He led an itinerant, often dissipated life but is not known to have possessed the visionary powers with which Yeats endowed Hanrahan. In fact, though Yeats at first adopted the name of his model and directly acknowledged (in a note to "The Devil's Book") his use of a historical figure, his character increasingly assumed an individual personality, and when the stories were published in book form he symbolically dissociated him from the real poet by changing his name to Owen Hanrahan the Red. The metamorphosis came to seem so complete to Yeats

31. Congal (Dublin: Edward Ponsonby, and London: Bell and Daldy, 1872), pp. 57–58.

32. Love Songs of Connacht, pp. 46–59.

33. "Irish Wonders," Scots Observer, March 30, 1889, p. 530. Yeats used it again later in The Dreaming of the Bones (Var. Plays, p. 766).

that years later, in "The Tower," he would boast, "I myself created Hanrahan." These examples show Yeats drawing upon a rich and varied body of sources and testing their literary potential. As Chapter 5 will illustrate in more detail, he was also using the method he had devised for giving viability to such materials.

In addition to the stories collected in *The Secret Rose,* Yeats wrote during this period four other stories. According to Allan Wade, one of them, "The Adoration of the Magi," was originally to have been included in *The Secret Rose,* but the publisher, Bullen, suddenly became afraid to include it, presumably because one of the central characters is a harlot who is paralleled with the Virgin Mary, and part of the action takes place in a French brothel (*Letters,* 280). It was published privately along with another story, "The Tables of the Law," which, since it has the same narrator as "Rosa Alchemica" and "The Adoration of the Magi" and similar subject-matter, was apparently also at one time intended for the collected volume. The time in both is contemporary, so that in their natural position following "Rosa Alchemica" there would have been no violation of chronological order.

The central figures in these stories, like those in *The Secret Rose,* are outside of conventional society. Owen Aherne is a wanderer and then a self-exile, and "The Adoration of the Magi" focuses upon a prostitute. A passage in the latter story explains the significance of such figures:

When people are good the world likes them and takes possession of them, and so eternity comes through people who are not good or who have been forgotten. Perhaps Christianity was good and the world liked it, so now it is going away and the immortals are beginning to awake.[34]

Here the positions of the outcast and of Christianity are aligned with spiritual and natural order, respectively. In "The

34. *The Tables of the Law/The Adoration of the Magi* (privately printed, 1897), pp. 44–45. Cf. also *Explor,* pp. 392–393.

Adoration of the Magi" the Christian dispensation is seen as about to yield to a return of an older one; "The Tables of the Law" reveals the potential painfulness for individuals of the transition. Aherne's suffering results from his having gained occult spiritual knowledge without having entirely freed himself of his original orthodox beliefs. Thus he is tormented by the thought that his new knowledge has made it impossible for him to sin, so that he is no longer "among those for whom Christ died." [35] In revising this story Yeats greatly expanded his revelation of Aherne's malady and also added an intrusion of the supernatural in the form of a vision of spirits experienced by the narrator. Such an intrusion occurs also in "The Adoration of the Magi," when the spirit of Hermes possesses the body of one of the old men. There was no periodical version of "The Adoration of the Magi," but "The Tables of the Law," which had appeared in *The Savoy* in November, 1896, underwent revisions as great as those in "The Devil's Book."

The other two stories not included in *The Secret Rose* were "Michael Clancy, the Great Dhoul, and Death" and "The Cradles of Gold." The former was published in December, 1893, but was probably written much earlier. In a letter Yeats revealed that he had heard the tale upon which it was based when he was about eighteen and had soon afterwards attempted to develop it into a long satirical poem. Discouraged by the work required and the number of enemies such a work might make for him, he turned the legend into a prose story.[36] This would seem to point to a date in the late eighties. It is noteworthy also that the story attempts to reproduce peasant brogue; as Yeats had used it in the first of the O'Sullivan stories to be written, but not in the second (published only a month later) or subsequent ones, it seems unlikely that the composition of "Michael Clancy" postdated that of "The Devil's Book." The story is set in Sligo and contains the intrusion of the supernatural typical of Yeats's stories, but it is

35. *Tables of the Law,* p. 28.
36. *Letters,* p. 307 (Christmas, 1898).

comic in tone and, as Yeats himself admitted in the same letter, little more than a trifle, so it is no surprise that it was excluded from *The Secret Rose.*

With "The Cradles of Gold," however, the reason for omission is not so clear. It was published very late, in November, 1896, and there are no internal or external indications of an early date of composition. It too is set in the Sligo area and is concerned with a struggle between mortals and the fairies, so that it harmonizes with the central theme of the collected volume. Its tone and atmosphere are similarly appropriate. It does not seem inferior in quality to some of the stories in *The Secret Rose,* but evidently Yeats felt differently. Another possibility is that inclusion was prevented by some technical publishing difficulty.

Yeats wrote one other piece of fiction during these years, the unfinished novel "The Speckled Bird." He probably began work on it in 1896, evidently had trouble from the start, and abandoned it around 1900 because (according to the account given in "The Stirring of the Bones") he was unable to achieve a satisfactory ordering of his materials (*Au,* 152). In genre it is related to the *bildungsroman,* reminiscent of Balzac's philosophical novel *Louis Lambert* (a long-time Yeatsian favorite) and anticipating Joyce's *Portrait of the Artist.* It is particularly interesting in relation to Yeats's own earlier fiction because it represents a compromise between the modes of *John Sherman* and *The Secret Rose.*

The earlier novel's concern with character is there: Yeats even wrote to Lady Gregory, at a time when the book was going well, "For the first time it is real novel writing and not essay writing or lyrical prose or speculative thought merely. It is now characterization and conversation" (*Letters,* 345). The conventional social elements are more numerous, embracing a wider range of social strata and involving such subjects as land agitation, emigration, the life of the Irish gentry in the eighteenth century, and a royal visit. In several scenes there are many characters on stage at once, and a comic element is interjected in the portraits of some of the minor figures.

On the other hand, Yeats's interest in folklore had received an added stimulus from his new friend Lady Gregory, and the book is full of folk elements, including a "folk" poem she translated for him.[37] Her influence is also felt in some "Irish" turns in the language of the peasant characters. Moreover, Michael Hearne, the central character, is, unlike Sherman, a visionary of the sort common in *The Secret Rose;* he moves in a sphere in which the occult and the supernatural are common. Thus, Yeats wrote late in 1896 that the book was to be among other things his "first study of the Irish Fairy Kingdom and the mystical faith of that time" before he returned to "more earthly things"; and he went on to observe that "there are certain preliminary studies in my new book *The Secret Rose*" (*Letters,* 268).

Michael endeavors, as Yeats himself was doing, to found a new spiritual cult, and his heterodoxy is opposed by various Catholic priests and by the religious orthodoxy of the girl he loves, another pattern often found in the stories. Furthermore, as indicated by the title—an allusion to the biblical "Mine heritage is unto me as a speckled bird: the birds round about are against her" (Jeremiah 12:9)—Michael is another of those "men apart" so common in the stories, separated from others by his higher vision. The language of the novel, so prosaic in the social scenes, often breaks into lyricism in passages involving Michael's visionary experiences and plans. Perhaps this attempt to unite his two previous approaches to fiction was an underlying cause of the difficulty Yeats experienced in writing the book. The excitement of participating in the founding of the drama movement also must have influenced his decision to abandon the novel.

In doing so he was in fact abandoning fiction, with the exception of a new first story for his revised version of the

37. The poem was later published in her *Poets and Dreamers* (London: John Murray, 1903), pp. 52–53.

Hanrahan group. Most of the material in his prose fiction reappears in his later work but embodied in poetry and drama: the queen and the severed head of "The Binding of the Hair," the old man and singing bird of "The Heart of the Spring," the "Magi" theme, and Robartes and Aherne are only a few of the more memorable examples. In a revealing comment Yeats himself pointed out another such connection, saying he had "planned out *The Unicorn* [*from the Stars*] to carry to a more complete realization the central idea of the stories in *The Secret Rose*" (*Letters*, 503). In the last analysis, fiction could serve him as proving ground but not as final form.

3. Propagandizing

Yeats was not content with merely letting his creative productions serve as *exempla* of the literary ideals he held in the 1880's and 1890's: he worked actively to transmit his ideals to others. He took this role quite seriously; in a letter of 1889 urging Katharine Tynan to confine her journalistic writing to *Irish* subjects, he said, "Much may depend in the future on Ireland now developing writers who know how to formulate in clear expressions the vague feelings now abroad—to formulate them for Ireland's, not for England's, use" (*Letters*, 138–139). And this commitment in turn made an important contribution to his own further development. It is still a commonly held belief that until he became involved with the drama movement, with "theatre business, management of men," he was an ineffectual romantic dreamer incapable of dealing with the workaday world: in fact, his emergence from the "Celtic twilight" into the harsher light of common day began during this earlier period, precipitated to a very great extent by his propagandizing and the controversies it stimulated; and even in these early activities he showed remarkable capability and toughness. He was later to observe, "We make out of the quarrel with others, rhetoric, but of the quarrel with ourselves, poetry," [1] yet in his own case the former sort

1. *Per Amica Silentia Lunae,* in *Mythologies* (New York: Macmillan, 1959), p. 331.

of quarrels definitely had a positive side: they helped create a literary movement and also formed an essential part of his personal maturation.

His literary propaganda had three distinct targets: the little group of Irish writers already at work, potential Irish writers, and the audience or potential audience for Irish literature—and he used extremely diverse methods to reach those targets.

At the most direct and immediate level Yeats exerted a strong personal influence. Often he simply lent books (as O'Leary had done for *him* at the beginning of *his* literary career). Thus, Yeats wrote in an 1895 letter, in regard to Eva Gore-Booth, that he was "always ransacking Ireland for people to set writing at Irish things. She does not know that she is the last victim—but is deep in some books of Irish legends I sent her and may take fire" (*Letters,* 256–257). While obviously trying to steer her towards Irish subjects, he was careful to avoid inculcating provinciality, and added that she would have to turn to English tradition in order to learn "a proper respect for craftsmanship." A second letter from this period, written to Katharine Tynan, shows Yeats acting as a one-man lending library and not hesitating to lend books that he himself, too poor to buy them, had borrowed:

Every new Irish writer will increase the public for every other Irish writer. Your copy of Miss Hopper is at this moment crusading at Lady Gore-Booth's and the whole family have taken to Irish things. They are now busy with O'Grady, and were a little while ago on the hunt for folklore among their tenants. *Maelcho,* despite my promise to return it at once, has only just returned from another Unionist household where it has carried on a not less efficacious evangel. They have got from me *The Wanderings of Cuculain* [O'Grady's *The Coming of Cuculain*]. A copy of Russell [*Homeward*] is also on the wander and one of the Gore-Booths has taken to your section of *A Book of Irish Verse* [edited by Yeats] and has asked many questions about you. These people are much better educated than our own people, and have a better instinct for excellence [*Letters,* 254].

This passage offers a perfect example of Yeats's propagandizing for his ideals and for those of his contemporaries who were already following them. O'Grady's works retold the Irish myths; Nora Hopper's *Ballads in Prose* drew upon myth and folklore; *Maelcho,* by Emily Lawless, was a historical tale of Elizabethan Ireland; Katharine Tynan wrote poetry on Catholic themes and used folk elements; and the spiritual constitutes the sole theme of AE's *Homeward.* Furthermore, none of these works were militantly Nationalistic—O'Grady and Lawless were themselves Unionists—and thus in attempting to develop an Irish reading public, Yeats could seek to transcend the bounds of parties and even welcome the Unionists as being more sensitive to "excellence" than the average Nationalist.

Correspondence was a second personal way in which Yeats exerted influence. As early as 1887 he made some "suggested emendations in the rhythm" of a poem by Hester Sigerson that was to be included in *Poems and Ballads of Young Ireland* (*Letters,* 43). By 1889 he was receiving for his criticism poems from writers he did not even know. His letter to the first such writer, Elizabeth White (sister of H. O. White, a professor at Trinity College), has fortunately survived:

The poems seem to me musical and pleasant. There are some really poetic phrases such as "breathing light" in the blank verse lines, and what the "Merrow" says about "The landfields, dark and still," and that other line about the sea lying dim ("dim" and "hill," by the way, are too nearly rhymes without being so, to come so close together as they do in this verse). I very much like the verse on the trees that saw naught beyond autumn "and breathed half timidly soft love songs through their crimson-stained leaves." It is the most poetic of your details perhaps, but I like the "Merrow's Lament" best as a whole. Blank verse is the most difficult of all measures to write well. A blank verse line should always end with a slight pause in the sound. Words like

[63]

"for" at the end of the eighth line of "A Mother's Dream" and "who" at the end of the second line on the next page are not good final words. Such words have no natural pause after them. There are not however more than two or three such lines in the poem.

You should send these poems to the *Irish Monthly,* the editor is the Rev Matthew Russell, St. Francis Xavier's Upper Gardener [*sic*] Street, Dublin. . . .

You will find it a good thing to make verses on Irish legends and places and so forth. It helps originality and makes one's verses sincere, and gives one less numerous competitors. Besides one should love best what is nearest and most interwoven with one's life [*Letters,* 103–104].

Clearly Miss White's poems were not strikingly promising: Yeats himself, in a letter to Katharine Tynan, said of the incident, "I spent a long time trying to say something pleasant about them without saying too much. They were not very good, though sincere and musical" (*Letters,* 107). His criticism was gentle, as he did not want to discourage a potential Irish writer, but he tried to be judicious as well. In addition, it was *good* criticism, detailed and specific, and reflected Yeats's concern with craftsmanship. The suggestion about using legends as subject-matter of course involved another of his ideals. And finally, his advice was practical, including as it did information about how the author could get her work published.

A decade later Yeats wrote a very similar letter to Dora Sigerson Shorter, who had sent him a volume of her work, *Ballads and Poems.* Yeats's criticisms were just as detailed and of course much more subtle than those in the earlier letter and—despite the fact that Mrs. Shorter was a more prominent and successful poet than Miss White—as often fault-finding as complimentary:

The *caesura* is wrong on line 5 of page 45. The word "come" is too strong a syllable. It takes the accent and so moves the *caesura* too far forward. "Upon" instead of "Come on" would be all right. . . . You build from the ground instead of starting like most writers of verse with an insincere literary language which they can apply to anything. Try however, I think, to build about a lyric emotion. I only learnt that slowly and used to be content to tell stories. "The Little Brother" lacks I think its lyrical emotion, and remains a merely painful little story. One must always have lyric emotion or some revelation of beauty.

In a postscript he wrote

You must not mind my having found so many little faults but I always myself think criticism is helpful just in so far as it is minute and technical. I have marked some other things which we can discuss when I see you [*Letters*, 321–323].

Yeats's literary relations with Katherine Tynan and AE, to be examined in detail in a later chapter, were extended instances of such influence, and there are probably other examples in letters that have not yet come to light.[2] Furthermore, the last sentence in the postscript of the letter to Mrs. Shorter serves as a reminder that the extent of his personal influence cannot accurately be gauged from letters alone.

Nevertheless, this sort of influence was clearly limited in scope. A more public form of Yeats's propagandizing during this period was the formation of Irish literary societies. He did not originate this idea. In 1880 a number of Young Ireland Societies had been founded in Ireland and had flourished for five or six years, until there were twenty or thirty branches throughout the country. But the central Dublin society had failed in 1885, and this in turn killed many of the branches and left the others moribund.[3] A Pan-Celtic Society was organized in Dublin in 1888,[4] but it attracted only mediocre minds. In England the Southwark Literary Club had been formed in 1883. Yeats later recalled that at the time he began his work, "It had ceased to meet because the girls got giggles when any

2. See, for example, "Hopes and Fears for Irish Literature," *United Ireland*, October 15, 1892, where Yeats refers to a letter from "a young man in a remote part of Ireland asking an opinion about some verses."

3. "The Young Ireland League," *United Ireland*, October 3, 1891.

4. See W. P. Ryan, *The Irish Literary Revival* (London: privately printed, 1894), pp. 39ff.

member of the Committee got up to speak. Every member of it had said all he had to say many times over" (*Au,* 121–122). This is probably an exaggeration, for according to the contemporary version of W. P. Ryan, the group had merely decided to abandon public lectures in favor of "solid literary work" and meetings in the homes of members; but all indications are that it operated at a very low level of literary culture and did not appear very promising.[5]

Yeats recognized the potential of such groups: they could cohere natural literary enthusiasm and by pooling resources could achieve ends unreachable by individuals; they could spread that enthusiasm, the presence of organized activity functioning as a magnet to attract others; and they could provide judicious criticism to fill the place left by the absence of decent periodical criticism. In addition to this perception he provided much of the practical energy required to make them working realities.

He began in the early autumn of 1891, during the fierce controversy in the Irish Party over support of Parnell. Not surprisingly, the organization he planned for Ireland was specifically designed to transcend the conflicts of faction and party. He had been interested in the Young Ireland Societies because O'Leary had taken him to some of their meetings,[6] and the idea he now conceived was to revitalize the Young Ireland groups still in existence, revive those that had perished (most importantly the central group in Dublin), and found new ones. These societies were to combat "ignorance and bigotry and fanaticism"; remaining neutral in the current political dispute, they would "welcome Parnellite and McCarthyite equally." Their program would include classes in Irish history and language, lectures upon Irish subjects, and the establishment of reading rooms to be stocked with appropriate reading-matter. Here Yeats would have an excellent means for devel-

5. Ryan, pp. 17ff, 34.
6. See *Au,* p. 60, and "The Young Ireland League," *United Ireland,* October 3, 1891.

oping an audience. The guidelines he set down for selecting the books definitely reflect his personal literary ideals: the Irish selections were to be books of imagination rather than scholarship, and they were to be national in subject; no writer would be included merely because he was Irish by birth. On the other hand, he hoped to see the collections of Irish books supplemented by "the masterpieces of other countries." [7]

Such a project sounds innocuous enough today, but at the time it aroused adverse comments from many sides. The English press scented Fenianism, the anti-Parnellite elements of the Irish press saw is as a Parnellite project, some of the extant societies were skeptical of the claim of nonfactionalism, and one critic wrote an article asserting that Ireland did not have any native literature worthy of support. Then, only a few days after Yeats's own article on the plan was published, Parnell died. Apparently because of the turmoil caused by that event,[8] Yeats for the time being transferred his major efforts to London.

In late December, 1891, he wrote that he was "busy getting up a London Irish Literary Society—to be a branch ultimately of Young Ireland League" (*Letters*, 188). On the twenty-eighth he held an organizational meeting with members of the Southwark "Committee" and T. W. Rolleston, who also played a major role in the project.[9] It was decided that the Southwark group "should be asked to merge itself in a new body with a new name, more central premises, and larger aims." [10] The new body, known as the Irish Literary Society, London, was formally founded on May 12, 1892, though the first public meeting did not take place until March, 1893.[11] In an article published at the time of the founding, Yeats outlined his conception of the Society's aim. It was to counter the threat of "de-

7. "The Young Ireland League," *United Ireland,* October 3, 1891.
8. Cf. *Letters,* p. 185.   9. See Ryan, pp. 36, 52ff.
10. Rolleston, "Twenty-One Years . . . ," p. 23; see also Ryan, pp. 35–36.
11. *Letters,* p. 200, note.

nationalization" by supporting Irish literature; that support would in turn lead to a greater interest on the part of Irish writers in their own country:

Irish authors who have been compelled to make their pens the servants of a foreign literature, and foreign inspirations, will come gladly to our help, and in doing so they will themselves rise to greater status, for no man who deserts his own literature for another's can hope for the highest rank. . . . Ireland has no lack of talent, but that talent is flung broadcast over the world, and turned to any rather than Irish purposes. Until it has been gathered together again and applied to the needs of Ireland it will never do anything great in literature . . . Let it be the work of the literary societies to teach to the writers on the one hand, and to the readers on the other, that there is no nationality without literature, no literature without nationality.[12]

This passage reveals Yeats's consciousness of the advantage of *group* effort and uses as its cornerstone the very formula Yeats had learned years earlier from O'Leary, with whom he kept in close contact while engaged in this work.

Paradoxically, after the initial shock of Parnell's death had passed, the ensuing uproar seems to have actually aroused enthusiasm for such projects. The utter collapse of the once powerful and united Irish Party, the bitter factional quarrels, and the end of immediate hopes for Home Rule could only stir disappointment and revulsion in sensitive minds. Consequently, as Rolleston recalled, many Irishmen made "the startling discovery that politics was only one branch, and perhaps not the most important branch, of patriotism, and that if Ireland could for the time achieve nothing at Westminster, there was in Ireland itself an immense and almost virgin field for work of national significance." [13] Yeats himself felt the same way: "It was the death of Parnell," he was to write in *Four*

12. "The Irish Intellectual Capital: Where Is It? The Publication of Irish Books," *United Ireland*, May 14, 1892.

13. Rolleston, "Twenty-One Years," p. 27; see also *Ideals in Ireland,* pp. 88–90.

Years, "that convinced me that the moment had come for work in Ireland, for I knew that for a time the imagination of young men would turn from politics." [14] Consequently, in the summer of 1892 he went to Ireland and began a period of feverish organizational effort.[15] His first action, as he later recalled it, was a conversation held ludicrously over a butter-tub in a Dublin back street (*Au,* 122), but everywhere he went he met with easy success, and he was soon writing optimistically to Edward Garnett that the society was "growing under our hands into what promises to be a work of very great importance" (*Letters,* 207–208). The same optimism imbued a contemporary passage in one of his Irish-American literary columns: "Men who are saddened and disgusted with the turn public affairs have taken have sought in our society occasion to do work for Ireland that will bring about assured good, whether that good be great or small. We have met more support than we ventured to hope for, and there is no sign of its falling off." [16]

But Yeats's declarations of success soon proved premature. In both Dublin and London all sorts of dissension began to appear, internally and even between the two groups. Though the societies were supposedly above party (and though the founders of the Dublin organization, known as the National Literary Society, had decided to remain separate from the old Young Ireland Societies in order to insure a nonpolitical atmosphere), there was much wrangling among various factions. And it became apparent that many of Yeats's recruits held literary principles antithetical to his own. The culmination was a lengthy controversy over a project to sponsor a series of cheap Irish books for popular consumption: it ended with both societies dominated by everything that Yeats despised (*EI,* 249).

Some good naturally came from the effort. The Dublin Society did support the theater movement.[17] There was the personal benefit to Yeats of encountering the ordinary world

14. Quoted by Wade in *Letters,* p. 193.   15. See Ryan, pp. 126ff.
16. *LNI,* p. 157 (dated November 6, 1892).
17. *Ideals in Ireland,* p. 89.

in all its ugly reality, though he came to feel that this advantage was counteracted by the harmful effects upon him of the intense animosities involved in such quarrels, and later wrote, "When I look back upon my Irish propaganda of those years I can see little but its bitterness" (*Au*, 141). In addition, if the organizations failed to promote greater coherence among the potential components of a literary movement, they at least attracted much attention, and this alone may have benefited Yeats and the writers with whom he was in sympathy: in 1899 he even credited the groups with having "awakened Irish affections among many from whom the old rhetoric could never have got a hearing." [18] But in general, as a means of spreading Yeats's literary ideals this propaganda endeavor was a disappointment.

Yeats's other major public means of literary propagandizing during this period was of course through the printed word. His noncreative writings of these years form a voluminous corpus. Much of this work owed its existence to economic pressures: as a young man Yeats was often pathetically short of money, and the few shillings he could make doing reviews and preparing anthologies constituted a vital part of his finances. These writings, however, cannot be dismissed as hack-work. He almost always related his subjects to his own central concerns. Thus, in 1893, faced with reviewing *Life with Trans-Siberian Savages,* he found in the beliefs preserved by those rude people "a creed which could have seemed almost entirely admirable to most of the great European mystics" and observed, "The savage looks upon naked eternity, while we unhappy triflers have built about us a wall of odds and ends." [19] During the same year he included, in a piece on "Two Minor [English] Lyrists," a reference to Allingham's sacrifice of Ballyshannon for "cosmopolitanism." [20]

His periodical publications ranged from brief letters to newspapers to elaborate formal essays in literary journals and

18. *Ibid.*   19. "The Ainu," *The Speaker,* October 7, 1893, p. 385. 20. *The Speaker,* August 26, 1893, p. 220.

encompassed book reviews and literary columns. A considerable portion were published in magazines and papers in Ireland; but Irish literary periodicals were few in number and paid poorly or not at all, and Irish journalism was unstable and given to intense partisanship, so that as Yeats became increasingly prominent and vocal he had to face even personal opposition in that quarter. For these reasons he contributed heavily to English journals. These contributions either dealt specifically with Irish subjects or else with subjects such as William Watson's meticulous craftsmanship or Villiers de L'Isle Adam's symbolic drama *Axël*, which by Yeats's standards ought to have been of interest to Irishmen: these articles too were a way of "getting at the Irish public." [21] Consequently he noted with pleasure that one of his articles in the London *Bookman* "was copied by the *Express* as well as *United Ireland*" (*Letters*, 258). The force of "as well as" derives from the fact that while a Nationalist paper such as *United Ireland* might be expected to quote him, the *Daily Express* was a strongly conservative Unionist organ. Yeats was delighted to see his audience broadened to include Unionists, whom, as already noted, he considered to be in general better educated and therefore potentially more capable of appreciating the increasingly esoteric work that he and others among the new writers were producing. Nor was he cut off from the Irish in America; between 1888 and 1892 he even published a series of pieces in the *Boston Pilot* and the *Providence Sunday Journal*.

As their titles often indicate, article after article reflected Yeats's own literary ideals: "Irish National Literature," "Dublin Mystics," "The Evangel of Folk-lore," "A Symbolic Artist and the Coming of Symbolic Art." Naturally he also propagandized for Irish writers, past and present, who had adhered to those ideals.

Past writers often helped to shape the taste of the contemporary audience, and all too frequently, it seemed to Yeats, the

21. *Letters*, p. 258 (July 31, 1895).

[71]

worst writers and books had had the greatest influence. He championed both Ferguson and Mangan and tried in the long run (with some success) to have them placed above the Young Irelanders as the best of the earlier poets. In the sphere of fiction the main subject of Yeats's critical writing, William Carleton, presented a yet more difficult problem. Yeats considered him the greatest Irish novelist because he had the "most Celtic eyes that ever gazed from under the brows of story-teller" [22] and unforgettably recorded the life of his day, a culture which already in Yeats's time had virtually disappeared. But because Carleton had for a short period marred his work with anti-Catholic feeling there was much hostility towards him, and the only books of his that had any popular sale in Ireland were those Yeats considered the poorest in artistic merit. Yeats sought to remove the obstacles to an intelligent appreciation of Carleton, but his anthology *Stories from Carleton* was harshly reviewed in the Irish newspaper *The Nation*, and when he wrote a letter of protest further explaining his position, the paper brushed it aside ("Mr. Yeat's [*sic*] letter does not increase our respect for his powers as a critic") and printed directly below it another letter to the editor beginning "My Dear Sir—As an Irishman and as a priest I cannot help thanking you for your outspoken, patriotic, and Catholic protest against the republication by an English popular publisher of the recent collection of Carleton's 'stories.' " [23] In a private letter Yeats showed himself irritated, but also amused and undaunted, by the incident:

At the foot of my letter they protest that they did not say anything against him as a whole but only against the anti-Catholic that was in him for a time. It is amusing to find printed after my letter a note from a Tipperary priest thanking them for their timely protest against this republication of Carleton's stories and wondering that I would edit such a book. He at any rate read them, as I did—O those Bigots—fortunately their zeal is not

22. *Stories from Carleton*, p. xvi.
23. "Carleton as an Irish Historian," *The Nation*, January 11, 1890.

equalled by their knowledge. I dare say I surprised some folk by reminding them of the numberless books full of the most ardent defense of the Catholic priesthood written by Carleton and by showing how very little there is of his anti-Catholic work and how early it was. I dare say, though, they are no bigots—people have so long passed on the calumny that unenquiring people might well come to believe that all he wrote was bitterly sectarian [*Letters*, 147].

Six years later he was still calling for new editions of the "good" Carleton.

Yeats made every effort to support those of his contemporaries in whom he discerned merit. On the other hand he openly criticized writers who were going astray: Elsa d'Esterre Keeling and Margaret Ryan, for instance, whom he took to task for failing to use Irish subjects (*LNI*, 90). He was always on the alert for new talent; as he wrote to Father Russell, who had offered to lend him a book of verse, "Anything that anybody may be doing in the way of Irish poetry interests me greatly," [24] though often, as in the case of Charles Weekes, whose *Reflections and Refractions* he had reviewed positively in 1893, the promise he discerned was never realized. In addition to treating individual writers of whose work he approved, he tried to give a sense of group activity, of a movement. He had anticipated a movement as early as 1886, in an article on Ferguson: "Whatever the future may bring forth in the way of a truly great and national literature—and now that the race is so large, so widely spread, and so conscious of its unity, the years are ripe," [25] and by the nineties felt that it had genuinely begun. He felt also that a consciousness of solidarity in contemporary Irish writing would not only encourage the writers already active but attract other writers and a larger audience.

Unfortunately, tags such as "The Irish Revival," the "Celtic

24. *Letters,* p. 130 (ca. July, 1889).
25. "The Poetry of Sir Samuel Ferguson," *Dublin University Review,* November, 1886, p. 940.

School," and "the Irish Literary Movement" underwent a rapid journalistic debasement, and in using them Yeats frequently indicated a degree of detachment from them by enclosing them in quotation marks. Once he even did this in a private letter.[26] In 1900, attacked in a newspaper for some of his propagandizing efforts, he defended himself against the charge of having misused such terms, asserting that his antagonist had been misled into supposing that he had "ever used the phrases 'Celtic note' and 'Celtic Renaissance' except as a quotation from others, if even then." He went on to declare that he had "avoided 'Celtic note' and 'Celtic Renaissance' partly because both are vague and one is grandiloquent, and partly because the journalist has laid his ugly hands upon them." [27] He did in fact occasionally use such terms without qualification, but it was the idea more than the name that chiefly concerned him, and there were other ways in which the idea could be suggested. He tried to create a sense of group effort through articles treating a number of writers together, and by listing, whenever possible, catalogues of names: "Mr. Stopford Brooke, Mr. Rolleston, Dr. Hyde, Mr. Ashe King, Mr. Alfred Percival Graves, Mr. Lionel Johnson, and other leaders of 'the Irish literary movement.' " [28] This passage illustrates one other problem Yeats had in playing up the movement and its achievements: he almost always had to leave himself out, though often he would have been his own best evidence.

In addition to the periodical publications, Yeats at various times wrote larger-scale works to mold public taste and conceived other projects of this sort that were never realized. In

26. Letter to Katharine Tynan of January 15, 1895, in the Houghton Library, Harvard University.

27. "Mr. W. B. Yeats," *The Leader*, September 1, 1900, p. 14. For the statement to which Yeats was responding, see D. P. Moran, "A Hundred Years of Irish Humbug," *An Claidheamh Soluis*, May 19, 1900, pp. 141–151.

28. "Professor Dowden and Irish Literature," *Daily Express* (Dublin), January 26, 1895.

1888 he published *Fairy and Folk Tales of the Irish Peasantry*, a collection intended as a "source book for Irish poets" (*Letters*, 88). *The Celtic Twilight*, a further gathering of folk material, appeared in 1893, and two years later he noted with pleasure that both books had affected Nora Hopper: "I am greatly delighted with her evident use of my two folklore anthologies as I compiled them that they might influence Irish literature and help lift it out of rhetoric." [29] He added later pieces to an enlarged edition of *The Celtic Twilight* that appeared in 1902, and still other material, intended for a third book, eventually went into Lady Gregory's *Visions and Beliefs in the West of Ireland*. Soon after *Fairy and Folk Tales* was finished, Yeats got the idea of compiling translations of the chief old Irish epic tales to aid experimental use of them.[30] This plan fell through, and it was not until Lady Gregory published her *Cuchulain of Muirthemne* (1902) and *Gods and Fighting Men* (1904) that he felt this need had been satisfied. His elaborate study of Blake presented an intelligent examination of a great poet and thinker whose mystic strain was, Yeats thought, the product of Irish ancestry. In addition to the *Stories from Carleton* he did a volume of *Representative Irish Tales* (1891), intended as a contribution to the re-evaluation of Irish fiction, and considered also writing a critical study of the Irish literary tradition up to his own day:

There is want for a short book . . . on Irish literature. Lives and criticism of all writers since Moore. It would sell largely, I hope, and do good work I am sure. . . . There is a great want for a just verdict on these men and their use for Ireland. I have often thought of setting about such a book and may when I have got on more with the novel-writers.[31]

29. Letter to Katharine Tynan of January 20, 1895, in the Houghton Library, Harvard University; quoted by permission of Mr. M. B. Yeats, Miss Anne Yeats, and the Harvard College Library. See also *Letters*, p. 81 and *Au*, p. 92.

30. See *Letters*, pp. 93, 128.   31. *Letters*, p. 133 (August, 1889).

Although he eventually began collecting some material, he never wrote the study; [32] but he performed something of the same task in his anthology *A Book of Irish Verse*, which appeared in 1895. In his introduction and in the selections he delivered his verdict about the writers of the past and to some extent about his contemporaries as well. He had a number of other plans for major propaganda efforts involving the other writers of the day. In 1892 he hoped for an entire series of books to be issued under his editorship; the next year he wrote to Lionel Johnson soliciting contributions for a "projected Irish Magazine which is intended to be the organ of our literary movement" (*Letters*, 228); and in 1899 he thought of "publishing translations of stories by O'Grady, Fiona Macleod and the rest of us in Gaelic at a very low price for the use of the peasantry" (*Letters*, 321), obviously an attempt to further expand the audience for the new literature. All of these ideas eventually came to something, but not until after the end of the period being examined, and then only in much-modified form.[33]

The question naturally arises of the extent to which the propagandistic motives of this work had a negative effect upon its quality. The answer is that the vast majority of his writing in this category is critically judicious. Yeats saw that one of the chief causes of the weakness of Irish literature was the lack of such judicious criticism. It had been all too customary to praise to the skies everything written by members of one's own faction and damn automatically the productions of one's enemies; the result was a complete distortion of literary values. Referring specifically to *A Book of Irish Verse*, Yeats wrote, "I felt my criticism would carry no weight unless I separated myself from the old gush and folly. I want people to accept my

32. See *Letters*, pp. 151–152. He entertained the idea as late as 1892, when it was one of the projected volumes of the New Irish Library.

33. The main vehicles were the Dun Emer and Cuala Presses and the various Abbey Theatre publications. At least one book of stories, George Moore's *The Untilled Field*, was translated into Irish.

praise of Irish books as something better than mere national vanity" (*Letters*, 252–253). And he knew that to draw Unionists into the audience for the movement he would have to "convince them that we were critics and writers before all else and not heady and undiscriminating enthusiasts" (*Letters*, 254). His own policy was therefore one of "sifting out and expounding what is excellent." [34] Thus, he tried to define the particular virtues of Ferguson's work, admitting that it lacked "the subtler forms of music" but finding compensation in the excellence of its larger outlines.[35] When AE's *Homeward* appeared in 1894, Yeats wrote to O'Leary, "George Russell has . . . published a little book of verse, which is exceedingly wonderful. I think we will be able to organize a reception for it. It is about the best piece of poetical work done by any Irishman this while back" (*Letters*, 231–232). The impulse to propagandize is sandwiched between bursts of enthusiasm about the book's literary merit and is in fact a product of that enthusiasm. And in the review that he wrote he did not let his desire to spread the fame of the book keep him from pointing out some areas in which it did not fully satisfy his stylistic ideals ("certain rhymes are repeated too often, the longer lines stumble now and again, and here and there a stanza is needlessly obscure").[36] To take one other example, Yeats had given almost unqualified praise to Douglas Hyde's *Beside the Fire* (1890), a volume of folk tales, and *Love Songs of Connacht* (1893), but openly indicated his disappointment with the poetic qualities of the versions of the "Three Sorrows" of Irish storytelling that Hyde published in 1895.[37]

Only on very rare occasions did he succumb to the temptation to put his goals or personal feelings before his critical

34. "Professor Dowden and Irish Literature," *Daily Express* (Dublin), January 26, 1895.

35. "The Poetry of Sir Samuel Ferguson," *Dublin University Review*, November, 1886, pp. 926ff.

36. "A New Poet," *The Bookman*, August, 1894, p. 148.

37. "The Three Sorrows of Story Telling," *The Bookman*, July, 1895, pp. 116–117.

honesty. The most striking instance was pointed out by Yeats himself. In 1895 he had published a short but very positive review of John Eglinton's *Two Essays on the Remnant*. Six years later, in another article on Eglinton, he admitted that he had disliked the book and only read a "few pages" of it, but then had "tried to make people read it." [38] A later chapter of this study will reveal that in the cases of Katharine Tynan and Nora Hopper he was not always as impartial as he should have been. And in at least one instance he included, in order to swell the role of current books of Irish fiction, a passing reference to a novel he had not read. The article alluded to "the authors [Edith Somerville and Violet Martin] of 'The Real Charlotte,' who have described with unexampled grimness our middle-class life." [39] Earlier in the same year he had written of the book in a letter "I have not read this but Henley [? or Healy] praises it greatly to me." [40] That he did not follow his friend's recommendation seemed highly likely, for he referred to the book nowhere else in his published writings, while its quality was so high—especially in comparison with other Irish fiction of the time—that he should have taken it up in a major way. Positive proof appeared in 1968 with the publication of a new biography of Somerville and Ross: the author quotes a letter written by Violet Martin in 1901 to the effect that Yeats, whom she had recently met "thinks *The Real Charlotte* very big, in the only parts he has read, which are merely quotations in reviews." [41] But these minor incidents only slightly vitiate the value of Yeats's propaganda criticism.

38. "Dublin Mystics," *The Bookman*, May, 1895, pp. 48–49; "John Eglinton," *United Irishman*, November 9, 1901, p. 3.

39. "Irish National Literature. Contemporary Prose Writers," *The Bookman*, August, 1895, p. 140.

40. Letter to Katharine Tynan of January 15, 1895, in the Houghton Library, Harvard University; quoted by permission of Mr. M. B. Yeats, Miss Anne Yeats, and the Harvard College Library.

41. Maurice Collis, *Somerville and Ross* (London: Faber and Faber, 1968), p. 129.

Yeats also participated in three major literary controversies during the 1890's; each of them involved one of his three central literary ideals, and each produced deliberate propaganda campaigns on his part. Thus, the story of those controversies is an essential component of the history of his efforts to affect the course of Irish literature.

The first controversy, which had at its center the problem of the proper relationship between art and politics, arose over the projected scheme to publish an inexpensive popular series of good Irish books. This plan, innocuous as it sounds, led to such bitter hostilities that W. P. Ryan, in his contemporary history of Irish literary activities, said as little about it as possible, excusing himself on the ground that the time had not yet come to write its full history ("secret much of it is"): "Coming to this part of our subject is coming to difficult and delicate ground, to matters on which some men who exerted all their energies to bring the cause to a successful issue entertain very decided feelings." [42] The publication of Yeats's letters written at the time of the affair has ended most of that secrecy and made it possible to understand precisely how the difficulty began.

Yeats first mentioned his version of the scheme in a letter to John O'Leary conjecturally dated late 1891 or early 1892: "I have a plan for a new 'Library of Ireland' which I have talked over with [Edward] Garnett" (*Letters*, 198). The original Library of Ireland had been part of the Young Ireland movement of the 1840's. Proposed by Sir Charles Gavan Duffy, it had consisted of shilling volumes of history, biography, literature, and other subjects intended to educate the populace of Ireland in the great traditions of their country so that they might better understand and support the cause of Repeal. Yeats's projected series was to be a "new" Library of Ireland in that it would be similarly inexpensive and widely educative of the sensibilities of Irishmen, and thus would help build up the audience for contemporary writers. The books were

42. Ryan, p. 65.

to sell for two shillings and to be distributed through the literary societies with which Yeats was working. Yeats had contacted Edward Garnett, the reader for the publishing firm of Fisher Unwin, about the possibility of Unwin publishing the series. Garnett's reply was encouraging, and Yeats hoped confidently that "Unwin would take up such a library, giving me a free hand and letting us couple an Irish publisher with him" (*Letters*, 198). The phrase "giving me a free hand" is important: Yeats wanted to control the content of the Library so that it would reflect his own ideals. In his next letter to O'Leary he indicated that his plan had already won support in the London Society ("our men are eager over the publication project") and that he had taken preliminary steps, including the lining up of several early volumes:

> Rolleston promises to do for the first volume a history of Fenianism of a popular nature and to fill it with sound national doctrine. I would myself do "a ballad chronicle of Ireland"—a Davis idea—selected from all the ballad writers and piece the poems together with short historical notes.
>
> For later volumes I have been offered "the Ossianic stories" by York Powell and Education in Ireland by Lionel Johnson. O'Grady would probably do a book also and I myself have a wish to write a manual of Irish literature in the present century.[43]

These titles, in addition to representing a variety of fields, would obviously be suitable vehicles for spreading Yeatsian concerns. O'Grady's book as well as York Powell's would probably deal with the old legends or early historical periods, and those by Rolleston and Johnson would strengthen national feeling. Yeats's two contributions would both enable him to carry on the work of "sifting out and expounding" what was excellent in the Irish literature of the century. The fact that the "ballad chronicle" was "a Davis idea" becomes extremely ironic in the light of later developments in the

43. *Letters*, p. 200. The eagerness Yeats speaks of is verified by Ryan, pp. 55, 58–59.

[80]

scheme, as Davis' ability as a writer was to become a central point of contention among the participants and Yeats would find himself on the anti-Davis side. It is important to note also that all these volumes were to be freshly compiled and involved living authors.

In this same letter Yeats spoke further of the structure of the project:

Such a series should have I think three directors who would show the various parties that it was national and not party—you and Sigerson might make two of them. I should myself be editor and have no Barry O'Brien [an Irish writer and journalist of whose imaginative abilities Yeats had a rather low opinion] or anyone else except the directors associated with me to hamper my action.

This passage, in addition to underlining Yeats's desire to control the series, is another example of his concern with freeing Irish literature from the constricting bonds of partisan politics and in doing so to increase the number of its writers and to broaden its prospective audience. O'Leary and George Sigerson were suitable as directors because, while both were appreciative of literature and moderate in temperament, they represented more or less opposite poles politically.

Meanwhile, Yeats's eventual antagonist, Charles Gavan Duffy himself, began once more to make his presence felt. After the collapse of the Young Ireland movement he had made another life for himself in Australia, and then in 1880 had taken up residence in the south of France and begun writing his memoirs. Despite the long years he spent abroad, his concern for his country had remained alive, and among the hopes he cherished was the re-establishment of his Library of Ireland. Ryan quotes a letter dated February 23, 1891, in which he expressed that desire, and to bring it to fruition he had gone to London and apparently spoken of it to some members of the Southwark group.[44] He and Yeats had in-

44. Ryan, pp. 32–33; and the unpublished "First Draft" autobiography, Section XII, p. 80 (photostatic reproduction in the Houghton Library, Harvard University).

dependently come up with the same idea, the only visible difference at this stage being that Duffy had thought to bring out the books through a company formed expressly for the purpose rather than through an established publisher.

When Yeats discovered the coincidence he decided to defer to Duffy,[45] feeling that his ends would be equally well served by the latter's version of the idea. This had occurred by late January of 1892, for in an article published on the twenty-third Yeats referred to the project *as Duffy's,* expressing the hope that it would "do much to foster a reading public in Ireland." [46] He continued, however, to consider himself an integral part of the endeavor. In July he sent Garnett a copy of a speech Duffy had recently made discussing the series in general terms and explaining the concept of the publishing company (*Letters,* 209); and on July 23 he wrote to Duffy himself, inviting him to chair the inaugural meeting of the Dublin Society and adding a significant postscript:

It seems to Mr. O'Leary and myself that it would be a good step towards ensuring circulation to fix as soon as possible upon the first 3 volumes of the proposed library. Mr. O'Leary and myself think that a good first volume would be a life of Wolfe Tone by T. W. Rolleston. . . . Mr. O'Leary thinks that my "Ballad Chronicle" would make a good second volume. For the third volume he suggests that Lady Wilde be asked to take up again the book on Sarsfield that had been projected for her. We of course wish to know if you think this a good selection or if you have anything to say in opposition or in modification [*Letters,* 212].

There were already some changes from Yeats's original line-up of early volumes: the shift in Rolleston's topic may have been the result of objections to his chosen subject by O'Leary, who had been one of the leaders of the Fenian movement; and Lady Wilde, although she had written for *The Nation,* was acceptable to Yeats because he had liked her re-

45. This is confirmed by Ryan, pp. 58–59.
46. "Dr. Todhunter's Irish Poems," *United Ireland,* January 23, 1892.

cent compilations of Irish legends and folk tales.[47] There was, however, no decrease in his confidence that he could still determine the character of the series and carry out his promise, in a May 14 article, that the new books would "be no mere echo of the literature of '48, but radiant from the living heart of the day."[48] But as early as the January 23 article he had qualified his optimism about the effect of the series: it could not do such work if it was to be "too exclusively a basket to gather up the fragments that remained after the feast of the old 'Library,' " and his "use" in the postscript of O'Leary, whose unimpeachable patriotism could shield them both from charges of self-interest and antinationalism, suggests that he saw the possibility of conflict ahead.

His concern was in fact well founded. Gavan Duffy's aim was to revive the Young Ireland movement. In an address to the London Society he made this explicit: "The thought that has long haunted my reveries . . . is this—that the young men of your generation should take up anew the unfinished work of their predecessors, and carry it another stage towards the end which they aimed to reach."[49] With this statement as a political and social goal Yeats had no quarrel; but Duffy was in literary ideas as well "still essentially a Young Irelander"[50] and felt that the job of preparing the people could be done with remnants from the original effort. In the letter in which he had revealed his plan for a new Library, the works he referred to specifically were by "men and women who have helped the national cause for the last generation or two": "Mary of Cork," John O'Hagan, and Charles Kickham.[51] The first two were minor Young Ireland poets, while Kickham,

47. See, for example, "Tales from the Twilight," *Scots Observer,* March 1, 1890, pp. 408–409; and *Letters,* p. 249.

48. "The Irish Intellectual Capital: Where Is It? The Publication of Irish Books," *United Ireland,* May 14, 1892.

49. *The Revival of Irish Literature* (London: T. Fisher Unwin, 1894), p. 11. See also *Au,* p. 137.

50. Ryan, p. 77.   51. Ryan, p. 32.

who had been associated with the Fenian movement, had some talent as a novelist but spoiled it by exaggerating to an incredible degree the virtues of the Irish peasantry. Yeats may eventually have seen this letter, possibly at one of the organizational meetings of the London Society. At least he knew somehow of the "Mary of Cork" material: in one of his autobiographies he recalled that Duffy "brought with him much manuscript, the private letters of a Young Ireland poetess, a dry but informing unpublished historical essay by Davis, and an unpublished novel by William Carleton into the middle of which he had dropped a hot coal, so that nothing remained but the borders of every page" (*Au*, 136). If and when he did see it he would certainly have disapproved of such choices, especially for the crucial early volumes of the series.

Yeats definitely knew Duffy's July, 1892 address to the members of the London Society, which contained some remarks on the volumes he had in mind. Nowhere in this speech did he say definitely that any specific book must be included. Instead he referred to a great number of possible selections, among them some that would have appealed to Yeats, for example, works culled from the vast stores of medieval Irish literature, and a gallery of studies of "representative Irishmen" by "the best men of this time." But almost lost in the bewildering variety of suggestions were some that would not be so palatable:

Davis's most remarkable achievement as a historian, "The Patriot Parliament" he calls it—not the Parliament of Grattan but the Parliament of Tirconnell, was prepared for publication by his own hand, and [because of his sudden death] it has remained without a publisher for two generations. Nothing of the miscellaneous writings of John Blake Dillon, John O'Hagan, Thomas Meagher, or Charles Kickham have been gathered into books.[52]

52. *The Revival of Irish Literature*, pp. 25–26, 38. Dillon and Meagher had been leaders of the abortive Young Ireland uprising of 1848; Dillon escaped to America, Meagher was transported to Australia.

Little more was heard of those "miscellaneous writings"; their unsuitability for a series intended to have a popular appeal and their profound contrast to what *Yeats* had in mind should be obvious. The Davis book, however, became a prime factor in the outcome of the affair. Duffy seemed also to have subsumed into his plan some of the books for which Yeats had originally gotten promises,[53] but when the series actually started appearing it became clear that he was never really interested in these books.

Considering the series mainly as a political tool and the quality of literature far less important than the quantity of its patriotic sentiment, Duffy took a position virtually antithetical to the conception of national literature towards which Yeats had been moving, and it is hardly surprising that the emerging conflict between the two began to involve disputes over the merits of Young Ireland literature and accusations of antinationalism.[54] While the question of national *versus* nationalistic literature was central, such arguments naturally brought in the matters of foreign influence (Yeats was considered to be too closely involved with the English "decadents") and the importance of craftsmanship.[55] Ryan's statement that "the claim that the hopes and aspirations of the risen generation should not be ignored for antique reprints and Young Ireland aftermaths, was emphasized in several quarters" provides evidence that Yeats had considerable support in both of the major literary societies.[56] The London group issued a statement of principles including an expression of the hope "that the unfinished schemes of '42 and '45 will be taken up; the aspirations of '92 fitly voiced and chronicled as well," and many of its members felt that "go-ahead

53. See *Letters,* p. 215.

54. See *Au,* pp. 123–124; "First Draft," XVIII, pp. 113–114; *Explor,* pp. 114–116, 200.

55. See preceding note, and also "First Draft," XVIII, p. 115.

56. Ryan, pp. 66–68.

policies and popular programs should be tried."[57] In the Dublin Society Yeats's backers were still more numerous, and it issued a statement:

Without an intellectual life of some kind we cannot long preserve our nationality. Every Irish national movement of recent years has drawn a great portion of its power from the literary movement started by Davis, but that movement is over, and it is not possible to live forever upon the past. A living Ireland must have a living literature.[58]

As Yeats described the situation later, "all the young men" were on his side in resisting Duffy's approach—"They might not want the books I wanted, but they did want books written by their own generation" (*Au*, 137).

By the end of the summer (sometime during which Duffy had personally consulted with the Dublin Committee and not been too warmly received)[59] Yeats had a good idea of Duffy's plans and made a determined effort to subject him to certain controls. In an article published on September 6, he asserted that the success of the company would depend upon "whether or no it keeps itself in touch with the young men of Ireland whom it wishes to influence, with those who represent them, and with the various organizations which they have formed or are forming throughout the country."[60] It would be possible to publish an excellent series of books that would be quite unsuited for "the Ireland of to-day," and the shareholders of the company should guard against this danger by seeing that Duffy would not be given sole authority over the scheme; as Duffy had agreed to work with an editorial committee situated in Dublin, Yeats urged that this committee be constituted as soon as possible, so that the writers could be selected and begin their work. The instructions were to be mainly in the hands of the committee, "for it should know best its generation and what that generation needs and is

57. Ryan, pp. 57, 61.   58. Ryan, pp. 127–128.
59. Ryan, pp. 66–67.
60. "The National Publishing Company. Should the Books be Edited?" *The Freeman's Journal*, September 6, 1892.

capable of." Yeats went on to suggest that the committee should consist of five members, chosen from among such men as Richard Ashe King, Douglas Hyde, George Sigerson, Robert Donovan, Count Plunkett, John Magrath, George Coffey, and O'Leary: "a 'library' so edited would be truly national, and would command the confidence of all sections and parties of the Irish race."

Yeats soon found out that he had been wrong about the universal acceptability of his suggestion. The very next day the *Freeman's Journal* attacked it and published a critical letter from John F. Taylor. O'Leary, who had inspired both Yeats and Taylor, wrote a letter gently chiding the latter,[61] and Yeats sent in a more vehement defense. He referred specifically to a newspaper interview of a few weeks earlier, in which Duffy himself had said "he would gladly accept such assistance," and questioned Taylor's right to speak for all the shareholders of the company.[62] Two days later both O'Leary and Yeats sent second letters. O'Leary gave further evidence that Yeats's view was shared by others and quoted a letter he had received that same day assuring him that Duffy "had no objection to make to the formation of any editorial committee in Dublin, it being understood that this committee will have no power except to advise and suggest." Yeats's letter said that the question had been "solved" by Duffy's acquiescence.[63]

The trouble, however, had only begun. Yeats's original proposal had been for the committee to have most of the power, with the editor-in-chief being largely a figurehead. But despite the softening of this demand, Duffy apparently did not in reality like the situation, for shortly afterwards he decided to abandon the idea of a publishing *company*. According to Ryan, the opposition he had received from Yeats was a major cause.[64] In a contemporary letter Yeats gave a somewhat

61. "The National Publishing Company," *Freeman's Journal*, September 8, 1892. The letter is dated September 7.
62. Yeats, "The National Publishing Company," September 8.
63. *Ibid.*, September 10.
64. Ryan, pp. 68–69.

different account: the members of the company, finding that a capital of three thousand shares would not be enough to support the necessary staff of manager and clerks, had decided to reorganize as a general publishing company with ten thousand shares and "were getting support when Duffy withdrew because it suddenly struck him that he could only control the Irish series and not the whole publishing work" (*Letters*, 226). Yeats's retrospective account in *Ireland After Parnell* gives yet another version of this incident:

Suddenly, when the company seemed all but established, and a scheme had been thought out which gave some representation on its governing board to contemporary Irish writers, Gavan Duffy produced a letter from Archbishop Walsh, and threw the project up. The letter had warned him that after his death the company would fall under a dangerous influence [*Au*, 138].

Presumably the Archbishop's allusion was to the religious heterodoxy of Yeats and some of his supporters.[65]

The company was dead, but not Gavan Duffy's desire for a series of Irish books, and soon he took a new step. Both he and T. W. Rolleston had been informed by Yeats himself of Fisher Unwin's interest in such a series. Yeats's later statement that "Gavan Duffy knew nothing of my plans, and so was guiltless" (*Au*, 138) is clearly contradicted by one of his contemporary letters, in which he explained that Duffy "only heard of these negotiations and of Unwin's views on the subject of Irish books from me. I wrote him a letter upon the whole matter when I began my work in Ireland." [66] Now, without a word to Yeats, the two went to Unwin and tried to negotiate a deal themselves.

Yeats's very involvement with the project was threatened by this "betrayal," and as soon as he learned of it from O'Leary, who had been sent word from London, he began to counter-

65. O'Leary may also have been included, as there had been considerable antagonism between the Church and the Fenian movement.

66. *Letters*, p. 215. Duffy is referred to by name just above the passage quoted.

attack. He at once wrote to Garnett about the problem, and his letter shows him still a little bewildered by the event but already trying to use his influence to prevent Unwin from coming to an agreement with Rolleston and Duffy:

Can you let me know what has really occurred? We have had for some time an offer from an Irish publisher [Sealey, Bryers, and Walker] who is ready to publish a series of books for us—for the National Literary Society, Dublin—on condition that we guarantee a sale of 1000 copies. Perhaps Unwin would make ultimately some arrangement whereby the Dublin publisher and himself could work together, as an Irish name upon the books is important. Do not make any arrangement for giving the editorship to Duffy, for there is the strongest possible feeling here against the series being edited from Nice. Duffy is also much too old and much too long out of touch to be a good editor. Count Plunkett, Douglas Hyde or myself would be the right people to choose from. At any rate as I practically planned and started this whole Irish literary movement I do not think that anything should be done behind my back. The National Literary Society here promises to be quite strong enough to make the success of a series of books but it certainly will not put its shoulder to the wheel to back up a series of Duffy's for he has enraged our members by such a complex series of false moves. If I can make arrangements such as will be required for the circulation of books among the literary societies and Young Ireland societies in the country I think that I should be consulted about the editorship. . . . I hope you will let me know about the whole matter for I am quite in the dark about it.

I should also say that many of the books proposed by Duffy for his Irish series were books which I got promised for the series I explained to you. I was quite ready to let the "Company" have them but now the "Company" appears to be abandoned I do not think that I should let Duffy and Rolleston—who is entirely under the influence of D at present—go with my scheme to Unwin as if it all came out of Duffy's head, or rather with my scheme mingled with his own ever changing plans, and not consult me about the proceeding to the slightest extent.

Do what you can to help me in this matter and believe me that I see in it no personal issue but one important for the literary movement here in Ireland. Remember that Duffy is so unpopular here in Ireland—for old reasons which I need not go into—that we were only able to partially suppress a disturbance got up against him at our inaugural meeting, and that we have more than once kept the papers from attacking him. . . . O'Leary feels even more than I do on these points [*Letters,* 215–216].

This letter was obviously calculated to suggest that a series edited by Duffy would fail commercially. Duffy is depicted as unlikely to choose the right books and as being so unpopular that the association of his name with the project would cost it much support, for political as well as literary reasons. The source of the political unpopularity to which Yeats alluded was Duffy's opposition, decades earlier, to the fiery John Mitchel. Yeats was later to describe graphically the "disturbance" that erupted in the Dublin Society:

At some public meeting of ours, where he spoke amid great applause . . . of his proposed Irish publishing firm, one heard faint hostile murmurs, and at last a voice cried, "Remember Newry," and a voice answered, "There's a grave there!" and a part of the audience sang "Here's to John Mitchell [*sic*] that is gone, boys, gone; Here's to the friends that are gone" [*Au,* 137].

It should be further noted that the course of action Yeats proposed would once again put him—or at least someone sympathetic to his ideals—in control of the enterprise. He made this clearer in a letter to O'Leary:

I have written a letter to Garnett asking for information about Duffy and Rolleston's negociations [*sic*] and putting our case in such a way as will I think stop all such treacherous dealing. . . . I suggest to Garnett that Bryers and Unwin might perhaps share the risk between them. I have however put the case very strongly against any dealing whatever with Duffy. This last action of his and R's simply means war and I think now that they have chosen Unwin's house for a battle-ground we rout them with ease, especially as Unwin makes all depend on the Irish organization [i.e., the National Literary Society, Dublin, predominantly on Yeats's side]. I am inclined to think that I should go to London in December or January and try to arrange the matter. . . . As soon as I return to Dublin I shall draw up a definite proposal for series of books, submit this to you and to Count Plunkett, and after modification send it to Unwin and ask him to agree, upon certain guarantees, to publish such a series uniting his name with Bryers' and appointing myself, Plunkett or Hyde editors.

But this optimistic note had given way to pessimism by the time he added a postscript:

The more I think over that Duffy and R. business the worse it looks. When I hear from Garnett I shall probably write to Unwin himself. Our point of view is clear—all depends on our organization and we will not work for a series ruled by Duffy [*Letters*, 216–217].

Although it did not appear obvious at the time, his latter mood proved to have been the more appropriate.

Garnett's reply called for a less extreme position. He asked Yeats "to examine what the differences are between your view and the rival schemes and see whether it is for the good of the idea *you* are working for that you and your party should be irreconcilable." He admitted that it seemed "absurd that Duffy should want to boss a national affair," but suggested that Duffy should be given the *"figure-headship"* so long as he could be kept from becoming *"Dictator."* As Garnett saw it, "the whole issue of the split" lay between Yeats and Rolleston, and he recommended to the former that if the two would "join hands," with Yeats representing the Parnellites and Rolleston the London Irish Literary Society, Yeats would find that "you and he are practically of the same mind about the books and that your own ideas would be carried through." [67] Garnett was trying to keep everyone happy, and his suggestion showed that he had underestimated Duffy's tenacity and the gap between the opposing sides.

Yeats, however, did his best to amend the situation: he responded by altering his proposal once again and writing of

67. Hone, *W. B. Yeats,* p. 98.

it to both Rolleston and Unwin. In its new form the plan called for the Duffy-Rolleston version of the scheme to be submitted to special committees in the Dublin and London Societies. These committees would suggest such modifications as they felt were called for and in turn would guarantee their support of the series. This idea would leave Duffy with more than the "figure-headship," but would also give Yeats and his followers a substantial measure of control. O'Leary had written to Yeats that if the plan involving Unwin fell through they would be "quite at liberty" to carry it out on their own, and seems soon afterwards to have actually suggested that they should throw their support behind a rival "Library" organized by Count Plunkett and to be published by Sealey, Bryers, and Walker; [68] but Yeats still preferred having Unwin. In his letter to Unwin himself he did however use the willingness of Bryers and O'Leary's position, as well as the strength of anti-Duffy sentiment, as levers:

If something such as I propose is not done Count Plunkett will conclude negociations [sic] which he opened months ago with his Irish publisher and our movement may split up on lines which the press will soon turn into a dispute of Parnellite Dublin and the Parnellite young men in the country parts, against what they will call "West British" and "Whiggish" Duffy and Rolleston. All the most ardent of the young men are Parnellites and would be only too ready to raise such a cry against Duffy, who is unpopular for Michellite [?] reasons [Letters, 222].

Yeats then wrote to Garnett, informing him of what he had done and excusing himself for having, as it were, gone over Garnett's head by saying that he had done so to make Duffy and Rolleston "feel his hand" in the matter as directly as possible (Letters, 222–223).

Following this he went to Dublin to make arrangements for the committee there. His next letter to Garnett revealed new difficulties. Steps were taken to set up the committee,

68. Ibid. O'Leary's letter is dated November 8, 1892.

and—apparently as a concession to Yeats's faction—Douglas Hyde had been given the position of subeditor of the series; but because the committee would have no power to *enforce* its decisions, the anti-Duffyites in the Dublin Society were dissatisfied with the idea and not mollified by Hyde's appointment. Yeats therefore suggested that a formal contract be drawn up by Unwin binding Duffy and Hyde to secure the cooperation of both societies in promoting the sale of the series (*Letters*, 224). Meanwhile, his stress to members of the Dublin group upon the power it would have over the scheme through this arrangement had freshly irritated Taylor and also aroused George Sigerson, Duffy's chief supporters there, and when news of the fresh flare-up reached Unwin he began to be "alarmed" about the project.[69] Yeats consequently once again urged the "clause" idea upon Garnett; something of the precarious nature of Yeats's own role in these activities can be seen in his postscript to this letter, in which he added the provision that "if it be needful to say who the suggestion about the 'clause' comes from, Mr. O'Leary says that his name may be mentioned. My name must on no account be mentioned to anyone" (*Letters*, 225). Similarly he wrote to O'Leary that *he* could not have taken the post of subeditor "as people would have been liable to accuse me of having fought for my own hand" (*Letters*, 226).

The year 1892 ended with Yeats still working diligently to arrange things satisfactorily, and as 1893 began it looked as if he might succeed. His next letter to O'Leary was quite confident in tone:

At the Committee last Saturday the following proposal was agreed to by those present, though a vote was not taken, that Sir Gavan Duffy be editor in chief with two sub-editors—T. W. Rolleston and Douglas Hyde (to represent us and have his name on all books) and, and this is the most important point, that the London Society elect a committee of three to draw up list of books, the Dublin Society to do the same. Then lists to be thrown into

69. *Letters*, p. 255, and "First Draft," XVIII, pp. 112–113.

one, each perhaps giving way in smaller matters, so that the final list represent both and yet be not too long. This final list to be sent to Gavan Duffy for his approval. If he agree to it or to the greater portion all will be well. If not we should have to do without him.

Duffy has accepted the Hyde proposal but has not yet been informed about the second one nor perhaps need be until the list is made. We should I think merely formally agree to the list of books I brought over (to the bulk of which Rolleston says Duffy makes no objection), the [Dublin] Society should approach you, Plunkett, and myself as committee. This will bring us all into harmony and establish our right to a voice in the matter [*Letters*, 226–227].

The sentence "If not we should have to do without him" is particularly interesting: Yeats still felt he had or could gain the upper hand in the dispute and guide the series to success. Apparently the plan in this most recent form was actually followed. A list of books was drawn up and was approved by everyone, including Duffy. Ryan lists as volumes announced in 1893 the Davis *Patriot Parliament,* a book of stories on Elizabethan Ireland by Standish O'Grady, *The New Spirit of the Nation,* "What Small Nations Have Done for Humanity" (Rolleston), "Irish Missionaries" (Sigerson), a life of Owen Roe O'Neill by Taylor, "Dr. Doyle" (projected for Michael MacDonagh), a book by Hyde on early Irish literature, Yeats's projected study of the Irish poetry of the century, "Ulster and Ireland" (John Magrath), a life of Sarsfield by John Todhunter, "Irish Songs and Airs" (A. P. Graves), Irish biographies by D. J. O'Donoghue, a volume on "Irish Technical Education" by Arnold Graves, an adaptation by Miss E. Lynch of a Balzac novel, and stories by Ryan himself.[70] This list obviously represents a mixture of items desirable to Yeats and his faction with those preferred by Duffy and his supporters. If Yeats had had any real control over the series it

70. Ryan, pp. 69–70.

[94]

might very well have succeeded with materials like these to draw upon. But Duffy, once his "concessions" had made the scheme operational at last, showed that he had in fact maintained controlling power: [71] the crucial early volumes of the series were mainly those that he had desired, *The Patriot Parliament, The New Spirit of the Nation* (an anthology of Young Ireland poetry), and the Lynch book, entitled *A Parish Providence;* of course neither of the two books Yeats had allotted to himself ever appeared. He had spoken of "doing without" Duffy, but it was he who was finally excluded. In addition, his efforts seemed to have brought him many enemies, even among those who had once supported him (*Au,* 139).

His loss of all power within the scheme itself was not, however, the end of his attempts to influence it. He simply shifted from private letters to the printed page. For over a year he maintained public silence about the project as he waited to see how it would turn out. (The "Irish magazine" intended to be "the organ of our literary movement" which he had written of to Lionel Johnson in February or March of 1893 may represent an early awareness on his part that the "Library" would *not* perform such a function.) [72] Early in 1894 he wrote, but never published, a review of a collected volume containing Hyde's "De-Anglicising" speech and two lectures by Duffy on the book scheme.[73] At this stage he was already severely critical of the literary weaknesses of *The New Spirit* and of the decision to begin the series with so unsuitable a volume as Davis' scholarly piece, but he liked the other early selection, O'Grady's *The Bog of Stars,* and was still hopeful that the canvassing system devised for selling the books would create great popular support for the literary movement. De-

71. Ryan refers obliquely to this fact, p. 70.   72. *Letters,* p. 228.
73. "The Revival of Irish Literature," holograph manuscript in the Houghton Library, Harvard University. I have dated it from internal evidence.

[95]

spite the doubts that Yeats had raised while fighting for a major role in directing the series, both societies apparently did give their support to selling the books.[74]

Unfortunately it soon became clear that the very success of the Davis book had done irreparable damage to the popular appeal of the Library: "so important had our movement seemed," and so intensive had the canvassing effort been, that "ten thousand copies had been sold before anybody had time to read it, and then came a dead stop" as many of the purchasers made up their minds to have nothing further to do with the series and spread the word to their friends.[75] By June of that year Yeats had decided to salvage what he could; he informed O'Leary that he had

written a severe article on "The New Irish Library" which will appear in the August *Bookman*. An inevitable re-organization of the scheme is at hand, and therefore it seems better to speak out. I believe that my article will only make patent the latent convictions of all the people here. Surely the world has not seen a more absurd "popular series" than this one, and the sale has very properly fallen steadily [*Letters*, 233].

The article to which he referred, "Some Irish National Books," showed how devastating he could be in "negative propagandizing":

Their first volume, "The Patriot Parliament," was an historical tractate which, if modified a little, had done well among the transactions of a learned society, but it bored beyond measure the unfortunate persons who bought some thousands of copies in a few days. . . . Pages upon pages of Acts of Parliament may be popular literature on the planet Neptune, or chillier Uranus, but our quick-blooded globe has altogether different needs.[76]

The New Spirit of the Nation he called "a gleaning from the same fields from which the editors of 'The Spirit of the

74. See also Ryan, p. 71.
75. *Au*, p. 138; "First Draft," XVIII, p. 113.
76. *The Bookman*, August, 1894, pp. 151–152.

Nation' reaped their not too golden sheaves" and asserted that instead of collecting Young Ireland leftovers Duffy should have included the "best work" of Callanan, Walsh, Davis, and other balladmakers and drawn heavily upon "the masters of Irish song," Ferguson, Mangan, Allingham, and de Vere. "Such a book could have been put into the hands of a cultivated man of any country without need of explanation," but the "jigging doggrel" chosen instead could appeal neither to the highly educated nor even to the peasantry. He felt the main fault was Duffy's, for having let didacticism "get the better of his judgment" and producing a series that, except for O'Grady's stories, was "little but a cause of blaspheming to mere mortals, who would gladly see the Irish reading classes discover the legends and stories and poems of their own country, instead of following at a laborious distance the fashions of London." After attacking in a similar vein *A Parish Providence* and even accusing Duffy of having many years earlier ruined William Carleton's talent by persuading him to do some moral tracts for the original Library of Ireland, Yeats went on to reveal that the "rival series" that Count Plunkett had been considering did actually appear, under the name "The Irish Home Library." But its first volume, *The Jacobite War*, also seemed to him too scholarly for a popular series: "Surely one needs something more picturesque, more vivid, if one would catch the general taste." Ryan's contemporary appraisal supports Yeats on this point:

The people did not care three straws for husks and shells, though we might call them history, nor for morals, however adroitly pointed, and in their crushed, sordid-ringed lives they had not the heart for industrial or statesmanlike problems. Something which brought back a little of the joys of the old times, the dew of Irish hills, the light of Irish hearths, the bonfire's light, the merry Christmas, some wand which waving showed them Rory's raids, or "Sarsfield's Ride," which opened the gates of the fairy world, or whose touch brought the ghosts to the night-lands: these

[97]

appealed to them, as did anything fresh and glowing with the new life and the new hopes of the old land.[77]

Except for the sentimentality permeating certain phrases, this was Yeats's view.

Throughout the article Yeats's own literary ideals are present, either directly, as in the reference to legends, or implicitly, as in the championing of Ferguson and de Vere (who had used myth and folklore in their work) and of Allingham and Mangan (the best craftsmen among the earlier Irish poets). In addition, he concluded with a bit of direct positive propagandizing for the new writers: "It is . . . books that can create an interest where there is none which are needed for a series of this kind, and if any publisher would set Mr. O'Grady, Dr. Hyde, Miss Lawless, Miss Barlow, Dr. Todhunter, Mrs. Bryant, and Mrs. Hinkson, to the making of such books, he would probably prosper." Except for necessary modesty he might also have included his own name.

At the same time Yeats also indirectly reflected his attitude toward the Library in his anthology *A Book of Irish Verse*, the introduction to which is dated August 5, 1894. In a note to the revised edition of 1900 he made the connection explicit:

I compiled [*A Book of Irish Verse*] towards the end of a long indignant argument, carried on in the committee rooms of our literary societies, and in certain newspapers between a few writers of our new movement, who judged literature by literary standards, and a number of people, a few of whom were writers, who judged it by its patriotism and by its political effect.[78]

The introduction was a brief survey of Irish literature in the nineteenth century. The Young Irelanders received some criticism that must surely have infuriated any "patriotic" Irishmen who happened to read it, such as the statement that

77. Ryan, pp. 71–72.
78. *A Book of Irish Verse*, revised ed. (London: Methuen and Co., 1900), p. xiii.

"in the main the poets who gathered about Thomas Davis, and whose work has come down to us in 'The Spirit of the Nation,' were of practical and political, not of literary importance." [79] Mangan and the nonpolitical poets of the next generation received sympathetic consideration, and Yeats also referred to a number of his contemporaries, though he made no strong claims for them. He ended his essay with a comment which revealed that he had designed this anthology for that more sophisticated portion of the potential audience for Irish literature which the New Irish Library in its current form could not possibly reach; the book was "intended only a little for English readers, and not at all for Irish peasants, but almost wholly for the small beginning of that educated and national public, which is our greatest need and perhaps our vainest hope." [80]

In the selections, too, Yeats reflected his criticisms of Young Ireland and propagandized for the writers, old and new, whose work was most in harmony with his own literary ideals. Of the contents he confessed,

This book is founded upon its editor's likes and dislikes, and everything it contains has given him pleasure. Several names familiar to Irishmen are excluded, and some quite unfamiliar included, and the selection may well be capricious and arbitrary. He might have partly avoided this by giving a little from every eminent writer, whether he liked him or not, but it did not seem possible to make a good book in this way.[81]

The most striking omissions involved the Young Ireland writers. Yeats did include Davis but avoided his propaganda verse; beyond that there were the handful of poems by Thomas D'Arcy McGee, Ingram's classic "The Memory of the Dead." [82] and a single poem by Doheny. Missing entirely were Denis Florence McCarthy, Richard D'Alton Williams, John O'Hagan, "Mary of the Nation," and many other figures associated with the movement.

79. *BV*, p. xviii.   80. *Ibid.*, p. xxvii.   81. *Ibid.*, pp. xxvi–xxvii.
82. Ingram was not, in fact, really a Young Ireland writer, his famous poem being decidedly a sport.

Other names the absence of which might have caused surprise were those of Swift and "Father Prout." The poems Yeats did choose fall roughly into two categories. In the first group are isolated pieces that he happened to like. Many of these, such as Charles Wolfe's "The Burial of Sir John Moore," could be found in almost any Irish anthology. Ellen O'Leary's "To God and Ireland True" may have been added to please her brother John, but she at least had some little reputation; Charles Weekes, on the other hand, must have been "quite unfamiliar" to most readers of the book. While for major representation Yeats demanded a major commitment to Irish subject-matter, in the isolated selections he relaxed this principle enough to accommodate what seemed to him pieces of particular excellence by such figures as Goldsmith, Sheridan, and even Emily Brontë.

The second and more important category is comprised of poets past and present who shared to a considerable extent Yeatsian interests and values in literature. The earlier writers, Ferguson, de Vere, Mangan, Allingham, Callanan, and Walsh are given the greatest amount of space; to avoid accusation of "log-rolling" Yeats rigorously limited the representation of his contemporaries. The ranks of the more modern writers would naturally have been considerably more impressive if Yeats could have included a selection of his own work, which he felt it particularly necessary to omit because he had "left out or criticised unfavorably in the introduction so many well known Irish poets" (*Letters*, 252). Nevertheless, he could rightly have claimed that this anthology was much more likely to win desirable readers for Irish literature than *The New Spirit of the Nation* and all its kind.

While Yeats was finishing up the anthology his August *Bookman* piece was already causing a reaction. An unfavorable consideration of it appeared in *United Ireland*, and in reply Yeats repeated his attack:

I recognize with deep regret, and not a little anger, that the "New Irish Library" is so far the most serious difficulty in the way of

[100]

our movement, and that it drives from us those very educated classes we desire to enlist, and supplies our opponents with what looks like evidence of our lack of any fine education, of any admirable precession [sic] and balance of mind, of the very qualities which make literature possible. Perhaps honest criticism, with as little of the "great day for Ireland" ritual as may be, can yet save the series from ebbing out in a tide of irrelevant dulness, and keep the best opportunity there has been these many decades from being squandered by pamphleteer and amateur. We require books by competent men of letters on subjects of living national interest, romances by writers of acknowledged power, anthologies selected from men like De Vere, and Allingham, and Ferguson [perhaps a bit of preparatory publicity for his own forthcoming anthology], and impartial lives of Emmet, Wolfe Tone, Mitchel, and perhaps O'Connell, and, if they are not to be obtained, let us bow our heads in silence and talk no more of a literary renaisance.[83]

This makes it clear that while he had by this point abandoned hope of popular influence for the series, he still desired to see it have some good effect, and this desire continued to live for quite some time. The following year the Library published a life of Patrick Sarsfield by John Todhunter, and Yeats, while he found a number of things in the volume to criticize, suggested to the management of the series (that is, to Duffy) that it print more books of this sort.[84] A. P. Graves's *Irish Song Book* and Hyde's *Story of Early Gaelic Literature* also seemed to him improvements. In 1896 he reviewed three further volumes, *Swift in Ireland* by Richard Ashe King, *Owen Roe O'Neill* by Taylor, and *A Short Life of Thomas Davis* by Duffy himself, and by this time thought he could discern a trend in the direction of the Library's publications:

The best of the Irish public, . . . having outlived the false ideals of Young Ireland, scouted prose and rhyme alike, and the library suddenly transformed itself and became vivid and scholarly. I

83. Untitled letter, *United Ireland*, September 1, 1894.
84. "The Life of Patrick Sarsfield," *The Bookman*, November, 1895, pp. 59–60.

praised at the times of their appearance "The Irish Song Book," "The Story of Early Gaelic Literature," and "The Life of Patrick Sarsfield," and the new volumes keep the same high level.[85]

But Duffy came in for further criticism, this time for continuing to call Davis (whom Yeats termed "the maker of three or four charming songs that were not great, and of much useful political rhyme that was not poetry") a great poet "and . . . seeking to prove it by quoting 'Fontenoy' and other savourless imitations of Macaulay."

As the century drew to a close, the trend that Yeats had discerned failed to materialize, and the series died a quiet death. Its over-all impact was much less powerful and beneficial than it should have been; as Ryan put it, as early as 1894, "It is interesting to consider what the young men would have done, if under the spell of the new spirit, they had gone to work upon their own lines. Some of them, such as W. B. Yeats, have since published independent books which, to put it mildly, challenge comparison with the best in the old Library of Ireland." [86] Yeats himself, meanwhile, was creating new vehicles to reach both the populace and the educated minority. The theater movement, which he though might achieve the former goal, became an active project by 1897. The means for accomplishing the latter was to be the series of books published by Yeats's sisters first as the Dun Emer and then as the Cuala Press. The antitype of the cheap volumes of the "Libraries" of '42 and '92, these books were expensive limited editions, nicely printed and bound. In them Yeats, wielding the power he had lost a decade before, presented selections from a number of the writers whose work he would have liked to have seen represented in the scheme of the nineties, including Hyde, Johnson, Katharine Tynan, Allingham, AE, and (as no modesty was needed in such an enterprise) himself. He also made up a volume of selections from de Vere and Ferguson,

85. "The New Irish Library," *The Bookman,* June, 1896, pp. 83–84.
86. Ryan, pp. 58–59.

[102]

though for some reason this was never published.[87] In 1912, by which time experiences such as the riots over *The Playboy of the Western World* had made him once again pessimistic about popular literature, he wrote an introduction to one of the Cuala books in which he exulted in the *un*popularity of his own "Library":

Now that we are unpopular we escape from crowds, from noises in the street, from voices that sing out of time, from bad paper made one knows not from what refuse, from evil-smelling gum, from covers of emerald green, from that ideal of reliable, invariable, men and women, which would forbid saint and conoisseur who always, the one in his simple, the other in his elaborate way, do what is unaccountable, and forbid life itself, which, being . . . the only thing that moves itself, is always without precedent. When our age too has passed, when its moments also, . . . seem scarce and precious, students will perhaps open these books, printed by village girls at Dundrum, as curiously as at twenty years I opened the books of history and ballad verse of the old "Library of Ireland." They will notice that this new "Library," where I have gathered so much that seems to me representative or beautiful, unlike the old, is intended for few people, and written by men and women with that ideal condemned by "Mary of the Nation," who wished, as she said, to make no elaborate beauty and to write nothing but what a peasant could understand. If they are philosophic or phantastic it may even amuse them to find some analogy of the old with O'Connell's hearty eloquence, his winged dart shot always into the midst of the people, his mood of comedy; and of the new, with that lonely and haughty person below whose tragic shadow we of modern Ireland began to write.[88]

With the reference to that "Mary of the Nation" whom Duffy had desired to publish, Yeats completed a full circle of the wheel and brought to an end the story of the book-scheme controversy.

87. *Letters,* p. 232, note.
88. *Selections from the Writings of Lord Dunsany* (Dundrum: Cuala Press, 1912), unpaginated.

Yeats's antagonist in the second of his major literary battles, which focused upon the question of national *versus* cosmopolitan literature, was Edward Dowden. He was an old family friend, having been at school with John Yeats, and, beginning in 1884, a close neighbor. He represented in many ways the antithesis of Gavan Duffy. A Protestant by birth, he had been educated at loyalist Trinity College, Dublin, and was affiliated with it for the rest of his life. In politics he was an ardent Unionist. Furthermore, Duffy's mind, while shrewd in practical matters, was not highly sensitive to literature, which he tended to see as a mere expedient for achieving national goals; Dowden, on the other hand, not only loved literature for its own sake but had a fine appreciation and an immense knowledge of it. In 1867, at the age of twenty-four, he had been appointed to the Chair in English Literature at Trinity, and within a decade his *Shakespere: a critical study of his Mind and Art* had earned him an international reputation. For the rest of his long life he continued to turn out quantities of perceptive scholarship.

Dowden's stature and abilities would naturally have been a tremendous asset to the nascent literary movement. Unfortunately, his exposure from childhood to the great masters of world literature, in combination with his loyalist upbringing and sympathies, made him in literary matters a conscious and determined cosmopolitan. The broad sweep of his interests encompassed most of the English writers (including such Yeatsian favorites as Shelley, on whom he wrote a book, and Blake [89]) as well as the major Continental traditions, and even Walt Whitman, of whom he was a friend and an enthusiastic champion; but it stopped at his own country. He knew personally Ferguson, de Vere, and Todhunter as well as the Yeats family and praised a number of Irish works including the Deirdre tale (which he called "one of the greatest tragic stories of the world"), de Vere's rehandling of the "Cattle

89. See, for example, *Fragments From Old Letters: E.D. to E.D.W.* (London and New York: J. M. Dent and Sons, 1914), I, 151–152.

Raid of Cualnge," and Yeats's own *Wanderings of Oisin* and *John Sherman;* [90] nevertheless he confessed himself "infinitely glad" that he had "spent his early enthusiasm on writers like Wordsworth and Spenser and Shakespeare, and not on anything that Ireland ever produced," [91] and in his few public utterances on the subject did his best to discourage interest in Irish literature. It is clear that personal prejudice, and not a lack of time caused by constant communion with the literary giants of France, England, and other countries, was mainly responsible for his avoidance of the Irish tradition: as E. A. Boyd observed, Dowden actually devoted a great amount of attention to extremely minor figures and to the minutiae of literary history. [92] Consequently, it was almost inevitable that he and Yeats would eventually become literary opponents.

Their controversy, though it culminated in 1895, after the book-scheme struggle, had begun long before. In fact its first manifestation came in a cosmopolitan act of kindness on Dowden's part. He had heard the young Yeats read his poetry, offered judicious criticisms of it, and seems to have taken a genuine interest in his literary future. Probably for this reason he offered to lend him some books by George Eliot, one of his own enthusiasms. Yeats did not like her work, [93] and apparently Dowden's interest in it irritated him. In his first major pronouncement on Irish literature, an 1886 article on Ferguson, Yeats began by asserting that Ferguson's unpopularity was due to his having courageously chosen to write on Irish subjects, and he singled out Dowden as a prime example of those responsible for the unfashionableness of such subjects:

It is a question whether the most distinguished of our critics, Professor Dowden, would not only have more consulted the inter-

90. *Letters of Edward Dowden and his Correspondents* (London and New York: J. M. Dent and Sons, 1914), p. 184; *Letters,* pp. 105–106, 180.
91. *Letters of Edward Dowden,* p. 184.
92. *Appreciations and Depreciations* (New York: John Lane, 1918), p. 151.
93. For his reasons, see *Letters,* p. 31.

ests of his country, but more also, in the long run, his own dignity and reputation, which are dear to all Irishmen, if he had devoted some of those elaborate pages which he has spent on the much bewritten George Eliot, to a man like the subject of this article. A few pages from him would have made it impossible for a journal like the *Academy* to write in 1880, that Sir Samuel Ferguson should have published his poetry only for his intimate friends, and that it did not even "rise to the low water-mark of poetry." . . . If Sir Samuel Ferguson had written to the glory of that, from a moral point of view, more than dubious achievement, British civilization, the critics, probably including Professor Dowden, would have taken care of his reputation.[94]

Thus, from the beginning of his propagandizing for national literature he saw Dowden and his influence as threats to his own goals.

Possibly in response to Yeats's criticism, Dowden himself directly confronted the problem of national literature in an 1889 article on "Hopes and Fears for Literature." The question, as he saw it, was "shall we in these islands of ours, who 'speak the tongue that Shakespeare spake,' nurse the dream of four separate streams of literature, or shall we have our pride and our joy in one noble river broadened and deepened by various affluent waters?" [95] His answer was that he preferred the alternative of variety within an encompassing unity, and

94. "The Poetry of Sir Samuel Ferguson," *Dublin University Review,* November, 1886, p. 924.

95. *Fortnightly Review,* Old Series LI (1889), 173. Dowden had originally delivered the essay in 1883 as a speech to the Trinity Historical Society. Yeats and Standish O'Grady both suggest that the passages about Irish literature were added later, O'Grady considering them a response to Yeats's criticism of Dowden in the Ferguson article. See Yeats, "Irish National Literature. IV.—A List of the Best Irish Books," *The Bookman,* October, 1895, p. 21; and O'Grady, "Irish Literature and Mr. Dowden," *Daily Express,* January 28, 1895, pp. 5–6. Dowden claimed that the offending passages had been in the original speech: "Literature in Ireland," *Daily Express,* January 29, 1895, p. 4. In any case he did choose to reprint them at a time when they *would* apply to Yeats and his associates.

that he could imagine and approve of an Irish literary movement in which "such differences of character as may perhaps exist should manifest themselves not of deliberate purpose, but naturally and spontaneously," but that if that "movement were to consist in flapping a green banner in the eyes of the beholders, and upthrusting a pasteboard 'sunburst' [representing Home Rule] high in air," he would prefer to stand apart.[96] He then gave a "literary" example of the sort of patriotism he found repugnant and ridiculed it with some witty ironies reminiscent of Matthew Arnold:

In a popular life of Lord Edward Fitzgerald, published in Dublin, I read the following poetical exordium: "Not Greece of old in her palmiest days, the Greece of Homer and Demosthenes, of Aeschylus, Euripides, and Sophocles, of Pericles, Leonidas, and Alcibiades, of Socrates, Plato, and Aristotle, of Solon and Lycurgus, of Apelles and Praxiteles, not even this Greece, prolific as she was in sages and heroes, can boast such a lengthy bead-roll as Ireland can of names worthy of the immortality of history." How partial, then, have been the awards of history! How true the saying that the world knows nothing of its greatest men! And how modest the writer of this life of Lord Edward Fitzgerald, to set forth the bead-roll of Greece in such ample detail, and to throw the veil of a general statement over the glories of his native land! If in the Irish literary movement we are to step to such a time as this, I think on the whole I should rather fall out of the ranks, or even step to music as paltry as that of "Rule Britannia." [97]

Although effective, this passage is profoundly unjust, for, while it does graphically illustrate the rightness of Yeats's insistence that only "impartial" biographies of the Irish leaders of the past would attract the more intelligent segment of the potential audience for Irish work, it hardly represents the point of view against which Dowden was arguing at its best.

96. "Hopes and Fears for Literature," p. 175.
97. *Ibid.*, pp. 175–176.

He then went on to explain in more detail his own conception of the relationship between literature and nationality:

If national character be really strong and vivid, it will show itself, although we do not strive to be national with malice prepense; it will show itself, whether we occupy ourselves with an edition of Sophocles or of Cicero, or with a song of the deeds of Cuchullain or the love and sorrow of Deirdre. No folly can be greater than that of fancying that we shall strengthen our literary position by living exclusively in our own ideas, and showing ourselves inhospitable to the best ideas of other lands. Nor is that hospitality the finest which constrains the guest to assume the garb and adopt the manners of his entertainers. . . . Surely any Irish man of letters may be engaged in work in the truest sense patriotic if he endeavours to bring into his country the best ideas from France, from Germany, from the old world of classical learning, from the living world of nature, or from some fresh exploration of the mind of man, even though the word "Ireland" be not for ever shrilling on his lips. We should be far better patriots if, instead of singing paeans about Irish genius, we were to set ourselves to correct some of the defects of Irish intellect. Let an Irish poet teach his countrymen to write a song free from rhetoric, free from false imagery, free from green tinsel, and with thoroughly sound workmanship in the matter of verse, and he will have done a good and a needful thing. Let an Irish prose writer show that he can be patient, exact, just, enlightened, and he will have done better service for Ireland, whether he treats of Irish themes or not, than if he wore shamrocks in all his buttonholes and had his mouth for ever filled with the glories of Brian the Brave.[98]

Dowden's position and Yeats's own coincided at several points: the need for correct judgments unblurred by patriotism, the desirability of infusing Irish culture with the "best ideas of other lands," and the goal of stylistic improvement in Irish literature. The two points Yeats could not accept were the explicit statement that Irish writers need not choose Irish subjects, and the implicit suggestion that no one in the Irish

98. *Ibid.*, pp. 176–177.

literary movement was aware of the faults Dowden saw, let alone had any concern with correcting them.

During the period of the Duffy controversy Yeats in a number of essays indirectly answered Dowden's charges. "Dublin Scholasticism and Trinity College" (July 30, 1892) turned the tables by attacking T.C.D. as a force impeding the intellectual development of Ireland, but one the deadening influence of which the book-scheme might successfully combat; "Hopes and Fears for Irish Literature" (October 15, 1892), the title of which may be an allusion to Dowden's article,[99] admitted the faults of Irish literature but expressed optimism about its future; and "Nationality and Literature" (May, 1893) argued that literatures in their primitive stages are naturally national and only become more cosmopolitan as they reach maturity. But a further direct confrontation between the two did not occur until 1895.

On January 20 of that year Yeats wrote to his sister Lily,

"The Irish Literary Movement" is flourishing. A lecture on Samuel Ferguson, which was read at the Irish Lit Society London by Roden Noel, was read in Dublin the other day by Miss Hickey, with the Archbishop in the chair and Dowden, Sir William Stokes, Prof Mahaffy, Judge Fitzgibbon, the Master of the Rolls and Prof Ingram all to make speeches about it; and the best of the joke is that it was described by one of the speakers as a lecture written for, and delivered to, an English audience—not one word was said about the Irish Lit Society and Prof Dowden expressed scorn for the Irish Lit movement and Irish lit generally, for which he has been catching it from all the Dublin papers— even the *Irish Times* which had a leader on him. He has written a rather feeble protest [*Letters*, 245].

99. It may be that Yeats did not know the 1889 article. In "Irish National Literature. IV.—A List of the Best Irish Books," *The Bookman*, October, 1895, p. 21 he says that the criticisms of the literary movement were added for the publication in volume form. As the offending passages *were* in the 1889 version, either Yeats never saw it, or he did read it but by 1895 had forgotten their presence.

It is fitting that it should have been Ferguson, the third figure in Yeats's first blast of criticism at Dowden, who precipitated the more extensive controversy between them which now began. In response to Dowden's criticisms Rolleston published a defense of Irish poetry, and Dowden in turn sent to the Dublin papers the relevant passages from his 1889 article, soon to be republished in a collection of his essays, *New Studies in Literature*. Rolleston replied again, and Yeats, along with Standish O'Grady and William Larminie, got involved.[100]

Yeats sent his reply to the Unionist *Daily Express,* where it appeared on January 26. He began by admitting what he himself had never denied, that Irish literature was full of faults; but he argued that this was to be expected of "a young literature, an experimental literature, a literature preoccupied with hitherto unworked material, and compelled to seek an audience for the most part among the poor and the ignorant" —so compelled because, as he had asserted in his Ferguson article of nine years earlier, the affluent and educated loyalists had turned their backs on it without ever giving it a chance. He then sought to show not only that there were many people striving to correct the faults of Irish literature, and in fact doing much more in that way than Dowden himself had ever done, but also that there was already a fair amount of Irish writing of high quality:

The only question at issue is whether we can best check these faults by carefully sifting out and expounding what is excellent, as Mr Stopford Brooke, Mr Rolleston, Dr Hyde, Mr Ashe King,

100. See the Yeats letter quoted in A. N. Jeffares, *W. B. Yeats: Man and Poet,* 2nd ed. (London: Routledge and Kegan Paul Ltd., 1962), p. 97; also Rolleston, "Professor Dowden and Sir Samuel Ferguson," *Daily Express* (Dublin), January 21, 1895, p. 5; the editorial reply to Rolleston, *Daily Express,* January 22, 1895, p. 4; Rolleston's second defense, "Professor Dowden and Irish Literature," *Daily Express,* January 23, 1895, p. 5; O'Grady, "Irish Literature and Mr. Dowden," *Daily Express,* January 28, 1895, pp. 5–6; and "Literature in Ireland," *Daily Express,* February 2, 1895, p. 5; Larminie, "Irish Literature," *Daily Express,* January 25, 1895, p. 3.

John O'Leary, from a sketch by John Butler Yeats. (By permission of Mr. M. B. Yeats.)

Edward Dowden. (From *Letters of Edward Dowden and His Correspondents,* London, 1914.)

Mr Alfred Percival Graves, Mr Lionel Johnson, and other leaders of "the Irish literary movement" are endeavouring to do; or by talking, like Professor Dowden, occasional vague generalities about rhetoric and sentimentality and bad technique. . . . And I think that the man who cannot find a distinct character in Callanan's "Outlaw of Loch Lene," in Walsh's "Mairgreed Ni Chealleada," in Davis' "Marriage" and "Plea for Love," in Mangan's "Ode to the Maguire" and "Woman of Three Cows," in Doheney's "A Cushla Gal ma Chree," in Allingham's "Winding Banks of Erin [sic]," in Ferguson's "Conary," in de Vere's "Wedding of the Clans," and in countless other poems, which are neither rhetorical nor sentimental, nor of flaccid technique, must be either prejudiced or a little lacking in artistic sensitiveness. I am sure that if Professor Dowden does not perceive this distinct character it can only be because he has given the subject too little attention; and if he does perceive it I ask him does he think he has quite done his duty by this new creative impulse. . . . Professor Dowden has been for years our representative critic, and during that time he has done little for the reputation of Ferguson, whom he admires, and nothing for the reputation of these others, whom Ferguson admired. Our "movement," on the other hand, has only existed three or four years [Yeats was probably thinking here of the "formalization" of the movement with the founding of the two literary societies], and during that time it has denounced rhetoric with more passionate vehemence than he has ever done. It has exposed sentimentality and flaccid technique with more effect than has been possible to his imperfect knowledge of Irish literature, but at the same time it has persuaded Irish men and women to read what is excellent in past and present Irish literature, and it has added to that literature books of folk-lore, books of history, books of fiction and books of verse, which, whatever be their faults, are yet the expression of the same dominant mood, the same creative impulse which inspired Ferguson and the poets I have named.[101]

Although the dispute with Dowden was essentially the opposition of a national writer and a cosmopolitan, Yeats's

101. "Professor Dowden and Irish Literature," *Daily Express* (Dublin), January 26, 1895.

ideals of increased craftsmanship and the precedence of the requirements of art over the needs of patriotism for the artist played an important part in the argument, for he countered Dowden's assertions of the poor quality of Irish literature with oblique references to his campaign against the rhetoric and sentimentality and stylistic weaknesses of Young Ireland verse. In addition, while the phrase "Irish literary movement" is set off in quotation marks (probably because of Dowden's derogatory use of the tag), Yeats's letter was clearly calculated to suggest that there was indeed a genuine movement in progress. Yet another interesting feature is the catalogue of good Irish poems. This catalogue had the dual functions of refuting by its very bulk Dowden's denial that there *was* any good Irish literature and serving as a guide to taste, suggesting to the prospective audience for Irish poetry the sort of work they ought to read. This device had been used by Yeats before and, in considerably more elaborate form, was to become a central feature of the later stages of the Dowden controversy. At this time he also wrote to Methuen asking him to publish *A Book of Irish Verse* (the selective principle of which had been national literature with stylistic excellence) as "a shot in the battle"; [102] it did not, however, appear at once.

Yeats was soon able to make a more direct use of his anti-Young Ireland propaganda campaign as evidence against Dowden. On February 7 he published in the *Express* the following account:

A very amusing proof of the unfounded nature of one of Professor Dowden's charges against the Irish literary movement has just reached me. At the very time Professor Dowden was sending to the Press an introduction, saying that we indulged in indiscriminate praise of all things Irish, and went about "plastered with shamrocks and raving of Brian Boru," a certain periodical was giving the hospitality of its pages to a long anonymous letter making a directly contrary charge. The writer of the letter accused some of the members of the Irish Literary Society of discouraging

102. Jeffares, *W. B. Yeats*, p. 97.

"worthy workers in the field," of endeavouring to substitute the pursuit of what he called "high art" for the old, easy-going days when every patriotic writer was as good as his neighbour, and even of making allegations against the literary merits of Young Ireland poetry. His feelings about one member, who had been rather active in criticism, so completely overpowered him that he could only say that this member's walk was ungainly, his personal habits objectionable, and his face dirty.[103]

The member involved may have been Yeats himself, in which case this public repetition would be partly cathartic in function. Such incidents surely had much to do with the indelible impression the quarrels of these years made upon Yeats's imagination.

During this period Yeats spent a considerable amount of time in Sligo, where he had been propagandizing for Irish literature among the Gore-Booths and other Unionist families, and their interest helped determine his ensuing action. His next letter to the *Express*, which appeared on February 27, began: "During our recent controversy with Professor Dowden certain of my neighbours here in the West of Ireland asked me what Irish books they should read. As I have no doubt others elsewhere have asked a like question, I send you a list of thirty books" (*Letters*, 246). As early as 1891, when Yeats was working on the plan to set up reading rooms in connection with the Young Ireland clubs, he had been interested in such lists: a list of one hundred had appeared a few years earlier in the *Freeman's Journal*, and Yeats criticized the cosmopolitanism of its principle of selection and gave (in ordinary paragraph form) his own list, from which he excluded those Irishmen who "did not make Ireland their subject matter." [104]

103. "Professor Dowden and Irish Literature," *Daily Express* (Dublin), February 7, 1895.

104. "The Young Ireland League," *United Ireland*, October 3, 1891. The earlier list, and some seventy-one letters of comment from figures ranging from Parnell to the Secretary of the General Post Office, appeared during March and April, 1886, and were reprinted in pamphlet form as *The Best Hundred Irish Books* (Dublin, n.d. [1886 or 1887]).

In the 1895 article he emphasized the list by having it set off as such typographically, and to elucidate both his choices and his omissions he added a lengthy commentary. (For the list itself, see Appendix A.) The general principles he followed were that the selections should be "books of imagination" or books necessary for understanding the imagination of Ireland and should be free of "strong political feeling." ("There is no book in it 'that raves of Brian Boru,' " he added for Dowden's benefit.) Among the fiction selections he included some books, such as *Charles O'Malley*, "Father Tom and the Pope," and the *Traits and Stories*, which he confessed did not bid their readers take Ireland quite seriously, but which were worth reading nevertheless for the "true records" they presented of certain aspects of Irish life. On the other hand, although he was partly concerned in this list with suggesting that there was enough good *national* writing so that one did not have to fall back upon Swift and Goldsmith and other cosmopolitan literature, he refused to uncritically include all the new writers. He listed Emily Lawless' *Essex in Ireland* only with great hesitation and excluded Jane Barlow entirely because both of these authors seemed to him to be inferior to the best Irish novelists, who created Irish character from within rather than merely observing it from without. He explained that he had listed comparatively few selections of poetry because most of the best Irish poems were so widely scattered, and, unless the reader would accept Yeats's own forthcoming anthology of them, would have to be hunted for through the many individual volumes in which they appeared. He could make this vague "pitch" for the collection because it contained none of his own work, but he was prevented by his position from including in the list itself such impressive items as *The Wanderings of Oisin* (the merit of which Dowden had privately admitted), *The Countess Cathleen*, and *The Celtic Twilight*. In the explanatory portion of the article he also named some other volumes of poetry that he had for various reasons not included in the list. One of these was AE's *Homeward,* which he termed "a very notable book, but not specially Irish in subject." He had already begun to believe that there was an essential connection between the visionary and the Irish and had decided to use some selections from the book in his anthology. But in his own work the mystical and visionary were found among much material that was clearly "Irish" by anyone's standards, and there was in fact *no* such material in *Homeward.* Thus, to include the whole volume in a list of *particularly* Irish books was further than he felt he could go.

In both the list proper and the commentary he expressed his unhappiness that some of the most desirable items were no longer in print while much poorer books, often by the same writers, were constantly being reprinted. This criticism was meant to include not only the case of Carleton, but also, at least by implication, that of the New Irish Library, which might have remedied such a situation. It was exceedingly frustrating for Yeats to try to use against Dowden the very quantity of good national literature while having to admit that much of it had found little favor with Irish readers; but while confessing that in the past the popular success or failure of Irish books had been controlled by prejudice, he concluded with the assertion that the new movement was succeeding in its effort to check this vice and "find an audience for whatever is excellent in the new or the old literature of Ireland."

By this time the controversy seemed to Yeats to be such a valuable propaganda device that he made a calculated effort to expand it. On the thirtieth he sent a copy of his *Express* list to O'Leary (one more instance of his constant closeness to all Yeats's work involving national literature) and added:

I wish you would write. It seems to me an excellent opportunity for getting a little information about Irish books into the heads of Dublin Unionists [who would be reading the *Express*]. The good effects of the Dowden controversy is [*sic*] shown by the debate and vote at a College Historical. I have written to a long list of persons, even to Stopford Brooke among the rest, asking them to contribute, in the hope of a long discussion like that in the *Freeman* on the best hundred.[105]

A contemporary letter to Lily Yeats clarifies the reference to the Trinity incident:

The Dowden controversy has had for one of its results a well attended debate in College Historical Society which passed almost unanimously the resolution "that the Irish Literary revival is worthy of support." Dowden was in the chair and had some more dabs at us.[106]

When Yeats was able to get a fairly accurate account of what those "dabs" included he issued a reply, again in the *Express*. Dowden had given his own definition of Irish literature—"It must be based on the old Celtic legends, must come from the Celtic people of the country, must have the basis and inspiration of race and racial tradition, and must not and cannot be divorced from the philosophy and influences of the Catholic religion"—and accompanied it with his own list of books. Yeats accepted the definition, with the crucial modifications that Ireland was neither wholly Celtic nor wholly Catholic; then he turned it against Dowden:

I . . . affirm that it covers every book upon my list. Are not "Beside the Fire," "The Coming of Cuchullin," and "Fin and his Companions" "based on the old literature and legends"? Are not "the Ballads and Lyrics" of Mrs Hinkson "full of the philosophy and influence and inspiration of the Catholic religion"? Are not "Fardorougha the Miser," "The Nolans," and "Castle Rackrent" informed with the inspiration of our "racial tradition"? On the

105. *Letters*, p. 251. Dowden's opinion had been solicited in regard to the earlier controversy, and he had sent a brief note confessing that his knowledge of Irish books was too slight to give him any basis for judgment (*The Best Hundred Irish Books*, p. 16).

106. *Letters*, p. 252 (March 3, 1895). An account of this debate is given in "The Irish Literature Movement," *Daily Express* (Dublin), February 28, 1895, p. 5.

other hand, does his definition cover a single one of the books selected from Ussher and Swift and Berkeley, which he desired us to consider our national literature? He named none but admirable books, certainly, but "Gulliver's Travels" and "Tristram Shandy" will be substitutes for the books I have named only when the books of Hume are considered Scotch literature in the same sense as the books of Burns or Barrie, or when the writings of Welshmen like Mr George Meredith and Mr William Morris are thought as full of the spirit of Wales as the triads of Taliesin. Professor Dowden must have been dreaming, or very eloquent, which comes to much the same thing, or he would never have included in the same speech so admirable a definition, so irrelevant a list.[107]

Yeats went on to defend the fact that the books in his own list were all "modern" and then explained that he had taken the trouble to answer Dowden's criticisms in order to show that while Dowden might be an " 'acknowledged authority' " on other literatures, on Irish work he was no authority at all, but rather a partisan ready to employ any argument in order to discredit it.

The controversy had even a greater effect than Yeats had expected upon public opinion, especially among the loyalists; he found himself "amazed" at the interest they had taken in the affair and predicted that within a year or two they would "begin to read Irish things greedily." [108] Because in his newspaper contributions he had been forced to spend a considerable portion of the limited space he had upon mere polemics, he planned to repeat the taste-making aspects of his argument on a larger scale in the *Bookman*. Between July and October, 1895, he published a series of four articles under the general rubric "Irish National Literature." [109] The first attempted once

107. "Irish Literature," *Daily Express* (Dublin), March 8, 1895.

108. *Letters*, p. 254 (March 25, 1895).

109. These articles were copied by the Irish press; see *Letters*, pp. 257–258, and "Irish National Literature. IV.—A List of the Best Irish Books," *The Bookman*, October, 1895, p. 21.

more to sift out and expound what was excellent in the poetry and fiction of Ireland up to Yeats's own time; not surprisingly, he was critical of the quality of Young Ireland work and gave most of his praise to Callanan, Mangan, Allingham, de Vere, Ferguson, and Carleton. Here and in the succeeding articles numerous references to "the Moods" and the importance of the "invisible life" illustrate the increasing prominence Yeats was giving to the connection between the spiritual and the Irish. Thus, he said of O'Grady, to whom he allotted first place among "Contemporary Prose Writers," that "multifarious knowledge of Gaelic legend and Gaelic history and a most Celtic temperament have put him in communion with the moods that have been over Irish purposes from the hour when, in the words put into the mouth of St. Dionysius, 'The Most High set the borders of the Nations according to the angels of God.' " [110]

In this same article he was again highly critical of all but a few parts of Emily Lawless' books, but a bit more positive than in the *Express* article in his comments on Jane Barlow. Nora Hopper he spoke of as highly as before and at much greater length. This survey ended with brief references to Irish writers who were helping denounce "rhetoric" and interpret Irish history and romance, and an optimistic assertion that there was in contemporary Ireland a "school of men of letters united by a common purpose, and a small but increasing public who love literature for her own sake and not as the scullery-maid of politics."

Among the "Contemporary Irish Poets," Yeats had kind words for Hyde and Rolleston (for their translations), Katharine Tynan, and Nora Hopper again. The highest and most extended praise, however, was given to AE. Because the latter had "begun to dig for new symbols" in Irish sources, Yeats could now confidently put him in a place of prominence

110. "Irish National Literature. Contemporary Prose Writers," *The Bookman*, August, 1895, p. 139.

among the national poets.[111] Yeats of course made no reference here to his own work.

The final article in the series, a sort of epitome of the preceding pieces, was another "List of the Best Irish Books." In some introductory paragraphs he made explicit the connection between these articles and his controversy with Dowden. He began by contrasting two unsatisfactory components of the Irish reading public, the Young Ireland enthusiasts and the majority of the Unionists. The former, despite their poor standards, had done no permanent harm, and their enthusiasm for Irish things had "kept Irish literature alive for better fortune." But the influence of the Unionists, prejudiced on principle against almost all things Irish, was much more deadly; and he took Dowden as his specific example. He referred again to the offensive essay from *New Studies in Literature,* calling it a type of criticism that "has done and is doing incalculable harm." Not only was it too lacking in knowledge and sympathy to have any positive influence upon the "ignorant patriotic masses," but also Dowden's name lent it enough authority with undergraduates and the educated classes to persuade them that their native literature and the "stories which are interwoven with their native mountains and valleys" were worthy only of contempt. Yeats conceded that this would "perhaps be no great matter" if it turned them to a deeper appreciation of Goethe, Shakespeare, and Milton, but it had no such effect and "by robbing them of the enthusiasm which lay at their doors" left them with no ideal enthusiasm at all. To capture the imagination of this group and to "overthrow and sack Dublin scholasticism" was therefore a major part of the business of " 'the Irish Literary Movement,' " and, in a small way, of such an admittedly artificial propaganda device as Yeats's list. Once more he asserted his national ideal against the cosmopolitanism represented by Dowden, explaining that his

111. "Irish National Literature. III.—Contemporary Irish Poets," *The Bookman,* September, 1895, pp. 169–170.

list contained "no book not upon an Irish subject, or written under some obvious Irish influence," for the time had "not yet come for Irishmen . . . to carry about with them a subtle national feeling, no matter when [for 'where'?], or of what they write." No "edition of Cicero" (or study of Shakespeare's "mind and art") [112] could qualify.

Despite its ampler dimensions, the list itself was very similar to that printed in the *Express:* only one book, Arbois de Jubainville's *Cycle Mythologique,* was dropped, probably because, while Yeats felt it essential for understanding the Irish legends, the author had absolutely no connection with Ireland. (For this list, see Appendix A.) Of the additions, Mitchel's *Jail Journal* and Tone's *Autobiography* had been excluded from the earlier article by its more strictly apolitical nature; virtually all the others had been referred to before in the sections of commentary in the articles involving the controversy.

To insure the full effect of this group of articles, Yeats sent them to Fisher Unwin to be published as a pamphlet under the title *What to Read in Irish Literature.*[113] He planned to restore some quotations omitted by the *Bookman* editors to conserve space, and to add some pages of introduction dealing with "the relation of such literature to general literature and culture and to contemporary movements" (such as, presumably, the Symbolist and "spiritual" movements). Unfortunately, despite the appropriateness of having such a work appear over the name of Unwin, the project was not carried out.

This marked the end of the controversy. Dowden, while never converted to Yeats's point of view, did find in the coming years a few more Irish books he liked, including AE's poems and Lady Gregory's *Cuchulain of Muirthemne.*[114] He

112. Dowden's famous *Shakespere* was in fact included in a list compiled by D. F. Hannigan, "The Thirty Best Irish Books," *Daily Express* (Dublin), March 16, 1895.

113. *Letters,* p. 258 (November, 1895).

114. *Letters of Edward Dowden,* pp. 273–274, 341; p. 318.

also continued to take an interest in Yeats's own career; when Yeats was engaged in the *Playboy* affair, Dowden expressed the opinion that he was perhaps devoting too much attention to "movements" and not enough to cultivating his own abilities; and he was even favorable to the idea that Yeats should succeed him in the T.C.D. Chair of English Literature.[115] On Yeats, on the other hand, their opposition left a permanent mark, and its importance grew in memory until by the time he began to write his autobiography he used Dowden to represent all that stood in his way at the start of his career (*Letters*, 603, 606).

"John Eglinton" (William Kirkpatrick Magee), Yeats's principal opponent in the third major controversy of the nineties, had much more in common with Dowden—whose writings attracted him so much that he regretted not having done a study of him [116]—than with Gavan Duffy. Like Dowden he was highly learned and had a sophisticated, cosmopolitan interest in literature. Furthermore, though not an active Unionist, he was no more enthusiastic about the political nationalism of Ireland. His stance towards both literature and national politics was determined primarily by his personal philosophy, the central tenet of which was the unfettered development of the individual human being's potential "divinity." [117] Art and the state were to contribute to this development, never to hinder it, and Eglinton's critical writings often judged literature according to whether or not it seemed likely to make such a

115. See *Letters*, pp. 550 note, 557; and *J. B. Yeats: Letters to his Son W. B. Yeats and Others, 1869–1922*, ed. Joseph Hone (New York: E. P. Dutton and Co., 1946), p. 160.

116. Boyd, *Appreciations and Depreciations*, p. 149; see also Eglinton's introduction to *The Letters of Edward Dowden* (1914).

117. Ernest A. Boyd, *Ireland's Literary Renaissance* (New York: John Lane, 1916), p. 246. For further remarks by Eglinton on the subject of national literature, see his introductory note in *Dana*, No. 1 (May, 1904), 1–3.

contribution. His objection on these grounds to the materials Yeats was proposing as the basis for the national literature began their controversy.

At first Yeats seems to have thought that Eglinton would be part of the movement and, conscious of his great acuteness of mind, welcomed the idea. From the appearance in 1894 of *Two Essays on the Remnant* (of which he did not like the style and could not make himself read, but the great intellectual promise of which he nevertheless perceived), he began to include Eglinton among the members of the "spiritual group," and in late 1897 he noted with pleasure that he had given his name as a guarantor for the projected theater.[118] But Eglinton had definite ideas about the nature of that theater, and his exposition of them, in an article published in the *Express* in September, 1898, revealed a considerable gap between his ideas and those of Yeats.

He began by asking where a writer of genius appearing in Ireland would seek the subject-matter for a national drama: "Would he look for it in the Irish legends, or in the life of the peasantry and folk-lore, or in Irish history and patriotism, or in life at large as reflected in his own consciousness?" [119] Yeats, if asked such a question, would have said that all four sources might be used; however, his own emphasis at the time was on the first two. But Eglinton had a different answer, different not only from Yeats's, but also from that which would have been given by Dowden, who had stated his opinion that the national literature must draw upon the old legends and upon the beliefs of the people:

The ancient legends of Ireland undoubtedly contain situations and characters as well suited for drama as most of those used in the Greek tragedies which have come down to us. It is, nevertheless, a question whether the mere fact of Ireland having been the scene of these stories is enough to give an Irish writer much

118. *Letters,* p. 289 (November 6, 1897).
119. *Literary Ideals in Ireland,* p. 9. Subsequent references to this volume, abbreviated *Lit Ideals,* are given in the text.

advantage over anyone else who is attracted by them, or whether anything but belles lettres, as distinguished from a national literature, is likely to spring from a determined pre-occupation with them. Belles lettres seek a subject outside experience, while a national literature, or any literature of a genuine kind, is simply the outcome and expression of a strong interest in life itself. The truth is, these subjects, much as we may admire them and regret that we have nothing equivalent to them in the modern world, obstinately refuse to be taken up out of their old environment and be transplanted into the world of modern sympathies. The proper mode of treating them is a secret lost with the subjects themselves [*Lit Ideals*, 11].

He applied the same principles implicitly to folklore and directly to history and patriotic themes: "Ireland must exchange the patriotism which looks back for the patriotism which looks forward" (*Lit. Ideals*, 12).

These statements seemed flatly to deny that the past could by literary means be brought viably to bear upon the present. Yeats, who had just completed an article praising the work of Nora Hopper (who made extensive use of legends and folklore), felt a challenge in Eglinton's assertion; at first, however, he sent no full rebuttal, but merely added a postscript to his article referring to the passage in which he had offered the examples of Ibsen's *Peer Gynt* and the works of Wagner as proof that a drama not only national but extremely influential as well could be made from the materials Eglinton had rejected (*Lit Ideals*, 17–19).

Eglinton himself then sent in a reply, which began by stating that he had had no intention of being "combative," and—a claim hardly borne out by the article—had only intended to raise the question, not to answer it. He added that he had not meant modern writers could not use the old legends, but that if they did so they had to "make them live again in a new way," the original modes of treating them no longer being available. After questioning whether Wagner, whom he saw as the artist of a coterie, could be thought of as the national

[123]

poet or dramatist of Germany, Eglinton concluded by arguing that all conceptions of poetry could be divided into two antithetical groups. On one hand was the position that saw poetry as philosophy (with the poet as "seer" and "spiritual force"), looking to man for its inspiration, and tending to be careless of form and artistic perfection. On the other he placed the conception of poetry as art (and the poet as a craftsman), finding its sources of inspiration in tradition—"old faiths, myths, dreams." It he characterized as stylistically more perfect, but cut off from "the source of all regeneration in art" and therefore diffuse and insincere. Eglinton clearly preferred the former (which he called "Wordsworthian" after one of his favorite authors) but felt the latter to be currently predominant, and suggested that it constituted a barrier to national literature because in it the poet, rather than coming to grips with himself and the age in which he lives, tries to escape from them; consequently his art "cannot be the expression of the age and of himself—cannot be representative and national" (*Lit Ideals,* 23–27).

Yeats's next article, "John Eglinton and Spiritual Art" (October 29, 1898), opened with the assertion that Eglinton was wrong about Wagner being the enthusiasm only of an elite minority, but that this fact was less important than Wagner's influence upon the "best intellects" of the day, upon men like Villiers de L'Isle Adam. Yeats's experience with the book-scheme had led him at least temporarily to the position that "the only permanent influence of any art is an influence that flows down gradually and imperceptibly" from the leading thinkers to the masses. He was pleased with the change in Eglinton's position regarding the use in modern literature of folklore and legend, for Eglinton's stipulation that they must be recreated by being infused with the author's own personality and milieu seemed to call for precisely the method that Yeats himself favored. He did, however, seize upon Eglinton's dualistic analysis of possible theories of poetry.

Yeats had been strongly affected by an essay on poetry by

[124]

Tennyson's friend Arthur Hallam and used it to restate Eglinton's distinction in terms much more flattering to the "aesthetic school" than to the "philosophical" poetry Eglinton preferred. According to this version, the works of the aesthetic writers always have a limited audience because, being the products of the most sensitive minds, they cannot be fully appreciated by ordinary men. The philosophic poets are more popular, for they mix with their highest perceptions various anecdotes, opinions, and moral maxims which "dull temperaments can understand." Furthermore, Yeats denied that there *was* any high philosophic content in the work of the philosophic school: it was the poetry of "the utilitarian and the rhetorician and the sentimentalist and the popular preacher," but not of the "seer," it was not a "spiritual force" (*Lit Ideals*, 33–35). The references to rhetoric and sentimentality echo the Dowden controversy and serve as reminders that for Yeats the poetry of Young Ireland would be part of the philosophical school.

Whether Yeats had yet managed to finish *Two Essays on the Remnant* is not clear; in any case he greatly overestimated the extent to which Eglinton shared his own contemporary spiritual world-view and therefore found it difficult to understand how Eglinton, as a "profound transcendentalist," could prefer art concerned with ordinary life, with the world of surfaces, "to a poetry which seeks to express great passions that are not in nature" (*Lit Ideals*, 35). To Yeats, Eglinton sounded like a Mill or an Arnold, and he himself could not accept such a position:

I believe that the renewal of belief, which is the great movement of our time, will more and more liberate the arts from "their age" and from life, and leave them more and more free to lose themselves in beauty, and to busy themselves, like all the great poetry of the past and like all religions of all times, with "old faiths, myths, dreams," the accumulated beauty of the age. I believe that all men will more and more reject the opinion that poetry is "a criticism of life," and be more and more convinced that it is a revelation of a hidden life, and that they may even come to think "painting, poetry, and music" "the only means of conversing with eternity left to man on earth" [*Lit Ideals*, 36].

Eglinton had placed philosophy above stylistic accomplishments, but for Yeats these were inseparable ideals: the extent to which art was spiritual depended directly upon its artistry, the ultimate standards for judging poetry were "the volume and intensity of its passion for beauty, and . . . the perfection of its workmanship."

The question of the reuse of ancient legends had still not been resolved to Eglington's satisfaction, as he made clear in the opening paragraph of his third piece; he did not feel that the examples suggested by Yeats really exemplified his stipulations for successful modern transformation of the originals. In truth, however, the choice of examples was really secondary; their difference of opinion was a function of their basic difference in world-view, a contrast that the rest of this article made more overt. Eglinton *was* closer to Arnold than to Yeats: he claimed that the poetry of the philosophical school was "more important than the poetry of art and artifice . . . because of its high seriousness [a direct quotation of a famous Arnoldian touchstone] and more universal appeal; because it is more concerned with the facts of life and is more inspired by faith and hope; because it expresses its age better and what is best in the age." He totally rejected the symbolist position:

What do the symbolists . . . mean exactly by saying that the "poetic passion is not in nature," and that art is to be "liberated from life." Life is nothing but what we make it, and we do not alter its substance by twisting it into an abnormality. If the transcendent realities do not exist in the normal human consciousness, they do not exist in "poetry, music, and painting," or at all [*Lit Ideals*, 45–46].

The "Editor's Note" to *Literary Ideals in Ireland*, the title given to the articles when published in collected form, states that the controversy was "not intended when the first article was written, but . . . spontaneously grew from week to week . . . and developed . . . a certain organic unity" (*Lit Ideals*, 5). The assertion of spontaneity is certainly true of the opening stages of the controversy, but not of the entire incident. Two years earlier AE had suggested to Yeats that they, along with Eglinton, Hyde, O'Grady, and Johnson, should do a book of essays dealing with the renewal in contemporary Ireland of the heroic past. Certain practical steps were taken, including the contacting of William Larminie as another possible contributor, but the project was not carried out.[120] Apparently the Yeats-Eglinton debate—on basically the same subject that AE had had in mind—led to the revival of the earlier plan. The week following the appearance of Eglinton's third piece, AE added a contribution in which he tried to show that Yeats and Eglinton were not as far apart as they thought, and in doing so pictured them as closer together than they really were. Perhaps there may have been a personal reason for this effort at mediation: Yeats later wrote of the affair that it "was a stirring row while it lasted and we were all very angry." [121] But several of the central issues were reopened by Larminie, who wrote the next week's essay; his own position, while definitely idiosyncratic and not a mere echo of Eglinton, differed primarily from Yeats's.

Meanwhile Yeats himself was now consciously expanding the controversy, in which he saw multiple propaganda values. In a November 6 letter to Lady Gregory he wrote,

I am going to try and widen the controversy if I can into a discussion of the spiritual origin of the arts. In this way we will keep people awake until we announce "The Irish Literary Theatre" in December and discuss that. . . . There have been some

120. Information from an unpublished letter from AE to Yeats, tentatively dated October, 1896 (microfilm of Alan Denson's collection of AE's letters, Harvard University Library).

121. Quoted in Allan Wade, *A Bibliography of the Writings of W. B. Yeats,* 3rd ed., revised by Russell K. Alspach (London: Rupert Hart-Davis, 1968), p. 286.

very good articles in the *Express* on the point of view that Ireland being poor must preserve the virtues of the poor, spirituality, ideality. . . . One last week called "Celtic Ideals" or some such thing was particularly good. I am trying to appeal to the writers of these articles in my controversy with "Eglinton" in hopes of gradually building up a school of spiritual thought in Ireland.[122]

His last article, "The Autumn of the Flesh," did widen the scope of the contention: it contained no specific references to Eglinton or even to Ireland, instead drawing from a survey of contemporary European art the conclusion that the apparent "decadence" was really a promise of the rebirth of "spiritual art." But the debate never returned to the subject of drama: the final essay, by AE, was on "Nationality and Cosmopolitanism in Literature."

An interesting postscript to the encounter was provided by a 1901 piece by Yeats on Eglinton's *Pebbles from a Brook*. By this time Yeats had definitely read *Two Essays on the Remnant* as well, and although he was full of praise for both books and found in them much that he agreed with, he now objected to them in a way that turned the earlier dispute inside out. While Eglinton had argued that art must concern itself with "the age," he also held that when the sensitive individual found that his duties to society no longer harmonized with his duties to his own self, he should withdraw from contact with that society. Yeats, who had placed far more emphasis on the invisible but "real" world than on the visible but illusory one, now argued that "the Remnant" (Eglinton's term for those sensitive individuals) should not withdraw from society, but rather should attempt actively to remake it, with "swords" if necessary.[123]

Despite their continuing disagreement, Yeats never came to consider Eglinton in the same hostile light as he did Dowden; in fact he seems to have prized that very disagree-

122. *Letters,* p. 304. For the article to which Yeats refers, see *Daily Express* (Dublin), October 29, 1898.
123. "John Eglinton," *United Irishman,* November 9, 1901.

ment, for when in 1905 he made a selection from Eglinton's work for a Dun Emer Press volume, he wrote in one copy of it, "John Eglinton is our one Irish critic. He is in permanently friendly opposition to our national literary movement. He has influenced us all I think even though we curse him at times." [124]

Both Gavan Duffy and Dowden also had, indirectly, a positive influence upon Yeats, the one by his opposition precipitating his necessary final break with Young Ireland, the other forcing him to think more acutely and discriminatingly than ever about the nature and quality of Irish literature. And all three controversies helped prepare him for the rigors of propagandizing for the theater movement (in articles, and in the theater organs *Beltaine, Samhain,* and *The Arrow,* which he edited) and defending its productions, from *The Countess Cathleen* to *The Playboy of the Western World.*

124. Quoted in William M. Schutte, *Joyce and Shakespeare* (New Haven: Yale University Press, 1957), p. 40.

4. Confrontations: Yeats and Other Irish Writers

The confrontations between Yeats and other Irish writers of the eighties and nineties reveal much about his ideals and how they were formed, his efforts to spread them to others, and the successes and failures of those efforts. The nature of the confrontations varied as widely as the principals involved; what was common to all of them was Yeats's desire to shape the course of Irish literature.[1]

1. A Group Effort

In 1888, John O'Leary and his sister Ellen, with the help of Yeats and Katharine Tynan, edited *Poems and Ballads of Young Ireland,* a small anthology of poetry by contemporary writers.[2] Of the contributors, Ellen O'Leary and Rose Kavanagh

---

1. I wish to acknowledge here a debt to Richard Ellmann's *Eminent Domain* (New York: Oxford University Press, 1967) and to my colleague D. N. Archibald, who is currently preparing a study of Yeats and such figures as Swift, Berkeley, and Burke; both have contributed to my awareness of the nature and complexities of literary influence.

2. See *Letters,* pp. 37 note, 43, 49, 70–71. *LNI,* pp. 121–122 suggests that Hyde, John Todhunter, and Rose Kavanagh may also have assisted. In the face of these references, Marcus Bourke can hardly be correct in asserting that Rolleston was the editor, though possibly he too had a hand in the project; see *John O'Leary* (Tralee, Ireland: Anvil Books, 1967), p. 189.

soon died, the importance of George Noble Plunkett and George Sigerson was not to be primarily creative, and Charles Gregory Fagan, Frederick J. Gregg, and Hester Sigerson all remained in literary obscurity; but Hyde, Todhunter, Rolleston, Katharine Tynan, and of course Yeats himself were to play significant roles in the literary activities of the next decade. Thus, the book can be considered the first anthology of the new movement.

The title embodied two almost antithetical associations. Along with the dedicatory verses (contributed by Rolleston) to O'Leary, modestly stating that the poems to follow would have "little chance to live with those that Davis' clarion blew," it evoked the specter of the Young Ireland tradition and hardly promised a revolutionary volume. But "Young Ireland" could also mean the Ireland of the present, of a new day, and its contents did in fact reveal significant departures from the literature of '45.

In the first place, as signaled by the epigraph from Allingham ("We're one at heart if you be Ireland's friend, / Though leagues asunder our opinions tend; / There are but two great parties in the end"), Nationalist politics occupy a much smaller place in *Poems and Ballads* than they did in the work of the poets of *The Nation*. Only one poem, Hyde's "Marching Song of the Gaelic Athletes," with its fulsome idealization of the Irish and warnings of rebellious might could be classed with the large body of Young Ireland verse having immediate political relevance and aimed at molding public opinion; and it is typical of only one strand of Hyde's work. Dr. Sigerson's "The Exile's Return" had been topical when originally written, at the time of Terence Bellew McManus' funeral in 1861, and makes use of some of the familiar Young Ireland diction. Hyde's "Death Lament of John O'Mahony" and "A Ballad of '98" bring in but are not centrally concerned with the political element, and the same is true of Todhunter's "Under the White-Boy Acts, 1800," Katharine Tynan's "The Grave of Michael Dwyer," and (very slightly) Rose Kavanagh's "St

Michan's Churchyard." None of these contain any of the bombastic rhetoric typical of Young Ireland. Rolleston's "The Flight of O'Donnell" recalls those Young Ireland poems on historical subjects that can be seen as having contemporary relevance. Todhunter's "The Coffin Ship" seems simply to be about an old woman crazed at the loss of her loved ones, but in the last stanza she is seen as a symbol for Ireland itself. The other two-thirds of the poems in the collection eschew politics entirely. For example, Yeats's "The Stolen Child" and Rolleston's "The Spell-Struck" are concerned with the fairies, Hyde's "St Colum-Cille and the Heron" is historical-religious, Rolleston's "The Dead at Clonmacnois," Hyde's "From the Irish," and Yeats's "Love Song" are renderings of Gaelic originals, and Rose Kavanagh's "Breasal's Bride" and Yeats's "King Goll" refer to the ancient Irish period. All of these subjects were outside what had come to be thought of as the central Young Ireland tradition, and thus their prominence represented a major shift in emphasis. Evidence that this shift was perceived at the time is offered by W. P. Ryan, who saw the collection as characterized by "sweetness and *fresh emphasis*." [3]

The book also revealed significant differences in quality from Young Ireland verse. Many of the contributions were indeed very bad, with the worst of all unquestionably Plunkett's "Hush Song":

> There's light in Heaven when the earth is dreary,
> Can we ever love you enough, my dearie?
> Wee hand, full of blessings, your father kissed it:
> My love of loves on my heart is feasted.

The pieces by Gregg, the Sigersons, Ellen O'Leary and Rose Kavanagh were also quite weak, though Yeats had kind words for Miss Kavanagh's and contrasted her "meditative and sympathetic" verse with the "stirring and energetic" Young Ireland tradition (*LNI*, 122–123). Hyde's poems, too, with the exception of "From the Irish," were undistinguished. But

3. Ryan, pp. 49–50 (italics added).

those by Todhunter, Rolleston, Katharine Tynan, and Yeats all revealed a definite concern with artistic craftsmanship and a mastery of technique greater than that of almost all the Young Ireland work (exclusive of Mangan). Ballad rhythms were used in some of the pieces, but there was a wide variety of other meters and stanzaic patterns: for instance, Todhunter's "Under the White-Boy Acts, 1800" was in blank verse, a meter not found in Young Ireland literature. The subtle rhythms of Rolleston's "The Dead at Clonmacnois"—

> In a quiet water'd land, a land of roses,
> Stands Saint Kieran's city fair;
> And the warriors of Erin in their famous generations
> Slumber there. . . .

—and the competence with which Yeats was already manipulating refrains, were virtually unmatched in the earlier tradition. Ryan's contemporary reaction is again relevant: he felt that there was perhaps "more finish" to *Poems and Ballads*, "more suggestion of real poetry" than in *The Spirit of the Nation*, with which he and others were directly comparing it.[4]

Poems and Ballads is an important document in assessing Yeats's role in inaugurating the movement. Although he had a hand in the editing, he was not primarily responsible for the "fresh emphasis" of the book: that distinction almost certainly belongs to O'Leary, who had been a major influence on nearly all the important contributors. The current of Irish literature had already begun to move in the direction Yeats would increasingly try to channel it. In fact, the literary success of the volume must have helped solidify his own developing ideals. The combination of shift in subject-matter with stylistic improvement graphically confirmed his feeling that if the Irish writers "had something else to write about besides political opinions, if more of them would write about the beliefs of the people like Allingham, or about old legends like

4. *Ibid.*

Ferguson, they would find it easier to get a style" (*EI*, 3–4). In this enterprise, then, Yeats was acting as part of a group, and he was as much a learner as a shaper; but in the following years he tried, with varying degrees of success, to bring each of his major fellow-contributors more into line with the principles their practice had helped to teach him.

2. *Katharine Tynan: A Working Relationship*

When Yeats first met Miss Tynan in 1885 she was already a poet of note, having published that year a volume of poetry, *Louise de la Vallière,* which had been favorably reviewed and had even won the commendation of Christina Rossetti. With the appearance of *Shamrocks* in 1887 she established herself as "the queen of Irish song." [5] Her acquaintance was consequently to be prized by an aspiring but still very obscure young poet. She was friendly, however, and he found it easy to talk to her about their craft. As their friendship grew he took an ever more active interest in her work. His interest is difficult to understand today, but when compared to other Irish literature of the eighties, her poetry unquestionably seemed better than it really was, and his personal sympathy and gratitude prejudiced him in its favor. But if he sometimes overvalued her work, his criticism was more often objective and highly penetrating. Furthermore, she recognized his genius very early (in an 1887 review of *Mosada* she predicted he would "take high place among the world's future singers") [6] and was therefore inclined to be receptive to his suggestions. Thus, his efforts to influence her met with considerable success, and they enjoyed for a number of years a close and fruitful working relationship.

His first recorded criticisms of her poetry date from 1887. He wrote two reviews of *Shamrocks,* one for *The Gael* and one

5. She was so called by F. A. Fahy, in a presentation copy of his *Irish Songs and Poems,* 1887 (recorded in List No. 272 of the Museum Bookshop, Dublin, Ireland [April–May, 1967], p. 26).

6. "Three Young Poets," *Irish Monthly,* October, 1887, p. 166.

for *The Irish Fireside*. No copies of the former paper are known to exist, but a contemporary letter from Yeats to O'Leary (who was, significantly, "literary editor" of *The Gael*) throws some light upon the contents of his review. O'Leary mistakenly believed that Yeats had evoked Christina Rossetti's praise of Miss Tynan to support his own, but Yeats revealed that actually he had quoted her as an opponent. He disliked the religious poems she cared for, such as "Sanctuary," preferring instead "St. Francis to the Birds" and "The Heart of a Mother," in which, more than in any other pieces in the volume, "the form and matter seem . . . in perfect unison and the simplicity the greatest." [7] In these poems Miss Tynan's always very simple ideas were expressed in a simple, unostentatious manner with plain, predominantly monosyllabic language, as in these lines from "The Heart of a Mother":

> You are so far away,
> And yet are come so near;
> On many a heavy day,
> I think of you, my dear,
> Safe in your shelter there,
> Christ's hand upon your hair.

Yeats contrasted this type of writing with her more ornate and elaborate style (dominant in *Louise de la Vallière* and never entirely abandoned during her career), characterized by artificial constructions and a literally glittering "poetic" diction featuring words like "chrysolite," "sapphire," "jacinth," "porphyry," "amber," "emerald," "azure," "pearl," and "gold." [8]

The *Irish Fireside* review emphasized stylistic improvement through a similar contrast, asserting that in *Louise de la Vallière* she had given "the metaphors of things," while in

7. *Letters*, p. 38. *Shamrocks* was dedicated to Christina and William Michael Rossetti.

8. Rolleston noted the presence of these two styles in her religious poetry and lamented the predominance of the latter ("Shamrocks," *The Academy*, July 9, 1887, p. 19); for Yeats on this review, see *Letters*, p. 45.

most of the poems in *Shamrocks* she gave the "things themselves." [9] In addition, Yeats here related that stylistic improvement to the problem of national literature: he claimed that
"the pre-Raphaelite mannerism and alien methods of thought
that obscured the nationality of Miss Tynan's first volume
are here almost entirely absent; and in thus finding her nationality she has also found herself, and written many pages
of great truthfulness and simplicity." It is true that there are
many more clearly Irish poems in *Shamrocks* than in *Louise
de la Vallière;* interestingly, however, none of the poems that
he used to illustrate the changes in style are specifically Irish
in subject-matter. A few weeks later Yeats was advising her
that "by being as Irish as you can, you will be more original
and true to yourself and in the long run more interesting,
even to English readers" and lamenting that she was doing
non-Irish articles for papers and magazines (*Letters,* 51).

Yeats's praise should not obscure the fact that *Shamrocks*
contains much poetry as bad as anything in *Louise de la
Vallière.* Katharine Tynan had a very strong sympathy for
babies, animals, and other small, delicate things, and
produced great quantities of mawkish verse about them. "A
Day of Frost," from *Louise de la Vallière,* may serve as an
example:

> Every bough's a-glitter. Hush! I hear
> From yon stark tree a gush of melody.
> Sing out, my birdie! I rejoice with thee.

This may be the worst of nineteenth-century bird songs, but
"A Nested Bird" in *Shamrocks* and many of her later poems
are almost as bad. About this vein in her work Yeats maintained a decorous silence.

During the next year (1888) he continued to be in general
highly complimentary about her "new manner," praising it for
"calm and temperance," naïveté and simplicity, and "a peculiar kind of tenderness" (*Letters,* 71–73). It should be noted

9. "Miss Tynan's New Book," *Irish Fireside,* July 9, 1887, p. 444.

that of these qualities, Young Ireland verse had only naïveté and simplicity, and those only in the uncomplimentary sense. She seems to have written to him about a "third manner" in which she would once more stress "colouring." Yeats replied with the warning that although her "colouring" was a "great power" she should "be careful to make it embody itself . . . in easily recognizable natural landscapes, . . . and keep it always secondary to the theme, never being a colourist for the mere sake of colour." [10] Later in the year she sent him a ballad in which, he felt, she had succumbed to this temptation, and he wrote back, "Your best work—and no woman poet of the time has done better—is always where you express your own affectionate nature or your religious feeling, either directly or indirectly in some legend; your worst, . . . where you allow your sense of colour to run away with you and make you merely a poet of the picturesque." He went on to advise her, "We should make poems on the familiar landscapes we love, not the strange and rare and glittering scenes we wonder at" (*Letters,* 98–99). Her poetic "specialties," he suggested to her elsewhere, ought to be Ireland and her Roman Catholic religion.[11]

There was nothing patronizing in these criticisms: he genuinely respected her abilities and was anxious for her comments on his work. Thus, he wrote to her, in regard to *John Sherman,* "How I long for your opinion on this little story of mine." [12] And she welcomed his advice and frequently followed it. For example, in 1888 she published a poem called "In the Cathedral":

> Up in the roof the carver wrought,
>   Creating many a lovely thing;
> His hand's true service shaped his thought,
>   He toiled to please no crownèd king,
> But the dear Christ whose image dim
> Gazed from the tall rood under him.

10. *Letters,* p. 84 (September 6, 1888).   11. *Letters,* p. 71.
12. *Letters,* p. 94 (November 14, 1888); see also p. 100.

Patiently, oh, patiently,
    His flowers unfolded from the wood;
His fruit grew on the long-dead tree;
    His elves took life, a sportive brook;
He fashioned many a singing-bird
Whose lovely silence praised the Lord.

He made a row of vines in fruit,
    And peaches on a southern wall,
And here a sad and stringless lute
    With dulcimers unmusical,
And roses red and lilies white,
And stars that lit no heaven at night.

His woodland creatures gazed at you
    Out from old boughs with lichen sere;
And flying birds that never flew
    Soared in the summer dusk up here,
Where a young angel prayed and smiled,
For all his wings a human child.

The patient carver toiled apart;
    The world roared on—a world away.
No earthly ties were round his heart,
    No passion stirred his quiet day;
His carvings in the cloister dim
Made home, and wife, and child to him.

He was so young when he began—
    A fair-haired boy, whose wistful eyes
Saw earth and heaven, and scarcely man,
    But weighed large issues and were wise:
The years that all unheeded sped
Shook their grey dusts upon his head.

And when this wilderness of shade,
    Far from men's eyes, made God's heart glad,
He woke from dreams, and, undismayed,
    Knew he was old, and cold, and sad;
He kissed his nerveless good right hand,
And died—his name was writ in sand.

In a far city whose walls are gold,
　　His hand regains its youth and strength;
His dreams more fair a hundred-fold
　　Meet him who gives them form at length:
Through pillared aisles of pearl and rose,
Heart-joyed the dreaming carver goes.

God's artists make His palace fair;
　　Where the vast arches glimmer and gleam
My carver shapes with happy care
　　The lovely visions of his dream;
And earns perhaps the fullest meed
God's praise,—"the work is good indeed!" [13]

He wrote to her that the poem was "harmonious and tender" and full of beautiful single lines, and that the "colouring" never overloaded and smothered the feeling. He felt, however, that the last two stanzas ought to have been omitted. While he predictably found the idea "especially pleasant," his objection was on stylistic grounds: these stanzas seemed less condensed and "magical in expression" than the rest of the poem, and their omission would strengthen it structurally and give "more unity and a better climax" (*Letters,* 114). She accepted the justness of the criticism, for when the poem was reprinted in 1891 the offending passage had been removed.

In January, 1889, there appeared in *The Irish Monthly* an article on the life and works of the Irish saint Óengus ("Angus the Culdee"), who had been associated with a monastery at Tallaght, near where Miss Tynan lived.[14] While Yeats had been pleased by the increased "Irishness" of the poetry in *Shamrocks,* he was by no means satisfied and even seems to have feared that she might backslide.[15] Consequently, he saw

13. *The Century Guild Hobby Horse,* III (1888), 114–115.

14. S.A., "The Rapt Culdee," *Irish Monthly,* XVII (January, 1889), 21–35.

15. For example, see *Letters,* pp. 138–139 (about October 10, 1889): "When you write, always tell me what you are writing, especially what poems, the journalism interests me more dimly of course, being good work for many people, but no way, unless on Irish matters, good work for you or me."

in the story of Óengus, who was both Irish and Catholic, a perfect subject for a national poem and especially so for her: "Do not forget to consider the 'Rapt Culdee.' You could make a poem out of him quite as charming as your St. Francis poems. Indeed, considering that he lived so near you, a poem upon him is clearly your duty." [16] His suggestion almost immediately produced results; within a few weeks he was saying, "I am delighted to hear about the 'Culdee.' How do you treat it? Will you bring in local scenery? I hope you will do that. It would be a fine thing to write a poem that always would be connected with Tallaght in people's minds. All poetry should have a local habitation when at all possible." [17] In the finished poem the only clearly *local* detail was a reference to "the Vale of Thrushes" (*Glen na Smole* in County Dublin), but the poem was at least definitely national. No record of his reaction to her treatment of the legend has survived, but in any case he did continue to see possibilities in the Óengus material, for he drew upon it himself in his story "Where There Is Nothing, There Is God."

He suggested experiments in genre as well as in subject-matter. In 1889 he wrote to Father Matthew Russell that he had "been trying to persuade Miss Tynan to write a Miracle play [because] it would be a new poetical form for her, and a new form often means a new inspiration." [18] The following year he proposed that they work together:

If I was over in Ireland, I would ask you to collaborate with me on that little miracle play I suggested to you on the Adoration of the Magi. I have already written so much in dramatic form that I could perhaps help by working a little prose sketch in dialogue to be turned into verse by you. Would collaboration make it hard for you to work or easy? [19]

16. *Letters,* p. 115 (end of February–March 8, 1889).
17. *Letters,* p. 120 (March 21, 1889).
18. *Letters,* p. 129 (July 13, 1889).
19. *Letters,* p. 152 (May, ? 1890).

The projected subject may seem rather an unexpected choice in view of his repeated emphasis on Irish subject-matter (and, if his later recollection was accurate, of the fact that she had once suggested he should use an Irish theme in one of his early closet dramas),[20] but it was one which was already of importance to him in relation to his occult studies. When, however, he started to think out the scenario, he discovered that he "could not get on without knowing the Catholic tradition on the subject" and did not immediately have time to look it up (Letters, 153–154). Perhaps because of this delay, nothing came of the suggestion; but the project was in a way realized independently by each of them. In Yeats's case a number of works, from The Countess Cathleen through the later dance plays, could be called miracle plays, and of course he wrote a story and a famous poem on the Magi.[21] Meanwhile Katharine Tynan did start writing such plays: "The Resurrection" appeared in 1894, and six Miracle Plays, all dealing with incidents in the life of Christ, in 1895. Unfortunately they showed absolutely no dramatic sense and the pathetic subject brought out the worst in her style, especially in her treatment of Mary and the infant Jesus. Before the appearance of Miracle Plays Yeats predicted that it might be her best work,[22] but he almost certainly would never have said this if he had already read the plays. The fact that he never mentioned them after their appearance helps confirm the supposition that he found them disappointing. Nevertheless, his suggestion that they collaborate reveals the regard in which he held her and anticipates his collaborations with Lady Gregory and others during the early years of the theater movement.

In 1890, Yeats, engaged in his intensive study of Blake, rec-

20. Letters, p. 476.
21. According to Ellmann (Yeats: The Man and the Masks, p. 128), The Countess Cathleen was actually subtitled A Miracle Play in the 1899 Irish Theatre programs.
22. "Irish National Literature. III.—Contemporary Irish Poets," The Bookman, September, 1895, p. 169.

ommended to Miss Tynan that she too should begin studying him: she would find it difficult, but it would open up for her, as it had for him, "new kinds of poetic feeling and thought" (*Letters*, 152–153). This suggestion was hardly likely to please, since her religion made her strongly opposed to heterodoxy of all kinds, but it indicates indirectly his awareness of perhaps the central defect of her poetry: she had only a few, very elementary things to say and repeated them again and again. Her religious poetry was full of simple piety with no doubt, no agonized groping for faith; while Nature was important to her, it was merely a beautiful surface without the profundity it held for poets like Wordsworth and Hopkins; and her love poetry only rehearsed the familiar. Developing thought, richness of implication, wit, irony, paradox were entirely absent. Yeats must have found her work increasingly unsatisfactory as his own grew more and more complex.

The fruits of her poetic efforts during the years since the publication of *Shamrocks* appeared in 1891 in *Ballads and Lyrics*. When Yeats read the volume in proof it seemed to him "much the most artistic" she had done (*Letters*, 180), and this perception provided the keynote for his formal review of the book. By then he had already begun to point out the stylistic weaknesses of Young Ireland verse, and he opened by criticizing the writings of that movement as a literature of emotion and impulse untempered by art and consequently, even when most powerful, blended with the flaccid and the commonplace. Against the Young Irelanders he set the poets of the following generation, Allingham, de Vere, and Ferguson, who had all been experimenters, "trying to find a literary style that would be polished and yet Irish of the Irish," and whose experiments had been of great benefit to the poets of the new movement, including Miss Tynan, whose poetry, in contrast to that of Young Ireland, was highly polished even at its worst. He in fact attributed the improvement he saw in her work largely to the study of the earlier Irish writers who had remained outside of the Young Ireland tradition. *Louise de la*

Katharine Tynan, from a portrait by John Butler Yeats. (By permission of Mr. M. B. Yeats and the Municipal Gallery of Modern Art, Dublin.)

George Russell, from a portrait by John Butler Yeats. (By permission of Mr. M. B. Yeats and the National Gallery of Ireland.)

Vallière had been "too full of English influences to be quite Irish, and too laden with garish colour to be quite true to the austere Celtic spirit." *Shamrocks* has been better, and now *Ballads and Lyrics* was "well nigh in all things a thoroughly Irish book, springing straight from the Celtic mind and pouring itself out in soft Celtic music." In studying "the master[s] of Celtic speech" she had found the world around her, and her landscapes were "no more taken from the tapestry-like scenery of Rossetti and his imitators, but from her own Clondalkin fields, and from the grey Dublin hills." [23] Yeats's opinion seemed authoritative enough so that when the "Irishism" of *Ballads and Lyrics* was challenged, O'Leary himself defended the book by quoting him. [24]

Yeats went on to say that from those same masters Miss Tynan had learned "nationality of style." This assertion offered a way of bringing into the Irish net such poems as "Sheep and Lambs," which, lacking specific references to *any* country, could be classified as Irish on stylistic grounds (whereas the St. Francis poems were inseparably tied to Italy). It is noteworthy that in a few of the poems Miss Tynan had even tried using "Irish" turns of speech: "'Tis I would know it . . ."; "It was you was the bitter day." After praising the naïveté of the religious poetry, which he argued was none the less genuine for being the product of art as much as of impulse, he admitted "here and there is a poem that leaves me cold, a song that does not seem to me to sing, a ballad where art has become artificial and has stifled impulse instead of guiding it." This seems mild enough criticism, but in previous reviews of her work, he had directed derogatory criticism primarily at the poetry in the volume preceding the one he was discussing. [25] He was so confident of the strength of this new collection that

23. "Poems by Miss Tynan," *Evening Herald* (Dublin), January 2, 1892.
24. "Miss Tynan, Irishism, and Other Things," *United Ireland*, January 16, 1892.
25. See also *Letters*, p. 120.

he felt its chances of success would not be damaged by a few adverse remarks. And indeed such remarks were fully justified, for there were several poems in the book which showed her at her worst, such as "Two in Heaven":

> Each had her aureole and gold gown;
> And each the long wings, rosy and sweet,
> Drifting from shoulder to bare feet.

By 1895, Yeats had published several volumes of his own and had become a more important poet than Miss Tynan, but his criticisms of her work continued to be mainly laudatory. He included *Ballads and Lyrics* in his two lists of the best Irish books and praised her for having given "distinguished expression" in it "to much that is most characteristic in Irish Catholicism."[26] Again there was an implicit contrast with Young Ireland verse, none of which could really be classified as religious poetry. In his introduction to *A Book of Irish Verse* he had alluded to the intellectual weakness of her work: "she has no revery, no speculation" (xxiii–xxiv). But in a letter to her he excused himself for this judiciousness, necessary if his criticism was to carry any weight as propaganda, and went on to compliment her work lavishly:

Your poems in *A Book of Irish Verse* seem to me by far the finest things in all the latter part of the book. I wish I were as certain of the immortalities of anything I have written or will write as I am of the immortality of "Sheep and Lambs." Now that Christina Rossetti is dead you have no woman rival. You, Ferguson and Allingham are, I think, the Irish poets who have done the largest quantity of fine work.

Of course he could hardly have referred to himself here, though he knew he had produced more "fine work" than she; he did, however, implicitly make room for himself by adding the word "woman" to what he had originally written.[27]

26. *Letters,* pp. 248–250; "Irish National Literature. IV.—A List of the Best Irish Books," *The Bookman,* October, 1895, p. 22.

27. *Letters,* pp. 252–253, and the original manuscript letter, in the Houghton Library, Harvard University.

His most extended discussion of Miss Tynan's work in 1895 appeared in the article on "Contemporary Irish Poets." Picking up the argument of his review of *Ballads and Lyrics,* he declared that "no living Irish poet has learned so much from the translators as Mrs. Hinkson [Katharine Tynan's married name], and the great change this knowledge has made in her work is an example of the necessity for Irish writers to study the native tradition of expression." (It will be recalled that one of his criticisms of the Young Irelanders was that, with the exception of the only peripherally involved Mangan, they had not studied that tradition.) *Shamrocks* was now grouped with *Louise de la Vallière* as only occasionally good. In those volumes her youthful inexperience had "kept her in a bondage of imitation of contemporary English poets," and "the turmoil of the time, and perhaps her own work for 'the Ladies' Land League,' continually drew her into rhetoric." This was the first time that he had used the term "rhetoric" in connection with her verse, and while she had been "nurtured" on patriotic poetry,[28] she had in fact never published, at least in her collected volumes, anything that might be mistaken for typical Young Ireland literature. But his view of her work, and of Irish literature generally, was now so intensely colored by his struggles over the merit of the poetry of *The Nation* that he thought he recognized in its development a dramatic breaking away from that type of writing. The Irish writers he now saw as responsible for that change were not those enumerated in the *Ballads and Lyrics* review:

The work of the Irish folklorists and the translations of Dr. Hyde and of an earlier poet, . . . Edward Walsh, began to affect her . . . soon after the publication of *Shamrocks;* and the best of *Ballads and Lyrics* and *Cuckoo Songs* [1894] have the freedom from rhetoric, the simplicity and the tenderness, though not the passion, of the Gaelic poets.

28. See her anthology *The Wild Harp* (London: Sidgwick and Jackson, 1913), p. xii.

His preference was not for the direct imitations, such as "The Red-Haired Man's Wife" and "Gramachree," but rather for "the poems in which she has assimilated the spirit, without copying the letter, of folk-song." He again cited "Sheep and Lambs," a poem that apparently seemed more and more Irish to him each time he read it.[29]

Naturally he could not in such discussions give *himself* any credit for the stylistic improvements in her work; twice, however, Miss Tynan later did so for him, on one occasion attributing to him the establishment (or re-establishment, if Celtic literature was to be considered) of "the artistic conscience and the artistic ideal in Irish poetry," [30] and on another crediting him with having delivered her from much "rubbish" by teaching the avoidance of false simplicity and insincere "rhetorical passion." [31]

In the years after 1895, Yeats quite understandably had very little to say about her work. From the time of her marriage in 1893 they had ceased to correspond regularly (though as late as 1895 he did take the trouble to send her books on Irish subjects),[32] and he was no longer in such close and immediate touch with her writing. Furthermore, financial necessities had forced her to turn out great quantities of hack-work, with the result that she did very little serious poetry and was no longer active in the movement. Meanwhile Yeats's own literary development had advanced far beyond hers; other, more exciting writers such as AE were increasingly occupying his attention; and then he became involved with the theater project. Thus, although he had had in her case a genuine and direct influence, she did not prove an important enough writer for such an influence to be of major significance.

29. "Irish National Literature. III.—Contemporary Irish Poets," *The Bookman*, September, 1895, pp. 167–169.

30. *The Wild Harp*, p. xiii.

31. *Twenty-Five Years: Reminiscences* (New York: The Devin-Adair Co., 1914), p. 290.

32. Letter to Katharine Tynan of January 15, 1895, in the Houghton Library, Harvard University.

Nevertheless, his few later comments on her work indicate that he did not forget her or minimize her contribution to the early development of the Renaissance. In 1898, for example, while admitting that her poetry, because uncritical and unspeculative, was often uninteresting, he asserted that the poems in which she expressed her "impassioned and instinctive Catholicism" would become "a permanent part" of Irish literature.[33] A decade later he edited a selection of her poetry for his book series, and in two essays of the same period she was one of the two writers Yeats singled out by name as having shared his early efforts to "reform Irish poetry."[34] Even if her active part in such efforts was not as great as Yeats suggested, the contemporary prominence of her poetry and the respect in which it was held surely helped turn attention in new directions and away from the Young Ireland mode.

3. Nora Hopper: Borrowings, Flattery, and "Log-Rolling"

On January 15, 1895, Yeats wrote to Katharine Tynan asking her to lend him Nora Hopper's *Ballads in Prose*.[35] She must have acted almost at once, for by the twentieth he had read the book, which was made up of alternating prose stories and short poems. His initial reaction was decidedly mixed, for he found in it many exemplifications of his own literary ideals coupled with wholesale borrowings from his work and Miss Tynan's. He wrote two letters on the twentieth, one to Miss Tynan and one to Lily Yeats. Their content and his subsequent attitude toward Miss Hopper's work suggest that he wrote to Miss Tynan first. In that letter his attitude appears to have been still in the process of forming. He began with a negative comment:

33. "Mr. Lionel Johnson and Certain Irish Poets," *Daily Express* (Dublin), August 27, 1898.
34. *Twenty One Poems by Katharine Tynan* (Dundrum: Dun Emer Press, 1907); *EI*, pp. 247–248; *Explor*, pp. 233–234.
35. Letter to Katharine Tynan of January 15, 1895, in the Houghton Library, Harvard University.

You are certainly very badly plagerized [sic] in "The Lay Brother" which amazes me. The only way I can account for it is that the author has by some freke [sic] of fancy, elected to consider you as a "document" an authority, and to use you much as I have used the Middle Irish "Oisin and Patrick" poems in "The Wanderings of Oisin." She has done this with me. For instance she quotes as a legendary authority a purely fanciful line out of "The Man Who Dreamed of Fairyland." She must have taken your Iona poem ["In Iona" from *Ballads and Lyrics*] as a versification, perhaps a translation, of some Gaelic original and never perceived the resemblance of her manner to the manner of yours.[36]

The poems were quite similar, and a direct relationship can hardly be doubted:

<table>
<tr><td>In Iona</td><td>Lament of the Lay Brother
(A.D. 598)</td></tr>
<tr><td>

O 'tis pleasant in Iona
  Whether in shine or snow!
Grand it is in Iona
  When the north winds blow.
The birds sing sweet in Iona,
  O very sweet and low!
But sore I miss in Iona
  A voice I used to know.

Iona hath the song-birds
  And the hum of the bees,
The distant bark of house-dogs,
  And the wind in the trees.
She hath the singing-cricket,
  And the moan of the seas,

</td><td>

Iona, O Iona,
  My days go sad and slow,
For mid your island meadows
  I hear no cattle low.
I miss the fields of Kerry,
  The green fields and the kine,
And in my brothers' chanting
  Is heard no voice of mine—
          Iona, O Iona.

Iona, O Iona,
  My mates are glad of cheer,
But I, the Kerry peasant,
  Dwell sad and lonely here.
I send an exile's sighing

</td></tr>
</table>

36. Letter to Katharine Tynan of January 20, 1895, in the Houghton Library, Harvard University; quoted by permission of Mr. M. B. Yeats, Miss Anne Yeats, and the Harvard College Library. The reference to Yeats's poem was as follows: "Quicken. This, the mountain ash, is one of the holiest trees of Irish tradition. It is sacred to the Gentle People, and in the Isle of the Blessed the happy dead dwell under 'woven roofs of quicken boughs' as W. B. Yeats has exquisitely described in 'A Man that Dreamed of Fairyland'" (*Ballads in Prose* [London and Boston: John Lane, 1894], p. 185).

But never the low of cattle
　My homesick heart to ease.

The wee brown cow of Kerry
　Is docile and kind,
The big-framed cow of Leinster
　Is much to my mind,
The wild little cow of the
　　　　　mountains
　Who shall loose or bind?
Sweet is the call of the milk-
　　　　　maid
　Borne upon the wind.

Columba he hath said it—
　"Wherever a cow shall be,
There shall be found a woman,
　Her wiles and witchery.
And in this Holy Island
　May God forbid that she
Should plague with sore temp-
　　　　　tation
　My holy men and me."

And since the kine are banished
　Heavy my heart doth go,
O sweet it is in Iona
　Whatever wind will blow
But I, the farmer-brother,
　My tears are sad and slow
For the low of the kindly cattle,
　The voice I used to know.

Across the sundering sea;
O would I were in Kerry
　Or the kine were here with
　　　　　me!

Iona, O Iona,
　The Saint sleeps well, I trow,
Nor dreams that one poor
　　　　　brother's
Heartbroke for Ireland
　　　　　now—
Heartbroke to be a herd-boy
　And watch the cattle feed,
And call the cattle homewards
　Across the darkening mead.

Iona, O Iona,
　All summer swallows stay
About your towers: the seagulls
　To Ireland take their way.
And would, I cry with weeping,
　The seagulls' road were
　　　　　mine—
To hear and see the lowing,
　The kind eyes of the kine!
　　　　　Iona, O Iona!

However, Miss Hopper's note to the poem makes it almost certain that she had other sources of inspiration as well.[37] Even

37. See *Ballads in Prose*, p. 185: " 'Where cattle are there are milk-maids, and woman is the root of all evil,' said St. Columba and he re-fused to allow his monks to pasture their kine in the green meadows of Iona: a refusal which the lay brothers must have lamented as they looked down on the empty meadows."

though Yeats apparently did not recognize the significance of this note, he gradually exonerated her and became more positive in emphasis:

I feel less inclined to be grieved [?] than you, for she seems to have great artistic feeling and very considerable imagination. Besides she has paid us "the sincerest form of flattery." I am greatly delighted with her evident use of my two folklore anthologies as I compiled them that they might influence Irish literature and help lift it out of rhetoric. I like the simplicity of her style too. "The Fairy Fiddler" and "Una of the West" and "The Silk of the Kine" among the verses are delightful and "Daluan," "The Gifts of Aodh and Una" (this has a wonderful scene in a temple) and "The Four Kings" among the prose.

All the works he named—indeed all the poems and stories in the book—draw heavily upon folk and legendary material and are suffused with a vague, misty effect that *could* be called spiritual. Naturally Yeats found this pleasing. He did note one defect in her style ("Her great lack is solidity and lucidity") but then he saw more positive potential: "However she is a fine new addition to [?] our little group and can only help to foster a taste for our Celtic wares." Once again there was some hesitation as he considered the fact that "she has unfortunately copied the title of my new book 'The Wind Among the Reeds' which has been mentioned under its name in several places, and made a poem out of it, and put a verse of it on her title page, which is exceedingly annoying but may be chance." [38] Finally he returned to a favorable judgment:

However there is no getting over the fact that she is an artist of considerable distinction and artists are few in Irish literature. Her next book will probably be quite her own. I wish this one had come in time for my anthology [*A Book of Irish Verse*]. She may

38. Yeats's projected title had been referred to in "An Interview with Mr. W. B. Yeats," *Irish Theosophist,* November, 1893, pp. 147–148; and "An Interview with W. B. Yeats," *The Sketch,* November, 1893, pp. 83–84.

have done all the iniquities [?] in the Newgate Calendar but she can write and that, in a writer, is the main matter.

Yeats could have listed many other likely borrowings in *Ballads and Prose*. Thus, "A Connaught Lament" seems to combine elements from Hyde's *Love Songs of Connacht* with an echo of "Innisfree":

> I will arise and go hence to the west,
> And dig me a grave where the hill-winds call;
> But O were I dead, were I dust, the fall
> Of my own love's footstep would break my rest!
>
> My heart in my bosom is black as a sloe!
> I heed not cuckoo, nor wren, nor swallow:
> Like a flying leaf in the sky's blue hollow
> The heart in my breast is, that beats so low.
>
> Because of the words your lips have spoken,
> (O dear black head that I must not follow)
> My heart is a grave that is stripped and hollow,
> As ice on the water my heart is broken.
>
> O lips forgetful and kindness fickle,
> The swallow goes south with you: I go west
> Where fields are empty and scythes at rest.
> I am the poppy and you the sickle;
> My heart is broken within my breast.[39]

All of her stories were very much like those Yeats had already published, in atmosphere and method as well as content: nine out of eleven of them contain some sort of intrusion of the supernatural, and in three she uses the "Countess Cathleen" motif of the person who sacrifices himself that others might be saved. And the trappings of the "Celtic Twilight" pervade the entire book, but with none of the underlying intellectual toughness that redeems them in Yeats's own case. Her craftsmanship and use of the subject-matter that he favored, in combination with his pleasure at his direct influence upon her, overcame the latent suspicion that she lacked originality.

39. Compare with Hyde's "If I Were to Go West" (*Love Songs of Connacht*, pp. 5–6).

The letter to Lily Yeats is consequently much more confident, beginning boldly "I have read Miss Hopper and like her" (*Letters*, 244–245). He still felt the appropriation of Katharine Tynan's poem to be "inexcusable," but termed the other borrowings "the plagiarisms of inexperienced enthusiasm" and found "amusing" her note about "The Man Who Dreamed of Faeryland." He repeated his judgment of her stylistic merits ("She has great artistic gifts, great gift for style") and also of her defects ("[she] is as yet lacking in solidity and clearness"), qualifying the latter with a suggestion of their temporary nature. Perhaps significantly, he did not here attribute to her the power of imagination. But he called "Daluan," "The Gifts of Aodh and Una," and "The Four Kings" "wonderful" and revealed that although it was too late for him to include her in *A Book of Irish Verse* he would try to propagandize for her anyway—"I am looking out for a place to review her in."

The Dowden controversy, which was heating up at this time, provided him with the desired opportunity. He included her book in the fiction section of his *Express* list of best Irish books and praised it extravagantly, calling it "an absolute creation, an enchanting tender little book full of style and wild melancholy" and singling out, in addition to the stories, its "many simple and artful verses about gods and fairies, which will probably outlive estimable histories and copious criticisms that the proud may be humbled" (*Letters*, 249). Later in the year he discussed it in both the "Prose" and the "Poetry" articles of his "Irish National Literature" series and placed it on his second list of best Irish books. In the "Prose" article he admitted the narrowness of her scope but considered it offset by her artistic care:

Miss Hopper is only interested in so much of life as you can see in a wizard's glass. She has less strength than those whose interests are more earthy, but more delicacy of cadence and precision of phrase, a more perfect lyric temperament. Her little book . . . has the beauty of a dim twilight, and one praises it with hardly a reservation, except perhaps that here and there is too much of filmy vagueness, as in visions in the wizard's glass, before the mystical sweeper has swept the clouds away with his broom.[40]

He said he had "been haunted all the winter" by "Daluan," "The Gifts of Aodh and Una," "The Four Kings," and (a new addition to his list of favorites) "Aonan-na-Righ." He then quoted at length his favorite passage, from "The Gifts . . .":

Then the door at which he was striving opened wide, and from the dark shrine swept out a cloud of fine grey dust. The door clanged to behind him, and he went up the aisle, walking ankle deep in the fine dust, and straining his eyes to see through the darkness if indeed figures paced beside him, and ghostly groups gave way before him, as he could not help but fancy. At last his outstretched hands touched a twisted horn of smooth cold substance, and he knew that he had reached the end of his journey. With his left hand clinging to the horn he turned towards the dark temple, saying aloud, "Here I stand, Aodh, with gifts to give the Fianna and their gods. In the name of my mother's god, let them who desire my gifts come to me." "Aodh, son of Eochaidh," a shivering voice cried out, "give me thy youth." "I give," Aodh said quietly. "Aodh," said another voice, reedy and thin, but sweet, "give me thy knowledge. I, Grania, loved much and knew little." There was a grey figure at his side, and without a word Aodh turned and laid his forehead on the ghost's cold breast. As he rested thus, another voice said, "I am Oisin; give me thy death, O Aodh." Aodh drew a deep breath, then he lifted his head, and clasped a ghostly figure in his arms, and holding it there, felt it stiffen and grow rigid and colder yet. "Give me thy hope, Aodh." "Give me thy faith, Aodh." "Give me thy courage, Aodh." "Give me thy dreams, Aodh." So the voices called and cried, and to each Aodh gave the desired gift. "Give me thy heart, Aodh," cried another. "I am Maive, who knew much and loved little," and with a shrinking sense of pain Aodh felt slender, cold fingers scratching and tearing their way through flesh and sinew till they grasped his heart, and tore the fluttering thing away.

40. "Irish National Literature. Contemporary Prose Writers," *The Bookman*, August, 1895, p. 140.

"Give me thy love, Aodh," another implored. "I am Angus, Master of Love, and I have none." "Take it," Aodh said faintly, and there was a pause. But soon the shivering voices began again, and the cold fingers clutched at his bare arms and feet, and the breath of ghostly lips played on his cheek as the cloudy figures came and went, and struggled and scrambled about him.

It is hardly surprising that he liked this passage so much, not only because of its use of Irish myth but also because its subject, "the sacrifice of Aodh in the temple of heroes, that the land might be delivered from famine," hit upon a central concern of his own and may in fact have been suggested to her by his work.[41] It must be admitted, furthermore, that here at least she was able to give a fresh and imaginative treatment to the sources of her inspiration. Even though Yeats's propagandizing for her was excessive, his specific appraisals were often quite judicious.

In his September article on "Contemporary Irish Poets" his treatment of Miss Hopper entered a new phase, as he for the first time linked her with AE. Her work, like his, was not Christian, but it was vaguely "religious": *Ballads in Prose* told, "with a symbolism drawn from mythology and folklore, of a pagan fairy world where good and evil, denial and affirmation, have never come," was "full of a perception of the spirit without any desire for union with the spirit," and created an effect of "beautiful, alluring, unaspiring peace." [42] As the references to "symbolism" and "spirit" indicate, he had begun to associate her with the "Dublin mystics" and other Irish writers whose work seemed to him to elevate the spiritual above the materialistic.

As implied in his statement that "her next book will probably be quite her own," Yeats had excused the derivativeness

41. Allen R. Grossman suggests that Miss Hopper's Aodh may have influenced in turn the character of the poet Aodh who appears in Yeats's story "The Binding of the Hair" and (as Aedh) as a *persona* in *The Wind Among the Reeds* (*Poetic Knowledge in the Early Yeats* [Charlottesville: the University Press of Virginia, 1969], p. 112).

42. "Irish National Literature. III.—Contemporary Irish Poets," *The Bookman*, September, 1895, p. 169.

of *Ballads in Prose* in part by the immaturity of the author. Ironically, when her next book, *Under Quicken Boughs*, appeared in 1896, it proved to be even more derivative than its predecessor. Two poems on fairies, "Finvarragh" and "The Dinny Math," were specifically dedicated to Yeats, and he was probably the person meant in "To a Poet," as it contains references to "Kathleen" and "the Rose." Furthermore, "The Passing of the Sidhe," which began "And did you meet them riding down / A mile away from Galway town," was very much like his "The Hosting of the Sidhe"; and each stanza of "The Dark Man" began "Rose o' the world." The very title of the volume echoed the phrase from "The Man who Dreamed of Faeryland" the allusion to which in *Ballads in Prose* had amused him. There was also a fairy poem dedicated to Katharine Tynan.

Yeats published nothing about the book when it appeared and alluded to it in the briefest way possible in his references to her during the rest of the decade. But a short introduction to her work which he contributed to Brooke and Rolleston's anthology *A Treasury of Irish Poetry* (published in 1900) indicates how he had explained away his disappointment with *Under Quicken Boughs:* he theorized that "a great part" of it "was probably written before *Ballads in Prose*." [43] The overt reason for this suggestion was that the poetry of the 1896 volume seemed to him generally to lack the "precise and delicate music" of its predecessor; obviously, however, he had found it in all ways a step backwards. It is not impossible that he was correct in his rationalization; Ernest Boyd, at least, was convinced.[44]

In articles of December, 1897 and August, 1898, he again included her among the writers of the Irish "spiritual group." [45]

43. *A Treasury of Irish Poetry in the English Tongue* (New York and London: Macmillan, 1900), p. 473.

44. *Ireland's Literary Renaissance*, p. 197.

45. "Three Irish Poets," *Irish Homestead*, December, 1897, p. 7; and "Mr. Lionel Johnson and Certain Irish Poets," *Daily Express* (Dublin), August 27, 1898.

Then in September, 1898, he discussed her work exclusively in a long piece at the end of which he made his first reply in the Eglinton controversy. His emphasis on this occasion was primarily upon the use of the Irish legendary materials, and in this respect he again quoted the passage dealing with the sacrifice of Aodh. He also gave an interesting new version of his personal response to *Ballads in Prose*, saying it had originally "haunted" him because "it spoke in strange wayward stories and birdlike little verses of things and persons I remembered or had dreamed of"—surely a humorous transmutation of her extensive borrowings. Also, he admitted that the "first enchantment" was gone, and he now saw faults to which before he had been blind, but affirmed that her work still affected him powerfully. At the end of the century he completed his propaganda efforts on her behalf and at the same time compensated for having missed the chance to include her in *A Book of Irish Verse* by giving her an important place in the introduction to the revised edition and including two of her poems.

Like many other writers in whom he had been interested, she was relegated to the back of his mind when he began devoting his primary energies to the theater, and he never made any reference to her last two volumes, *Songs of the Morning* (1900) and *Aquamarines* (1902). He may, however, have been conscious of the later work, for after her death in 1906 he wrote to Katherine Tynan agreeing with her suggestion that "our Irish fairyland came to spoil her work" (*Letters*, 483). But the implication of "came" is obscure, for in fact her succeeding volumes had been less, rather than more, heavily dependent upon "Irish fairyland" material. Boyd suggested that her Irish poems were the result of a patriotic impulse and that when her slight vein of Irishness was exhausted, the "encroachment" of her life in England completely triumphed over the national element in her work.[46] Thus, it is possible that Yeats had forgotten his earlier theory about *Under Quicken Boughs* and was referring to *it* as having been spoiled. Whichever explana-

46. *Ireland's Literary Renaissance*, pp. 198–199.

tion is correct, the central fact remained the same: Nora Hopper, like Katharine Tynan, was not as talented as he had wanted to believe and had not lived up to his early expectations.

The positive value of her work and Yeats's writings on her behalf is suggested by an article by "Fiona Macleod" (William Sharp) which appeared at the end of the period, in 1899. Sharp also had a very high opinion of her work and was seeking to vindicate it against the charge of derivativeness:

I have often seen allusions to Miss Nora Hopper's work in prose and verse as though it were only an echo of that of Mr. Yeats. This is certainly unjust. I do not know whether Miss Hopper began to write before or after she came under the influence of Mr. Yeats, but from internal evidence I should say that she found her own way by following in the direction where the elder writer had preceded her.[47]

Sharp was giving her more credit than she deserved, but he shows that the issue was frequently discussed, and the debate itself was excellent propaganda for the literary movement. The possibility that a writer is beginning to be imitated by others draws attention both to the master and to his school, and the resultant sense of "something new going on" in Irish literature—a sense absent for half a century—probably helped turn toward their own country the eyes of writers more able than she.

4. Todhunter, Rolleston, Armstrong: The Danger of Cosmopolitanism

Although John Todhunter (1839–1916) had studied medicine and for a time practiced, he had had since his youth a deep love of literature, and in the early 1870's he had decided to devote all his energies to writing.[48] He had been born in Dublin and grew up there, but had been educated at T.C.D.;

47. "A Group of Celtic Writers," *Fortnightly Review*, LXXI (January, 1899), 47.

48. Yeats contributed a biographical note on Todhunter to *The Magazine of Poetry*, Buffalo, New York, I, No. 2 (April, 1889), 143–144.

consequently, when he wished to become a writer he left Ireland for London, and all his early work was on English, Continental, and Classical subjects. Only in the middle eighties, after he had published half a dozen volumes, did he begin to direct his literary attention to Ireland. One reason for this change may have been his reading of Standish O'Grady's inspiring *History of Ireland*.[49] Also, in London he was a neighbor of the Yeats family, and Yeats's own fresh enthusiasm for things Irish may have been influential. By 1887 he was writing poems on Irish subjects, ballads and retellings of the "three sorrows" of Irish legend.[50] Because of his education and his interest in the Celtic past, he was a promising addition to Irish literary activity and thus Yeats, more than twenty-five years his junior, took a considerable interest in him. At one period they worked quite closely together, Yeats listening to Todhunter read out his poems, and Todhunter helping him correct the proofs of the *Wanderings of Oisin* volume and reviewing it sympathetically in *The Academy*.[51] When Yeats gave a lecture on fairies to the Southwark Literary Club he got Todhunter to go along and take the chair (*Letters*, 74–75); Todhunter developed an active interest in the group and was present at the meeting in which the decision to form the Irish Literary Society was made.

Yeats had a generally favorable opinion of Todhunter's Irish poetry, which employed subject-matter of which he approved and was free of rhetoric (*LNI*, 190), but what attracted him most were Todhunter's playwriting activities. Before the emergence of his Irish interests he had done a play on Helen of Troy which had been elaborately staged; in 1890 he again began dramatic work and turned out, perhaps at Yeats's suggestion, a pastoral drama called *A Sicilian Idyll*.[52]

49. See the dedication to *The Banshee and Other Poems* (London: Kegan Paul and Co., 1888).

50. See *Letters*, p. 33.

51. *Letters*, p. 90; "The Wanderings of Oisin and Other Poems," *The Academy*, March 30, 1889, pp. 216–217.

52. See *Letters*, p. 151; *Au*, p. 73; *LNI*, p. ix.

Yeats was highly pleased with the project. In the first place the play was in verse, a poetic drama. Furthermore, it had several successful performances in an attractive private theater, with good acting and music and the appreciation of an intelligent audience. He could not, however, feel satisfied with the Classical subject (drawn from Theocritus), and in his first article on the play he expressed the opinion that "Greek" plays did not seem to him "quite the most valuable work Dr. Todhunter might do just now." [53] Yeats had liked the idea of a pastoral drama, but he felt that Todhunter could have chosen a "pastoral incident" from Irish legend or history that would have been "newer and not less beautiful than anything in Tempe's fabled vales." Todhunter was unaffected, and when his next play, *The Poison Flower,* appeared in 1891, it proved to be based on Hawthorne's story "Rappaccini's Daughter." Yeats tried again, ending his review of the new work with the statement that he would "very much like to see what Dr. Todhunter could do with an Irish theme written for and acted before an Irish audience." [54]

The effort was bound to be futile. Although it was not then apparent, Todhunter's flirtation with national literature was virtually over, at least as far as creative work was concerned. He remained active in the Irish Literary Society, and Ryan, writing in about 1894, referred to him as a writer from whom much was expected.[55] In fact, his only subsequent Irish publications were the *Life of Patrick Sarsfield* (1895) which he contributed to the New Irish Library and *Three Irish Bardic Tales* (1896), not new work, but rather a reprinting of his versions of the "Children of Lir" and "Sons of Turann" myths along with a "Deirdre" he had finished in 1888 but decided not to include in his volume of that year.[56] The other literary efforts of the remainder of his life were contributions to the two "Books" of the Rhymers' Club (1892 and 1894), of which

53. *LNI,* p. 106 (May 17, 1890).
54. "Plays by an Irish Poet," *United Ireland,* July 11, 1891.
55. Ryan, p. 98.
56. See *The Banshee and Other Poems,* pp. vii–viii.

he was a member, a volume of poems on music (1905), and some translations of Heine (1907). He ended his writing career as he had begun it, a "cosmopolitan." Yeats had wanted to consider him "one of the national writers of the Irish race" (*LNI*, 177), but he later recognized that "with him every book was a new planting, and not a new bud on an old bough" (*Au*, 72). Consequently, by the time he made his survey of "Irish National Literature" in 1895 he had to link Todhunter with de Vere, both poets "but slightly related to the Irish lyrical movement of to-day, for the bulk of their work is of a past time, and but little of it is Irish in subject or temperament, or written under an Irish influence." [57]

The case of T. W. Rolleston was similar, except that instead of moving once from cosmopolitanism to nationalism and then going back, he repeatedly oscillated between the two: he was extremely well trained intellectually, but the very catholicity of his interests prevented him from devoting sustained attention to any one field, and he was by Yeats's standards only intermittently an Irish national writer.

Like Todhunter he had been educated at T.C.D., and his early activities were cosmopolitan. He shared Dowden's devotion to Walt Whitman (with whom he frequently corresponded) and did much to further his reputation, most notably a German translation of *Leaves of Grass*, which he projected in 1881 and completed three years later.[58] A classical scholar as well, he published in 1881 a translation of the *Encheiridion* of Epictetus. About 1884 he, again like Todhunter, read and was profoundly impressed by O'Grady's *History*, and in 1885 he came under the combined influences of O'Leary and the writings of Davis.[59] Predictably, he began to take an interest

57. "Irish National Literature. III.—Contemporary Irish Poets," *The Bookman*, September, 1895, p. 169.

58. See *Whitman and Rolleston: A Correspondence*, ed. Horst Frenz (Bloomington: Indiana University Press, 1951), p. 10. The translation was not published until 1889.

59. C. H. Rolleston, *Portrait of an Irishman*, p. 18; Ryan, p. 84.

in Irish activities. His most important contribution to national literature at this time was his editorship of the *Dublin University Review,* which during its short life published Yeats, O'Leary, Hyde, Katharine Tynan, Jane Barlow, and others who were to play roles in the development of the Renaissance; he even printed an article on "Esoteric Buddhism" by Charles Johnston, which E. A. Boyd saw as an important event in the growth of the Irish spiritual movement.[60] A few years later he had several poems on Irish subjects in *Poems and Ballads of Young Ireland.* He continued to pursue his other interests, however, writing a life of Lessing which appeared in 1889. Yeats, noticing the appearance of this book and of the German *Leaves of Grass* and a reprint of the Epictetus, commented in one of his *Boston Pilot* columns "He is a fine Greek scholar and quite the handsomest man in Ireland, but I wish he would devote his imagination to some national purpose. Cosmopolitan literature is, at best, but a poor bubble, though a big one" (*LNI,* 74).

In justice to Rolleston it should be pointed out that in this same year he did an edition of the prose writings of Davis, and in 1890 wrote an introduction to Shelley's *An Address to the Irish People.* But later in 1889, Yeats heard a story that Rolleston was trying to obtain a professorship in Australia and gave a valedictory opinion of him that revealed continued skepticism about his national activities: "He will be a loss in many ways. I was always hoping he would drift into things—do something for nationalism, political or literary, though indeed I feel the scholastic brand was too deep in his heart. He is a loss, anyway, however" (*Letters,* 145). He did not mean that Rolleston was too *scholarly* (indeed he felt that Rolleston's scholarly talents would be particularly useful): "scholasticism" he associated with T.C.D. and its cosmopolitan dismissal of native culture.

Yeats's farewell proved to have been premature, for Rolleston did not go to Australia at all. When the Rhymers' Club

60. *Ireland's Literary Renaissance,* p. 214.

was formed in late 1890 or early 1891, Yeats brought him into it, intending, he afterwards recalled, "to set him to some work in Ireland later on" (*Au,* 104). At this time Rolleston also contributed an introduction to a posthumous collection of Ellen O'Leary's poems, and Yeats apparently began to think of him once more as part of the movement. Graphic testimony of this is provided by a July, 1891 letter to Katharine Tynan in which Yeats spoke of editing an anthology of Irish poetry that would give him a chance "to include you, Rolleston, and the rest of our little school of modern Irish poets" (*Letters,* 173). Rolleston was obviously prominent in his contemporary plans.

To involve Rolleston more fully in literary nationalism, he invited him to the December 28, 1891, meeting at which the London Society was planned. Ryan, who was also present, relates that before Rolleston's arrival the others, including Yeats, discussed what share he might take in the operations of the group; someone—perhaps Yeats himself—expressed the opinion that he had "lost faith" in such enterprises, but that if he could be shown any "reasonable hopes of success, his enthusiasm would be speedily rekindled, and the movement have no more resourceful supporter." When he did arrive he seemed "to be much more the critic than the enthusiast," and although "genuinely anxious for a movement to popularize or promote Irish literature, . . . he was not the less disposed to examine the initial ideas and the initial ground as with a microscope." [61] But soon his enthusiasm *was* kindled; he became a leader of the Society, and Yeats wrote to O'Leary that helping to found it had "stirred up Rolleston's Irish ardour again" (*Letters,* 199). Unfortunately, that ardor, once aroused, took a direction inimical to Yeats, as became apparent in the book-scheme controversy.

Yeats never did forgive Rolleston for what he considered his treachery in the matter, but there was no open breach and they continued to keep track of one another. When the Dow-

61. Ryan, pp. 52–55.

den controversy began in 1895, Rolleston abandoned his early ties by defending Irish literature, and Yeats in turn named him as one of the leaders of the Irish literary movement and in the introduction to his *Express* list referred to him, along with O'Grady and Ashe King, as capable of "filling in the gaps" in the list.[62]

Rolleston meanwhile continued to oscillate, his productions during the nineties including an edition of Plato (1892), extensive writings on German literature, and a "Deirdre" that was the *Feis Ceoil* prize cantata for 1897. By the close of the century, however, Yeats was finding his personality exceedingly annoying, as indicated by two memorable comments in letters of 1899. In regard to Rolleston's inability to cope with George Moore, who was beginning to thrust himself upon the Irish literary scene, Yeats depicted him as "an old lady with a lot of parcels in the middle of a crowded crossing" (*Letters,* 314); and later in the year he remarked sarcastically, "he grows more and more a country clergyman's daughter's dream of a perfect gentleman every day. He is the flawless blossom of Irish gentility" (*Letters,* 326). More seriously, by this time he seems to have felt that Rolleston had failed to maintain a significant involvement with the movement, for when he revised the introduction to *A Book of Irish Verse* he eliminated the reference to him. At that very time, however, Rolleston was engaged with Stopford Brooke in editing his own Irish anthology, *A Treasury of Irish Poetry,* which proved to be an excellent book and one of his major contributions to Irish literature.

But Yeats had been right, for in the twentieth century Rolleston's literary endeavors followed much the same pattern as in previous years: *The High Deeds of Finn* (1910) and *Myths and Legends of the Celtic Race* (1911) had to share his attention with such projects as translations of Wagner and

62. "Professor Dowden and Irish Literature," *Daily Express* (Dublin), January 26, 1895; and *Letters,* p. 246.

even a book called *Parallel Paths: A Study in Biology, Ethics, and Art*. He did not become a major force in Irish literature either as a creative artist or as a man of letters.

George Francis Savage-Armstrong (1846–1906) was yet another T.C.D. man and fit the stereotype much more completely than either Todhunter or Rolleston. He was a prolific writer, almost always on cosmopolitan themes. His volumes included *Poems* (1869), *Ugone: A Tragedy* (1870), *The Tragedy of Israel* (three parts, 1872–1876), *A Garland from Greece* (1882), *Victoria Regina et Imperatrix. / A Jubilee Song from Ireland* (1887), *Mephistopheles in Broadcloth* (1888), and *One in the Infinite* (1891). His only effort during this period to write of Ireland was *Stories of Wicklow* (1886), a collection of descriptive-reflective poems. While national writers like Ferguson and O'Grady were having great difficulties in finding publishers, Armstrong's work had a ready market, and by 1892 he achieved the "distinction" of a nine-volume uniform edition.

This edition occasioned Yeats's first literary encounter with him. In July he wrote a short notice of it for *United Ireland,* and later in the year he contributed a somewhat more substantial review to *The Bookman*.[63] He began his first discussion with a description of the edition itself, contrasting its bulk with what he considered its utter lack of importance. He gave Armstrong credit for "genuine poetic feeling" and "obvious intellectual forces" but was irritated that he had not brought those qualities to bear upon national concerns, and he rejected as worthless the eight cosmopolitan volumes:

Mr. Armstrong has cut himself off from the life of the nation in which his days are passed, and has suffered the inevitable penalty. He has tried to be an Englishman and to write as an Englishman, instead of reflecting the life that is about him, the history of which every hillside must remind him, and the legends the women murmur over the fire in the cabins by the roadside. An Irishman might possibly succeed in writing and thinking as the best English-

63. "Some New Irish Books," *United Ireland,* July 23, 1892, p. 5; "Noetry and Poetry," *The Bookman,* September, 1892, p. 182.

men do if he left Ireland in his childhood and threw himself wholly into the life of his adopted country; but if he lives here he must choose between expressing in noble forms the life and passion of this nation, or being the beater of the air all his days.

He was quite generous in his commendation of *Stories of Wicklow*, the one volume he felt deserved any attention; but he infused even his praise with negative criticism of Armstrong's neglect of his own country:

Despite an obvious unfamiliarity with the Celtic feeling and the Celtic traditions of this country he has written in this one book many pages for which we feel heartily grateful. Ever at his best in blank verse he has made the dialogue on the top of Lugnaquilla entirely moving, glowing, and beautiful. The more humorous parts of the book are a little touched with that conventionality of feeling which seems inseparable from West Britonism.

The *Bookman* review, generally similar in import, did show one interesting variation from Yeats's earlier survey. Again he brushed aside the greater portion of Armstrong's work, but this time *A Garland from Greece* was added to *Stories of Wicklow* as volumes he considered to possess some merit. He praised both for their concern with "weighty themes" and their use of "lofty metrical forms." It was perhaps not coincidental that the more extremely national view was expressed in a Nationalist paper, but Yeats may simply have taken a second look at the Greek volume and found that it was considerably above the level of the other non-Irish work.

Yeats was objective enough to admit Armstrong's talents, but because of his separation from the emerging movement would not propagandize for him. Naturally he never entered into Yeats's—or anyone else's—conception of the book-scheme; he was excluded from *A Book of Irish Verse* and from all of Yeats's lists and discussions of "National Literature." Rather ironically, while continuing to show his allegiance to the "loyal minority" through such productions as *Queen-Empress and Empire, 1837–1897*, he also began to write much more poetry on Irish subjects; he did a number of poems using Ulster traditions and dialect and even some rehandlings of early Irish legends such as the story of the Celtic smith-god Goibniu and a "St. Patrick and the Druid." [64] Much of the material for these works came from his extensive researches into his own family history, but while Yeats's direct criticisms almost certainly did not provide an impetus, it is possible that in using that material poetically Armstrong was to some degree responding to the spirit of the times in his country.

These poems were not published in collected form until 1901, and Yeats may well have been unaware of their very existence. Armstrong, however, was quite aware that he was being intentionally ignored by the national writers, and he saw in their increasing power a threat to his own popularity. This awareness led to his second, more personal, encounter with Yeats, which took place in 1898. Yeats described the incident to Lady Gregory:

I had a great battle with George Armstrong at the Irish Lit Society last Friday. He lectured on "The Two Irelands in Literature" and his whole lecture was an attack on "the Celtic movement" and was full of insinuations about conspiracies to prevent his success as a poet and to keep him out of anthologies etc. He spoke for two hours. I replied with a good deal of fierceness and described the barrenness of the so called educated intellect of Ireland and traced it to the negations of Armstrong's "Ireland" and told how all the cleverer of the young men were leaving him and his and coming to us. I then attacked Armstrong's scholarship and showed that his knowledge of Irish things was of the most obsolete kind. I believe I was unanswerable, at any rate Armstrong made no attempt to answer but excused himself because of the lateness of the hour, which was weak as he had sought the contest himself and made the hour late by speaking for two hours. Father Barry, who was in the chair, said to me afterwards "thank

64. See *Ballads of Down* (London: Longmans and Co., 1901). In a prefatory note he says that most of the dialect poems were written between 1892 and 1899.

[166]

you for your speech. I agreed with almost every word of it." I was glad of this as it was probably the fiercest speech the society has heard and I was afraid my hearers may not have understood that conspiracy insinuation enough to understand why. The whole thing delighted me as it shows how angry we are making our enemies, how seriously they are feeling our attack. Armstrong has lectured a number of times like this before I believe.[65]

Obviously Armstrong still represented to Yeats all that was most harmful in cosmopolitanism and Trinity College scholasticism, with none of Todhunter's and Rolleston's mitigating national efforts. Consequently he was harsher than he had ever been with either of them. Armstrong's severance from the movement was symbolically completed by Rolleston himself, who in *A Treasury of Irish Poetry* included him only in the special selection devoted to such cosmopolitans as Dowden, Lecky the historian, and a number of obscure contributors to the T.C.D. college magazine, *Kottabos*.

5. Lionel Johnson: A Successful Conversion?

The formation of the Rhymers' Club brought Yeats into the company of Lionel Johnson, yet another well-educated Irishman whose literary activities were cosmopolitan. Unlike Todhunter and Rolleston, however, Johnson had the excellent excuse of not really having considered himself Irish. Yeats was drawn to him, and he seems to have liked Yeats in return. In education they were antitypes, Johnson having been at Oxford, where he had sat at the feet of Pater; Yeats long remembered Johnson's suggestion that he needed "ten years in a library" (*Au*, 184). But they had much in common. Both were endowed with what might be called a "transcendental" cast of mind.[66] (Johnson, though able, as Yeats was not, to accept

65. *Letters*, pp. 300–301; also *Au*, p. 248.
66. See Barbara Charlesworth, *Dark Passages: The Decadent Consciousness in Victorian Literature* (Madison and Milwaukee: University of Wisconsin Press, 1965), p. 84.

orthodoxy in religion, had even flirted briefly with "Esoteric Buddhism" around the same time as it was affecting Yeats); [67] and both cherished the ideal of stylistic perfection in art.

Yeats's confrontation with Johnson seems to have brought out the latent Irish side of Johnson's nature. He had from youth been interested in things Celtic as they involved Wales, but he developed an interest in Irish national subjects only shortly after the beginning of his friendship with Yeats. In November of 1891, Yeats wrote to O'Leary, "Lionel Johnson who is an Irishman talks of being in Ireland next Spring and of lecturing if we like to the Young Ireland League or to our Dublin Social and Literary Club" (*Letters,* 181). This project was not realized for two years, but meanwhile Yeats was careful to fuel the spark of enthusiasm he had kindled. At the December 28, 1891, meeting that gave birth to the Irish Literary Society, Yeats pledged to secure Johnson's aid in the project and kept his promise. Ryan related that Johnson

was to the fore at the first general meeting, and made good suggestions. Later on he was elected on a literary sub-committee, and it did not take long for the guides of the Society to discover that a valuable recruit had been found. Whenever hard work was to be done, or a graceful, hopeful speech to be made, Johnson was ready for the task.[68]

In early 1892, Yeats named as a promised volume for his "Irish Library" a study by Johnson, "Education in Ireland." Sometime in February or March, 1893, Yeats solicited contributions from Johnson for the "Irish magazine which is to be the organ of our literary movement." During the year Johnson began writing poetry on Irish subjects, and in September he made his first visit to Ireland. Yeats began to consider him the potential critic and "theologian" of the movement: his ability to "see as one sacred tradition Irish nationality and Catholic religion"

67. *The Complete Poems of Lionel Johnson,* ed. Iain Fletcher (London: Unicorn Press, 1953), p. xx.
68. Ryan, pp. 95–96.

(he was a recent convert) would place him at the heart of Irish culture and would also be useful for defending art before audiences containing parish priests who tended to consider good literature immoral (*Au*, 134, 221). When Ryan at this time made his survey of the movement he described Johnson as one of its most active and most promising members. In 1894, Johnson again visited Ireland and lectured widely on Irish literature. One of these lectures has survived and shows the extent to which his position corresponded with that held by Yeats.

"Poetry and Patriotism in Ireland" reflects the conflict over the relative merits of Young Ireland and contemporary literature which had begun to heat up in 1891 and 1892, with the founding of the literary societies and the development of the book-scheme controversy, and which was in full blaze at the time of the lecture. Johnson was more lenient toward Young Ireland literature than Yeats tended to be, but in essence they agreed, for both wanted a literary mode radically different from the earlier one. He affirmed that the patriotic verse typical of *The Nation* was a legitimate form of literature, and very competent work of its kind: "I do not know, in any language, a body of political and social verse at once so large and so good." [69] But he reminded his audience that, being work "done in the rapture and heat of a great enterprise," it had "the defects of its qualities" and even when not marred through hastiness "had no pretentions to being work of the highest order" (*PP*, 169). Just as, despite those considerations, he did not want to reject it, so he urged its supporters not to let their patriotic love for it blind their critical judgment and keep them from recognizing the merits of other kinds of poetry: "Let us have our ringing rhetoric, strong verse with the clash of swords in it; our sorrowful dirges for the dear and dead of to-day, and of long ages past; our homely songs of laughter and of tears; but let us welcome all who write for

69. "Poetry and Patriotism," p. 168. Subsequent references to this essay, abbreviated *PP*, will be included in the text.

the love of Ireland, even if they write in fashions less familiar."
(*PP,* 172). And to support this broadening of the scope of Irish literature he argued for the Yeatsian principle that it was possible for a writer to be national even though he did not propagandize in his work for the Nationalist cause, either because he was by nature unfitted to do so or because he was politically a Unionist (*PP,* 174–175).

Johnson could thus find a place even for "rhetoric"; but because he was himself so deeply concerned with artistic craftsmanship (his concern in this case perhaps helping to strengthen Yeats's own), he sought to counter the Young Ireland supporters' distrust of stylistic perfection. Their criticism, as he stated it, asked:

Why trouble about minute proprieties or delicate graces of art, so long as our verse go with a ring and a swing, celebrating the glories of Ireland, or with a sigh and a cry, lamenting her griefs? Is there not something cold-blooded and slow-pulsed in writing without vehemence and a rush of sentiment? Leave metre-mongering to the young decadents and aesthetes of Paris and London: and let Irish verse sweep unfettered as the Irish winds, and surge as free as the Irish seas, and satisfy the Irish people [*PP,* 167].

Johnson's first answer was that concern with craftsmanship was genuinely Irish, was even part of the "true Irish note":

The intricacy and delicacy, the artfulness and elaboration, of Gaelic and Cymric verse, are unparalleled in European literature. . . . Music and poetry were held by our forefathers in an almost religious veneration: the poet passed through a long discipline of the strictest severity before he reached the high dignities of his profession. There is no modern cultivator of arduous poetic forms . . . who endures half the labour that was demanded by the ancient laws of Irish and Welsh metre. An Irish poet of to-day may lack a thousand Irish virtues: but if he give a devoted care to the perfecting of his art, he will have at least one Celtic note, one characteristic Irish virtue. While he is intent upon the artful turns and cadences of his music and the delicate choice of his words, striving to achieve the last graces and perfections possible

[170]

to his work, he is at one in spirit with the poets of old Ireland [*PP*, 166–167].

He used this argument to defend Katharine Tynan, whose work, in the eyes of one Nationalist critic, had shown from volume to volume "a notable decrease in the true Irish spirit of poetry." As Johnson saw it,

what the critic meant was that in Mrs. Hinkson's earlier work there were a greater fluency and flow of sentiment, less restraint and careful finish, more obvious rhetoric and impulsiveness. The dainty delicacy of the later work, its mastery of rhythm and curbing of haste, were lost upon him: the idea that all art implies discipline and austerity of taste, a constant progress towards an ideal perfection, though his earliest ancestors knew it well, seemed strange to him. . . . This passion for perfection seems to me as truly Celtic a thing as the ready indulgence of sentiment.[70]

Yeats had similarly viewed her development as an increase in artistry, but he had not yet seen that increase as involving a corresponding movement away from "rhetoric." Possibly his use of the term in that connection in the following year owed something to Johnson. Neither before nor after this time, however, did Yeats use the "Gaelic artistry" argument itself.

For his second answer Johnson did utilize a Yeatsian position—a position involving the distrust of cosmopolitanism: "A cosmopolitan artist, a citizen of the world, with no local patriotism in his heart, has never yet done anything memorable in poetry, or in anything else" (*PP*, 176). Furthermore, while he was an enthusiastic supporter of the Gaelic movement (on one occasion even offering a prize for an essay in Irish on what Wales had taught Ireland in respect to a national language revival)[71] and agreed with "every word" of Hyde's "de-Anglicising" speech (*PP*, 180), he, like Yeats, felt that Irishmen

70. *Ibid.*, pp. 173–174. Johnson's copy of *Shamrocks*, dated "Dublin, 1893," is now in the Olin Library, Cornell University.

71. *Irish Literature*, ed. Justin McCarthy (Philadelphia: John D. Morris and Company, 1904), V, 1693–1694.

could know and make use of foreign traditions without losing their nationality: "We need not fear lest an Irish poet should cease to be Irish, if he study and borrow and adapt the best achievements of foreign art to the service of the Irish Muses" (*PP*, 167). Hence, he urged Irish writers to "make raids upon other countries, and bring home the spoils, and triumphantly Celticize them, and lay them down at the feet of Ireland."

His illustration of this principle in regard to Young Ireland metrics is particularly interesting. He began by pointing out the popularity among the Young Irelanders of the "swinging measures," anapests and dactyls. (He believed that in using them they were at least in part imitating Celtic poetry, but Yeats was probably more nearly correct in suggesting the influence of such writers as Scott and Macaulay.) These measures, Johnson believed, were not conducive to poetry of the highest kind; in fact they constituted a barrier to it. One of the examples he gave was the very "Come, Liberty, come . . ." passage from Denis Florence MacCarthy that Yeats was to quote in the same connection in his essay on the New Irish Library finished shortly before or after Johnson's lecture,[72] and if there was any influence here it might have been in either direction. Rather than attempt to work in such measures, Johnson went on, Irish writers could legitimately concentrate upon "the less rhetorical, and more delicate or stately rhythms," combining the virtues of the best English metrics with Irish "spirit and effect."

In discussing this subject Johnson also referred directly to Yeats, but in doing so revealed that in his own conception the boundaries of national literature were far broader than Yeats himself acknowledged. He rejected the criticism that because Yeats's "style and . . . themes" were not those familiar from the patriotic literature of the country he must be "treading in the footsteps of some English poet, despising Irish art."

72. "Some Irish National Books," *The Bookman*, August, 1894; see *Letters*, p. 233, where in a June 26, 1894 letter Yeats refers to this article as having been accepted for publication.

"Themes" is the key word, for while Yeats could accept the idea that Irishness of style genuinely existed even though not precisely definable, he held stricter views about Irish subject-matter. Johnson wanted Irish themes, but did not demand them:

Unquestionably, we would rather have our poets choose Irish themes, and sing of Tara sooner than of Troy; of Oisin sooner than of Orpheus: but if they went to China or to Peru for their inspiration, the result would be neither Chinese nor Peruvian, but "kindly Irish of the Irish" still. Our race is not lost by spreading itself over the world, and our literature would not lose its Irish accent by expeditions into all lands and times. Let Irish literature be de-Anglicized, by all means: away with all feeble copies of the fashionable stuff that happens to amuse London Society for a season, and even with mere copies of distinctly good English work! It is neither national, nor patriotic, to wait eagerly and humbly upon the tastes and the verdicts of the English public and of the English press. But if we are to foster, encourage, and develop Irish literature, and not least of all, Irish poetry, it must be with a wise generosity; in a finely national, not in a pettily provincial spirit (*PP*, 176).

He thus included among national writers such figures as Farquhar, Steele, and Sheridan. Yeats agreed with the importance of avoiding provinciality, but not with the first part of Johnson's statement, for such a position could be—and was— used by Dowden and other figures not sympathetic to the national literature as an excuse for neglecting their homeland. It was the major difference in position between the two men, but since the principle was not coupled, on Johnson's part, with any defense of cosmopolitanism, it apparently did not lead to any tension.

In both his judgments of individual Irish writers of the past and his conception of the preoccupations of the new writers, he was very close to Yeats. While he spoke in more positive terms about Young Ireland, and in one passage even used their phrase "racy of the soil" (which Yeats found annoying and avoided),[73] the two writers he referred to specifically were Davis, whose competence Yeats always recognized, and of course Mangan. He also praised such Yeatsian favorites as de Vere, Allingham, Callanan, Walsh, and Ferguson. He characterized the literature of their successors as "displaying in fresh forms, under new aspects, the glory and the beauty, the deeds and the dreams, the legend and the history of our country" and predicted confidently that the age was almost past "in which Irishmen could disdain the Irish language, laugh at the Irish legends, and devote themselves entirely to English literature." What vitality there was in contemporary Irish literary endeavors lay in "their freedom from that spirit of ignorant contempt, and in their determination to cherish our rich inheritance" (*PP*, 181–183). Here was a sanction for the unworked sources of subject-matter, and the new ways of treating them for which Yeats was propagandizing.

Thus, in 1894, Johnson's attitudes toward Irish literature were in close harmony with Yeats's and probably in part derived from them. Yeats himself seems to have felt a special interest in and sympathy with the "Poetry and Patriotism" lecture, for he later published it, along with an essay of his own, in a Cuala Press volume. But it is equally clear that E. A. Boyd was wrong in his assertion (based specifically on this lecture) that "in their literary theories they were at one, so far as Ireland is concerned," and that Johnson's arguments were "the same" as Yeats's.[74] Johnson had too strong a mind to be overwhelmed by even so dynamic a figure as Yeats, and he preserved his originality and may have exerted some influence of his own.

On the strength of this and similar lectures, Yeats twice in

73. The only instance I know of in which he used it was in "Dr. Todhunter's Irish Poems," *United Ireland*, January 23, 1892, an early review in which he was addressing an audience whose literary sympathies would be founded for the most part upon the work of the Young Irelanders; see "Mr. W. B. Yeats," *The Leader*, September 1, 1900, p. 3 for a direct expression by Yeats of his dislike for this "trying phrase."

74. *Ireland's Literary Renaissance*, p. 193.

1895 included Johnson in his lists of those leaders of the Irish literary movement who were helping the Irish reading public to discern what was excellent in Irish writing.[75] Johnson, meanwhile, continued to produce Irish poetry of his own. His earliest specifically Irish poems date from 1893; his last was written in 1899.[76] During that period, however, the total quantity of Irish work was quite small, less than twenty poems altogether. But the Irish content of his two collections, *Poems* (1895) and *Ireland and Other Poems* (1897), seemed greater than it was because of the title of the second volume and because he had dedicated many poems, several of which were not specifically Irish, to Irish literary figures: Yeats, Hyde, O'Leary, Katharine Tynan and her husband Henry Hinkson (a minor T.C.D. poet), Rolleston, Todhunter, Charles Weekes, AE, George Sigerson, O'Grady, Ashe King, George Moore, Dora Sigerson Shorter, Allice Milligan and Father Matthew Russell.

In "Poetry and Patriotism" Johnson had written sympathetically of the poet who,

though he be intensely national in temperament and sympathy, may be unfitted by nature to write poetry with an obvious and immediate bearing upon the national cause. . . . Upon occasions of great emotion, a leader's death, a national victory, what you will, odes and songs may be forthcoming by the score from others: he will feel as deep a sorrow, or as wild a joy, but his Muse will be silent. He will talk of these things as much as others, or write as much about them in prose; but in poetry he has not the necessary gift [*PP*, 174–175].

This was not a personal apologia; the great majority of Johnson's own Irish poems *were* patriotic, and some contained sentiment very much in the Young Ireland vein. A poem com-

75. "Professor Dowden and Irish Literature," *Daily Express* (Dublin), January 26, 1895; and "Irish National Literature. Contemporary Prose Writers," *The Bookman*, August, 1895, p. 140.
76. His last poem was the prologue he contributed for the opening performance of the Irish Theatre; see *Letters,* p. 318.

memorating the second anniversary of Parnell's death concluded with a call to action:

> Her son, our brother, lies,
> Dead, for her holy sake:
> But from the dead arise
> Voices, that bid us wake.
>
> Not his, to hail the dawn:
> His but the herald's part.
> Be ours to see withdrawn
> Night from our mother's heart.

Of course Yeats too had tried to express his feelings about this incident ("Mourn—and Then Onward!"), but his poem remained a sport. This was not the case with Johnson. For example, his "Ninety-Eight" used as the first line of each stanza the "Who fears to speak of Ninety-Eight" of Ingram's famous poem; and some of the language and imagery in "Ireland" is highly reminiscent of the *Nation* school:

> Ah, tremble into passion, Harp! and sing
> War song, O Sword! Fill the fair land, great Twain!
> Wake all her heavy heart to triumphing:
> To vengeance, and armed trampling of the plain!

In two major ways, however, Johnson's patriotic poetry departed significantly from the tradition. First of all, as might be expected, his work showed far greater stylistic care and subtlety than almost all Young Ireland verse. The manipulation of rhythm and sound in a stanza like the following, from "Ireland's Dead," was unparalleled except by Mangan:

> For thy dead is grief on thee?
> Can it be, thou dost repent,
> That they went, thy chivalry,
> Those sad ways magnificent?

Secondly, in a number of the poems he combined his Irish nationalism and his Roman Catholicism, producing a blend very untypical of the earlier writers:

[176]

Golden allies are thine, bright souls of saints,
Glad choirs of intercession for the Gael:
Their flame of prayer ascends, their stream of plaints
Flows to the wounded Feet, for Innisfail.
Victor, the Angel of thy Patrick pleads;
    Mailed Michael with his sword
Kneels there, the champion of thy bitter needs,
Prince of the shining armies of the Lord:
And there, Star of the Morning and the Sea
    Mary pours prayer for thee:
And unto Mary be thy prayers outpoured.
O Rose! O Lily! O Lady full of grace!
O Mary Mother! O Mary Maid! hear thou.
Glory of Angels! Pity, and turn thy face,
Praying thy Son, even as we pray thee now,
For thy dear sake to set thine Ireland free:
    Pray thou thy little Child!
Ah! Who can help her, but in mercy He?
Pray then, pray thou for Ireland, Mother mild!
O Heart of Mary! pray the Sacred Heart:
    His, at whose word depart
Sorrows and hates, home to Hell's waste and wild.[77]

This combination would have satisfied almost anyone's criteria for national literature.

He wrote one poem, "Saint Columba," on an early Christian story, but used the main cycles of Irish legend only as occasional imagery ("Thou hast no fear: with immemorial pride, / Bright as when Oscar ran the morning glades; / The knightly Fenian hunters at his side, / The sunlight through green leaves glad on their blades"), and, while he praised *The Celtic Twilight,* did not draw upon folk or fairy lore.[78] In addition his corpus included many poems on Welsh themes, on Catholicism, and on personal subjects, which could, because he had

77. "Ireland"; cf. also "Christmas and Ireland" and "To the Dead of '98."

78. See "Ireland" and "To Samuel Smith," in *The Complete Poems of Lionel Johnson.*

also done the specifically Irish pieces, be considered appropriate work for an *Irish* poet.

Yeats, of course, wanted to consider Johnson a national writer and succeeded in doing so, but not primarily on the strength of the patriotic poems. His comments on Johnson's work from the time he became connected with the movement make this quite clear. In June, 1894, he praised Johnson's contributions to the *Second Book of the Rhymers' Club* (*Letters*, 232), but "Celtic Speech," the only one of them that contained any Irish references, was written in 1887 and was actually a product of his period of Welsh enthusiasm. During 1894, Yeats also saw some of Johnson's Nationalist poems and included two of them, "Ways of War" and "The Red Wind," in his *Book of Irish Verse*. (The other two selections he chose were "Celtic Speech" and the Welsh "To Morfydd.") In the introduction Johnson was listed among the leading contemporary poets, but Yeats avoided specific judgment on the ground that it was "too soon to measure the height and depth of Mr. Johnson's impassioned eloquence" (*BV*, xxiii).

At the end of the year he read Johnson's *Poems* in proof (*Letters*, 244); his response was generally favorable, but tinged with reservation, for while he found the book "exceedingly stately and impressive" and likely to "make a stir," he had to confess that it was "monotonous and will scarce be very popular." In April, 1895, he wrote to Olivia Shakespear that the poems in the collection were "delightful and curiously distinguished" (*Letters*, 256). Although Johnson was Mrs. Shakespear's cousin, Yeats was definitely not being insincere: many years afterward he was still praising several pieces in the volume, and later in the year he gave further proof of his artistic sympathy with Johnson by dedicating to him the "The Rose" section of his own *Poems*. But still later in 1895 it became clear that he did not in general like the patriotic poems as well as the others.

In his survey of "Contemporary Irish Poets" he said of Johnson, "He has written a few Irish poems of distinguished beauty, but, unlike Mr. De Vere and Dr. Todhunter, is best when he writes on subjects, and under influences, which have no connection with Ireland." This seems like a dangerous admission, for it suggests that either Johnson's work violated the "law" that there is no great literature without nationality, or that he was not *really* Irish. But Yeats did not recognize the problem or decided to gloss it over, for he went on immediately to restore Johnson to the main stream of contemporary national poetry:

All of these poets [Johnson, Todhunter, de Vere, and AE, Katharine Tynan, Hyde, Rolleston, and Nora Hopper], however, . . . are examples of the long continued and resolute purpose of the Irish writers to bring their literary tradition to perfection, to discover fitting symbols for their emotions, or to accentuate what is at once Celtic and excellent in their nature, that they may be at last tongues of fire uttering the evangel of the Celtic peoples.[79]

Despite this claim, however, some doubts may still have remained, for he did not include Johnson's *Poems* in his next month's list of best Irish books.[80]

During the following two years, as he became increasingly convinced of the spiritual nature of contemporary Irish writing, he found a more satisfactory way of linking Johnson's best work with his Irish commitment. In "Three Irish Poets," which appeared in December, 1897, Johnson was treated as one of those spiritual poets who "touch our deepest and most delicate feelings and believe that a beauty, not a worldly beauty, lives in worldly things," and as being all the more Celtic because of his Catholicism.[81] The title of another such article, "Mr. Lionel Johnson and Certain Irish Poets," might

79. "Irish National Literature. III.—Contemporary Irish Poets," *The Bookman,* September, 1895, p. 170.

80. He did include Johnson among those poets whose work ought to be anthologized; see *Letters,* p. 250.

81. "Three Irish Poets," *Irish Homestead,* December, 1897, p. 7. For a document relevant to Johnson as a spiritual writer, see his review of the Ellis-Yeats *Blake* in *Post Liminium,* pp. 81–90.

seem to exclude him from a national role, but in fact the article itself clearly treated him as Irish and as part of the school of Irish poets who "believe . . . in a spiritual life, and express this belief in their poetry." [82] Nor did he hesitate, in his discussion of Johnson's work, to refer to a number of poems on such subjects as Lucretius, the Medieval Church, and Leo XIII. A third article, also published in 1898, applied to Johnson's poetry the categories from the essay by Hallam that he would soon use in the controversy with John Eglinton; not surprisingly, the Nationalist pieces were included in the group in which "pure poetry" was mixed up with opinions, but in his last paragraph Yeats redeemed them by predicting that they would "become part of the ritual of that revolt of Celtic Ireland which is, according to one's point of view, the Celt's futile revolt against the despotism of fact or his necessary revolt against a political and moral materialism." [83] Yeats's own point of view on the issue was obvious, and his feeling that Johnson shared it later received support from Santayana, who believed that Johnson's conversion to Irishness was itself a rejection of the materialistic English ethos.[84]

The beginning of Johnson's subjection to drink and the physical deterioration that followed coincided very closely with the start of his Irish activities.[85] He visited Dublin as late as 1898 [86] and even contributed a prologue for the opening performance of the Literary Theater, but as his infirmity increased he became less and less active in the movement. It has been suggested that if he had lived, he, like Todhunter and Rolleston, would eventually have revealed himself to be a cosmopolitan.[87] The possibility is undeniable, but since it was

82. "Mr. Lionel Johnson and Certain Irish Poets," *Daily Express* (Dublin), August 27, 1898.

83. "Mr. Lionel Johnson's Poems," *The Bookman*, February, 1898, pp. 155–156.

84. Quoted in Charlesworth, p. 89.

85. See *The Complete Poems of Lionel Johnson*, p. xxviii.

86. *Ibid.*, p. xxvi.   87. Boyd, *Ireland's Literary Renaissance*, p. 194.

never realized Yeats continued in later years to remember Johnson as a key figure in the movement. In addition to the limited editions he prepared of Johnson's poems and of "Poetry and Patriotism," he named Johnson and Katharine Tynan, in a 1907 essay, as his co-workers in the reform of Irish poetry (*EI*, 247–248), and in one of his autobiographies, describing how he had wished to express the national spirit as the Young Irelanders had, but in literature of higher quality, he declared, "Lionel Johnson's work . . . carried on the dream in a different form." [88] In his eyes, at least, the conversion was a success, and a decided gain for the development of the national literature.

6. AE (George Russell): Old Friend Turned Co-Worker

AE had been Yeats's "earliest friend" (*Letters*, 838), and they had written closet dramas in friendly rivalry and discussed religion together as men in their early twenties.[89] But whereas Yeats soon became an Irish writer, AE remained for some time detached from national concerns. In one 1887 letter he referred to the work of a number of Irish authors,[90] but the bulk of his contemporary correspondence shows that he was at the time much more interested in the Sacred Books of the East. His friend John Eglinton later recorded that for AE the major event of 1891 was not the death of Parnell, but rather that of Madame Blavatsky.[91]

Yeats, however, was at that very time beginning to see him as an integral part of the national scene. In October, 1891, he published an account of AE entitled "An Irish Visionary" in which he stressed how "Celtic" his "mysticism" was, how representative of the Celtic twilight. The following year AE be-

88. *Au*, p. 300; see further positive reference on p. 301.

89. See Jeffares, *W. B. Yeats*, p. 24.

90. February, 1887 letter to Carrie Rea, Alan Denson manuscript. The writers referred to were Katharine Tynan, Mangan, Yeats, Davis, Lover, and Ferguson.

91. *A Memoir of AE* (London: Macmillan, 1937), pp. 24–25.

gan editing the *Irish Theosophist,* thus bringing closer together his national and his religious concerns. He was also writing much poetry in which he gave expression to his personal faith, but it was in no tangible way Irish. Nevertheless, when the poems of this period were collected in *Homeward,* Yeats did his best to see them as part of the movement. In 1895, AE joined the National Literary Society [92] and finally— as Yeats noted almost with relief—began to write specifically Irish pieces,[93] first prose and, the following year, poetry.[94] Yeats does not seem to have been responsible for this development: AE later gave the credit to his reading of O'Grady's *History,* though unfortunately his account of the incident contained no precise indication of when it took place.[95] In any case, the Irish materials he chose and the methods he employed were very much in harmony with Yeats's own ideals.

As early as 1891, Yeats had typed AE as an "Irish visionary," and from the day that *Homeward* (which bore as a preface the statement "I know I am a spirit") was published, he became for Yeats the center of the "spiritual group" of Irish writers, and was given primacy of place in almost all his references to such a group.[96] In some of these cases AE's name functioned

92. *Letters from AE,* p. xxxii. According to Yeats, he had for a time refused to join "because the party of Harp and Pepperpot had set limits to discussion" (*Au,* pp. 145–146).

93. "Irish National Literature. III.—Contemporary Irish Poets," *The Bookman,* September, 1895, p. 170.

94. See "The Enchantment of Cuchullain," *Irish Theosophist,* November 15, 1895, pp. 32–35 and following issues; and "The Children Awoke in Their Dreaming," *Irish Theosophist,* July 15, 1896, pp. 190–192, which AE says was his "first definitely Irish poem" (*Letters from AE,* p. 18).

95. "A Tribute to Standish O'Grady," in *Standish O'Grady: The Man and the Writer,* ed. Hugh Art O'Grady (Dublin: The Talbot Press, 1929), p. 72.

96. See, for example, "A New Poet," *The Bookman,* August, 1894, pp. 147–148; "Three Irish Poets," *Irish Homestead,* December, 1897, p. 7; "Mr. Lionel Johnson and Certain Irish Poets," *Daily Express* (Dublin), August 27, 1898; "A Symbolic Artist and the Coming of Symbolic

partly as a surrogate for Yeats's, but he undoubtedly did deserve the position attributed to him. Both men entertained essentially the same conception of the universe: they saw the material world as a veil concealing a spiritual world that, despite its ethereality, was much more "real" and desirable. "The visual world is the shadow of the invisible," wrote AE in 1898; [97] Yeats had discerned in *Homeward* a "continual desire for union with the spirit, a continual warfare with the world" [98] and dedicated *The Secret Rose,* which had as its theme "the war of spiritual with natural order," to AE. [99] But in other ways the two men were, as they themselves saw, opposites; [100] most notably, while Yeats could never for long give full commitment to that world-view and repeatedly sought empirical evidence for it, AE preserved a much more stable and unquestioning faith. Thus, he was far more suited to the role of religious prophet and teacher and attracted many young men and women seeking a replacement for the lost orthodoxy of their childhood.

Furthermore, at the very time he was beginning to use Irish elements in his work, Ireland itself assumed a new importance for him philosophically. In June, 1896, he wrote to Yeats, "The gods have returned to Erin . . . and the universal heart of the people will turn to the old druidic beliefs." [101] He soon shared Yeats's conviction of the essentially spiritual and visionary nature of Ireland and Irish tradition, and Yeats even invited AE to take part in the development of rituals for his

---

Art," *The Dome,* December, 1898, pp. 233–237; and the revised introduction to *A Book of Irish Verse,* p. xxix.

97. "In the Shadow of the Gods," *The Internationalist,* March 15, 1898, p. 106.

98. "Irish National Literature. III.—Contemporary Irish Poets," *The Bookman,* September, 1895, p. 169.

99. See also *Literary Ideals in Ireland,* pp. 53, 84–85.

100. See, for example, *Letters,* p. 345: "He and I are the opposite of one another"; *Au,* pp. 147–148; *EI,* pp. 412–413; and AE's 10·6·35 letter to Sean O'Faolain (Alan Denson manuscript).

101. *Letters from AE,* p. 17.

projected Irish spiritual order (*Letters*, 295). AE saw the old Irish myths and the fairy beliefs of the people as full of reflections of the faith in which he believed, and interpreted them that way in his work. He too came to see contemporary Irish writing as dominated by the spiritual; in an 1899 article he noted the spirituality of Edward Martyn's plays *The Heather Field* and *Maeve* and saw him as illustrating through such works

the tendency of the most serious minds of to-day, who more and more wander in thought by the margin of the great mysteries, and who are feeling their way half unconsciously to spiritual certitude through impalpable things and visionary longings, and the sights and sounds which penetrate to our world from a world unseen. . . . Almost all the later Gaelic writers exhibit this tendency.[102]

Naturally he listed Yeats as chief among those writers. It was he who originally proposed the discussion of heroic values in Ireland that was eventually realized in the Eglinton controversy, and he himself contributed to the discussion a defense of spiritual interpretation of the Irish past.

AE's "The Gates of Dreamland" (1898) exemplifies the sort of Irish spiritual poetry he was writing:

It's a lonely road through bogland to the lake at Carrowmore,
And a sleeper there lies dreaming where the water laps the shore;
Though the moth-wings of the twilight in their purple are unfurled,
Yet his sleep is filled with music by the Masters of the World.

There's a hand is white as silver that is fondling with his hair:
There are glimmering feet of sunshine that are dancing by him there:
And half open lips of faery that were dyed to richest red
In revels where the Hazel Tree its holy clusters shed.

102. "The Irish Literary Drama," *Daily Express* (Dublin), January 28, 1899, p. 3.

"Come away," the red lips whisper, "all the earth is weary now;
'Tis the twilight of the ages and it's time to quit the plough.
Oh, the very sunlight's weary ere it lightens up the dew,
And its gold is changed and faded ere its falling down to you.

"Though your colleen's heart be tender, a tenderer heart is near,
What's the starlight in her glances when the stars are shining here?
Who would kiss the fading shadow when the flower face glows
    above?
'Tis the Beauty of all Beauty that is calling for your love."

Oh, the mountain-gates of dreamland are opened once again,
And the sound of song and dancing falls upon the ears of men,
And the Land of Youth lies gleaming, far beyond our earthly
    strife,
And the old enchantment lingers in the honey-heart of life.[103]

Here the Irish folk belief that the fairies have the power to
carry off human beings is seen by AE as embodying his own
vision of the spirit that, having long dwelt in clay, hears a
summons from on high and returns to the Ancestral Self from
which it originally came. The imagery and rhythms are designed to suggest a mood of weariness and a sense of the tenu-
ousness of all material things and thereby to evoke by implication a spiritual realm beyond.[104]

Such poetry was the antithesis of Young Ireland: for patriotic subject-matter it substituted "the spiritual side of nationality," [105] and its style bore no resemblance to the bombastic
rhetoric, cliché language, and galloping cadences of the *Nation*
school. AE's emergence as a poet coincided closely with the beginning of Yeats's attacks on Young Ireland, and his friend's
work must have been doubly pleasing to him because of the
contrast, which was far greater than in Johnson's case. Thus,
he praised AE for having "a subtle rhythm, precision of phrase,
an emotional relation to form and colour, and a perfect under-

103. Text from "In the Shadow of the Gods," *The Internationalist,*
March 15, 1898, p. 104.
104. See *Literary Ideals in Ireland,* p. 72 for Yeats on this effect.
105. *Letters from AE,* p. 50.

standing that the business of poetry is not to enforce an opinion or expound an action, but to bring us into communion with the moods and passions which are the creative powers behind the universe; that though the poet may need to master many opinions, they are but the body and the symbols for his art, the formula of evocation for making the invisible visible." [106] And in 1900 he asserted that despite the absence in AE's work of the more familiar elements of Irish poetry, it was "more Irish than any of those books of stories or of verses which reflect so many obviously Irish characteristics that every newspaper calls them, in the trying phrase of 1845, 'racy of the soil.' " [107]

AE himself was highly critical of the Young Ireland school: in 1896 he wrote to William Sharp, "I feel in a frenzy when I see the 'Spirit of the Nation' referred to as literature," [108] and later he praised *The Wind Among the Reeds* (which represented the fullest flower of Yeats's own spiritual work) as "the most extreme reaction from the old popular poetry with semi-political aims, which Davis, Mangan, and the '48 men made popular, and . . . the most complete escape from the tyranny of the ephemeral passions of the hour into the world of pure art, idealism, and beauty." [109]

By the beginning of the new century AE had begun to develop a substantial following among the younger Irish writers, and when in 1903 he edited *New Songs,* an anthology of their work, he introduced it as representing "a new mood in Irish verse. There is no sign that the tradition created by the poets of *The Nation* which had inspired so many young poets in Ireland has influenced the writers represented here." [110] In a letter to Yeats he put it proudly and more bluntly: "There

106. "Irish National Literature. III.—Contemporary Irish Poets," *The Bookman,* September, 1895, p. 169.

107. "Mr. W. B. Yeats," *The Leader,* September 1, 1900, p. 3.

108. Letter dated "? April, 1896," Alan Denson manuscript. This and all subsequent quotations from AE's unpublished letters are made with the permission of Mr. Diarmuid Russell and Mr. Denson.

109. *Letters from AE,* p. 32.

110. *New Songs* (Dublin, 1904); see also *Letters from AE,* p. 50.

is not a patriotic poem in the book." [111] Yeats did not in fact like most of the poetry in *New Songs* (*Letters,* 434–435), but at least its defects were not those of the earlier tradition, and AE certainly played a key role in turning Irish literature permanently away from that tradition. There is no need to suppose that AE got his attitude towards Young Ireland from Yeats: granted the general similarities in their world-views, he could be expected to have a similar dislike for such an unsympathetic poetic mode. Very probably, however, Yeats's extensive negative propaganda reinforced his own feelings.

In emphasizing AE's artistry Yeats was again constantly drawing or implying a contrast with Young Ireland, but also to some extent casting him in a role that he could not fill. Because of his full commitment to a spiritual vision, he was less inclined than Yeats to consider craftsmanship as an ideal. He was by no means without stylistic skill, nor did he fit the image of spontaneous composition associated (incorrectly) with such writers as Wordsworth. In fact he often labored at revision. The "idea" of "The Gates of Dreamland" was present in the first, rudimentary version:

It's a lonely road through bogland to the lake at Carrowmore:
And a sleeper there lies drowsy where the water laps the shore:
Tho' the moth wings of the twilight in their purple are unfurled,
Yet his sleep is filled with gold light by the masters of the world.

Far more tender than your colleen is the heart we'll bring you
 near.
What's the starlight in her glances when the stars are shining here?
And who would kiss the shadow when the flower face glows above.
Tis the Beauty of all beauty that is calling for your love.

And the mountain-gates of dreamland close behind his spirit's
 feet,
And a heart enraptured meets him, and a music far and sweet,
And a cry exultant ringing over cabin bog and shore,
Say a spirit's leaped to dreamland from the lake at Carrowmore.[112]

111. Letter of early January, 1904, Alan Denson manuscript.
112. *Letters from AE,* p. 25; quoted by permission of Mr. Diarmuid Russell, Mr. Alan Denson, and Abelard-Schuman, Limited.

The alterations were all concerned with increasing the efficacy with which the "idea" was expressed. Thus "drowsy" was changed to "dreaming," and the second stanza was added to clarify the physical situation and especially the identity of the "caller." The other new stanza was designed primarily to strengthen the poem's effect of that *fin de siècle* mood which was really, as AE and Yeats saw it, a herald of the triumph of the spirit. The change to "Who would kiss the fading shadow" improved the rhythm and heightened one of the alliterative patterns, while the ludicrous image of "spirit's feet" leaping to dreamland was wisely eliminated. The poem underwent still further revision before its next appearance, primarily in matters of language and sound. Thus, "earth" was changed to "world" to increase the onomatopoetic effect of weariness, the cliché "far beyond our earthly strife" was replaced with "flushed with rainbow light and mirth," and (somewhat less felicitously) "mountain gates of dreamland" became "great gates of the mountain." [113]

Nevertheless, AE did not really share Yeats's passion for artistic perfection, and his writing often suffered from carelessness and obscurity. But he was very conscious of Yeats's own artistry, and his awareness may have strengthened his impulses in that direction. At least in later years he gave Yeats credit for having by precept and example improved the quality of Irish literature as a whole. On one such occasion he spoke of "a general tendency to write carefully which grew up around Yeats who was the great theorist," [114] and elsewhere he called him "the pivot around which Irish literature turned from instinctive to conscious art, . . . the first artist in Irish literature," so that "after his verse began to find readers, there came a shrivelling of the resounding and empty rhetoric in which so many had been content to express themselves." He added the interesting speculation that if Yeats had antedated Moore, Ireland would have had much greater poetry from Moore,

113. See *The Divine Vision and Other Poems* (London: Macmillan, 1904), pp. 3–4.

114. Letter of July 8, 1922, Alan Denson manuscript.

Mangan, and Ferguson "because so scrupulous a craftsman had preceded them." [115] Yeats *did* precede AE, at least as a professional poet, and provided both precept and example. AE even happened to be present at an 1893 lecture in which Yeats stressed craftsmanship as the great need of Irish poets.[116] And having almost all Yeats's poetry by heart, he was acutely aware of—though he often did not like—his friend's ceaseless revisions.

Yeats also showed a more direct concern by making specific suggestions for improvement of various poems. AE welcomed Yeats's opinions and sometimes even solicited them. Such was the case with "The Gates of Dreamland," the earliest version of which he sent to Yeats in a letter. Among the changes due to Yeats's influence were the elimination of the repetition of "Carrowmore" and the replacement of "gold light" (which Yeats said put the verse "out of the usual accentuation") with "music" (which would give "a full sound").[117] In another letter, however, AE rejected a similar attempt to alter what he had written. Yeats had objected to his use of the word "planets," which he felt was too scientific a term for a poem dealing with a time when the heavenly bodies were deified. AE wrote back: "I don't agree with you about 'planets.' . . . change it I will not. . . . I am obstinate about words which are part of my idea and which cannot be altered without altering my meaning. I do not care whether another word is more beautiful if it does not convey the idea." [118] Of course Yeats

115. *The Living Torch,* ed. Monk Gibbon (New York: Macmillan, 1938), pp. 257–258.

116. "Nationality and Literature," *United Ireland,* May 27, 1893; this was a lecture to the National Literary Society, and AE is among those listed as attending.

117. See the letter quoted in Ellmann, *The Identity of Yeats* (New York: Oxford University Press, 1964), p. 53; for another example, see *Letters from AE,* pp. 21–22. AE gave as well as took advice: see *Letters,* p. 327, *Letters from AE,* pp. 44–45.

118. Quoted in *The World of W. B. Yeats,* ed. Robin Skelton and Ann Saddlemyer, revised edition (Seattle: University of Washington Press, 1965), p. 197.

believed that his suggestion provided a word that did convey the idea and was more beautiful as well, that the beauty was even essential to the successful conveyance of the idea. AE's misrepresentation was revealing in regard to his attitude toward art, for it implied that he considered beauty to be separable from and secondary to the thought of the poem. This seemed to Yeats artistic heresy, and he remonstrated with his friend accordingly:

I do not understand what you mean when you distinguish between the word that gives you your idea and the more beautiful word. Unless you merely mean that beauty of detail must be subordinate to general effect, it seems to me just as if one should say "I don't mind whether my sonata is musical or not so long as it conveys my idea." Beauty is the end and law of poetry. It exists to find the beauty in all things, philosophy, nature, passion,—in what you will, and in so far as it destroys beauty it destroys its own right to exist. If you want to give ideas for their own sake write prose. In verse they are subordinate to beauty which is their soul. Isn't this obvious? [119]

Yeats may ultimately have had his way, for AE seems to have changed the poem after all.[120]

This exchange took place at the end of the early phase of the movement. During that phase Yeats's comments on AE's work credited it with a high degree of stylistic competence. He did refer to a few flaws in *Homeward* [121] and in the introduction to *A Book of Irish Verse* called him "an exquisite though still imperfect craftsman" (*BV*, xxiv), but even at this stage the praise far outweighed the negative criticism, and he called the next volume, *The Earth Breath* (1897) AE's "best

119. *Letters*, pp. 342–343. For another example of AE's attitude towards the relation between "beauty" and "idea," see *Letters from AE*, p. 19.
120. The poem in question was "The Master Singer"; see *Some Passages from the Letters of AE to W. B. Yeats* (Dublin: Cuala Press, 1936), pp. 21–22. When published in 1904, it did not use the word "planets."
121. "A New Poet," *The Bookman*, August, 1894, pp. 147–148.

work" and saw in it "an enormous advance in art" (*Letters*, 295). In 1898 he called his poems "the most delicate and subtle that any Irishman of our time has written." [122] It was perhaps indicative of a shift in attitude early in the new century that in revising *The Celtic Twilight* Yeats added to his discussion of AE's earliest poetry a reference to "careless writing." [123]

About this time, at any rate, he began to grow dissatisfied with the democratic AE's refusal to pick and choose among the numerous young writers whom he encouraged, to demand excellence rather than trying to give everyone a chance. [124] By 1906, in a letter in which he surveyed recent Irish poetry and, in spite of the positive influence he had generated, still found it unsatisfactory stylistically ("they play at words and have no organic structure"), he was quite harsh in his criticism of AE's attitude:

I once hoped a great deal from George Russell's influence . . . but he has the religious genius, and it is the essence of the religious genius, I mean the genius of the religious teacher, to look upon all souls as equal. They are never equal in the eyes of any craft, but Russell cannot bear anything that sets one man above another. He encourages everyone to write poetry because he thinks it good for their souls, and he doesn't care a rush whether it is good or bad.

He went on to accuse him of almost wrecking the theater movement with such ideas and even of having tried to democratize the Dun Emer (Cuala) Press, which Yeats very strongly wanted to be devoted to only the *best* writing; then Yeats the artist characteristically concluded by speaking of

122. "The Poetry of A.E.," *Daily Express* (Dublin), September 3, 1898; cf. also " 'A. E.'s' Poems," *The Sketch*, April 6, 1898, p. 476.

123. *The Celtic Twilight*, p. 38. Yeats says that in about 1891, AE had sent him some poetry which, as Edwin Ellis pointed out to him, was full of technical flaws, but that the next work he saw was "clear in thought and delicate in form" (*Au*, p. 146).

124. See *Au*, p. 273, where Yeats says that for a time after 1900 the circle of AE's followers "seemed to lead the opposition."

plans of his own "for improving our new poets." [125] By the time he wrote *The Trembling of the Veil* his appraisal of AE's work had been altered enough so that *Homeward* seemed his one "perfect book," never equaled afterward (*Au*, 148).

In addition to his efforts to keep the ideal of artistic perfection always before AE, Yeats made at least one important and successful attempt to strengthen his national commitment. That commitment needed strengthening for the same reason as did his dedication to art: there was a basic tension between it and his religious faith. As AE himself later described the dilemma,

birth in Ireland gave me a bias towards Irish nationalism, while the spirit which inhabits my body told me that the politics of eternity ought to be my only concern, and that all other races equally with my own were children of the Great King. . . . If I advocated a national ideal I felt immediately I could make an equal plea for more cosmopolitan and universal ideas. [126]

In 1897 he seems to have been in one of those periods in which he was out of sympathy with national impulses; in an April letter he wrote Yeats that he feared it would be a "futile task" for him to "try consciously for the Celtic traditional feeling. A certain spirit I have of it but I am not Celt inside, not for many lives." [127] In November of the same year he gave up his place in Pim's and was considering taking a position writing for the American Theosophists. At this same time Horace Plunkett, with whom Yeats had been working for a permit to put on theater performances in Dublin, was looking for someone to help organize agricultural banks in rural Ireland, and Yeats suggested AE. [128] Yeats wrote Lady Gregory,

125. *Letters*, p. 477, supplemented by the original letter in the Houghton Library, Harvard University. Wade made some major omissions in this letter in order to make the harsh criticisms less offensive.

126. *Imaginations and Reveries* (New York: Macmillan, [1916?]), pp. ix–x.

127. *Letters from AE*, pp. 19–20.

128. Alan Denson, in *Letters from AE*, p. xxxii, says AE was recommended by P. J. Hannon, but in a contemporary letter Yeats said plainly "I suggested him" (*Letters*, p. 291).

"It would give him a great knowledge of Ireland and take him out of the narrow groove of theosophical opinion" (*Letters,* 291).

AE was reluctant to leave his little circle of mystical followers, but Yeats brought some of them to him and they promised to carry on during his absence, so he took the post. At first he found the work depressing, and Yeats had to cheer him up:

Remember always that now you are face to face with Ireland, its tragedy and its poverty, and if we would express Ireland we must know her to the heart and in all her moods. You will be a far more powerful mystic and poet and teacher because of this knowledge. . . . Absorb Ireland and her tragedy and you will be the poet of a people, perhaps the poet of a new insurrection [*Letters,* 294–295].

Yeats's invitation to AE to join in devising rituals for the Irish spiritual order was probably also calculated to tie him firmly to national activities.[129] AE's new experiences did begin to produce positive results. On one of his trips for the agricultural movement he heard the legend he used as the basis for "The Gates of Dreamland," and the essay in which he first published it was an enthusiastic affirmation of Ireland as a stronghold of spirituality.[130] He probably picked up in a similar manner many of the other folk elements that appeared in his next volume of poetry. Within a year his general outlook had changed enough for Yeats to write, "Dublin is waking up in a number of ways and about a number of things. Russell is doing a good part in the awakening." [131] His new involvement with the country led in fact to a long-range commitment to Irish problems: while the conflict was not permanently resolved, his interest in his country remained strong. So much so that in 1903 he was rather disturbed by its strength

129. *Letters,* p. 295. AE was somewhat concerned that such pursuits would cause Yeats to neglect his own poetry (*Letters from AE,* p. 30).

130. *Letters from AE,* pp. 26–29; and "In the Shadow of the Gods," *The Internationalist,* March 15, 1898, pp. 103–107.

131. *Letters,* p. 306 (December 25, 1898).

and informed a friend "don't suppose that I do not love Ireland. I am only afraid of liking it too much and of making its history and traditions too much a part of my soul to have anything to carry back to the stars when I go"; [132] and he never gave up participation in national activities.

It was probably not coincidental that his fullest theoretical statement concerning the national and cosmopolitan alternatives came shortly after he had begun his new work, in his contributions to the Eglinton controversy. He took advantage of the controversy to promote his earlier plan for a symposium on the revival in Ireland of the heroic ideals, especially in the second of his two essays. He saw Ireland at a "parting of the ways," faced with a choice between two paths: "One path leads, and has already led many Irishmen, of whom Professor Dowden is a type, to obliterate all nationality from their work. The other path winds spirally upwards to a mountain-top of our own, which may be in the future the Meru to which many worshippers will turn." [133]

The terms here were Yeatsian, with Dowden on one hand and the holy mountain on the other; and the projected spiritual cult had as one of its objects the "sanctification" of the landscape of the country. AE did not explicitly advocate either course, but indicated where his primary sympathy lay by devoting most of the essay to explaining how to follow the latter path and especially what role literature should play in conveying the country along it. He granted a limited validity to the position that "nationality may express itself in many ways; it may not be at all evident in the subject matter, but may be very evident in the sentiment." [134] But literature written in accordance with such a conception would never perform the main function of a national literature, which was to create a soul for the country, to give adequate expression to its native ideals. Using a metaphor that anticipated Yeats's poem "The

132. Letter to Stephen Gwynn of May 1903, Alan Denson manuscript.
133. *Literary Ideals in Ireland*, p. 87 (November 12, 1898).
134. *Ibid.*, p. 80.

Statues," he compared the current state of Ireland to that of "Greece before the first perfect statue had fixed an ideal of beauty which mothers dreamed of to mould their yet unborn children." But nationality as a spiritual force was at the present time very strong in Ireland and if focussed could create a national ideal in a generation. The two main aspects of that ideal which needed fit literary embodiment were the mystical and visionary, and the heroic; he saw the former as already adumbrated by many writers (he referred specifically to the "Dark Rosaleen" of Mangan and to Yeats's "Apologia addressed to Ireland in the coming days") and named O'Grady as one who had partially accomplished the latter. His analysis of this process, and especially his prediction that O'Grady's Cú Chulainn might become "to every boy who reads the story a revelation of what his own spirit is," looked forward to Padraic Pearse and 1916.

Throughout their friendship with each other, Yeats and AE had frequent differences of opinion, but it was not until after the end of the early phase of the Renaissance that Yeats came to feel that some of his friend's goals were destructive of his own; their relationship up to that time was a fruitful one.[135] There were currents of influence in both directions, but each writer preserved his integrity, and the reconcilable, often harmonious, but always individual positions of each made significant contributions to the emergence of the new literature.

7. Douglas Hyde: An Incorrect Evaluation

Douglas Hyde's career might have been similar to that of Edward Dowden: a brilliant student while at T.C.D., he had earned his LL.D. by 1887 and could have become a cosmopolitan scholar of considerable reputation. The life he actually chose was antithetical to Dowden's. The son of a Protestant clergyman in the West of Ireland, he had as a child become fascinated with peasant life and haunted the cabins, absorbing

135. Thus the prominence given to AE in the revised (1900) edition of *A Book of Irish Verse*, p. xxix.

the language and the tales that were told in it. Shortly after its establishment in 1877 he became an active member of the "Society for the Preservation of the Irish Language," and between 1879 and 1884 he contributed over one hundred original poems in Irish to various periodicals.[136] He preserved these interests while living in the hostile atmosphere of Trinity: he wrote poetry and collected folklore throughout his college years. In 1891 he had a chance to emulate Dowden, being appointed Professor of Modern Languages in the University of New Brunswick, Canada; but any temptation towards cosmopolitanism was dissipated by this experience, and he soon resigned. Although he did not need to be "converted" to national concerns, he became one of O'Leary's disciples, and Yeats made his acquaintance through that connection.

Yeats at first took him for a peasant and was surprised to learn his real background (*Au,* 131). He soon discovered their common interest in folklore and began to watch his work attentively. Hyde already showed promise of becoming a major contributor to the new literary movement. Yeats praised some of his English-language poetry, and in 1888, when he was compiling *Fairy and Folk Tales,* Hyde not only helped him with the notes but also allowed him to include his own translations of three tales he had collected. Yeats saw that Hyde, with his combination of scholarship and imagination, had real ability as a folklorist and could aid greatly in making such material available for literary use.

Those translations also engendered thoughts about the possibility of a native style in literary prose. The "Irish" dialect employed by the nineteenth-century novelists and folklorists, which had attempted to reproduce the pronunciation of the spoken language, had always something of the ludicrous about it. It was used only in dialogue or in narration by *personae,*

136. This and much of the other information about Hyde's life is taken from Brian Ó'Cuív's introduction to Hyde's *Literary History of Ireland* (London: Ernest Benn Limited, and New York: Barnes and Noble, 1967), pp. xiv–xv and *passim.*

and limited to the rustic characters; elsewhere the writers had fallen back upon standard English, often stilted through striving for "elevation." John Mitchel had written frequently powerful prose, but based it upon the model of Carlyle. And for a "grand style" in which to retell the ancient Irish legends, Standish O'Grady had had to blend Carlyle with Homer. In translating his folk tales Hyde used as his prose medium a simple, lucid English that did not attempt to represent pronunciation or brogue but occasionally contained idioms and constructions derived from Irish and used by the country people in speaking English: for example, "there was a man in it," "in it" meaning "there," "in existence," from the Irish *ann*. Yeats had been "troubled because Scottish dialect was capable of noble use, but the Irish of obvious roystering humour only." [137] His readings for the anthology had made him aware of how much better Hyde's language was than that of the earlier writers, and almost at once its impact upon him began to appear. Later that year he wrote, "Hyde is the best of all the Irish folklorists. His style is perfect—so sincere and simple—so little literary" (*Letters*, 88), and in 1889 he asserted that Hyde "understands perfectly the language of the people, and writes it naturally, as others do book-English. . . . The three stories he translated for *Fairy and Folk Tales of the Irish Peasantry* show what a master he is of dialect" (*LNI*, 79). At this same period, while criticizing another folklorist's handling of Irish dialect pronunciation he noted with approval that the author's sentences often had "an Irish turn in them." [138]

Meanwhile Hyde had published his *Leabhar Sgeuluigheachta*, a large collection of tales in Irish. Yeats was tantalized by this work he could not read and anxious to see it translated. He was soon to have his wish: the publisher David Nutt had liked Hyde's contributions to Yeats's anthology and sent through Yeats an offer to publish a book by him.[139] The trans-

137. *EI*, p. 335 (1910).
138. "Irish Wonders," *Scots Observer*, March 30, 1889, pp. 530–531.
139. *Letters*, p. 136 (September, 1889).

lation seemed to Yeats "a great event" (*Letters*, 136), and he predicted it would be "the most completely Irish folklore book, both in manner and in matter, that has yet come from any press." [140] In making his English versions, Hyde used his special style much more than he had in the earlier tales, and when the book appeared, under the title *Beside the Fire,* Yeats reviewed it very enthusiastically, calling it "incomparable" and crediting Hyde with having "caught and faithfully reproduced the peasant idiom and phrase." [141] For the first time, he recalled in *The Trembling of the Veil,* an Irish form of English had been used viably for the "expression of emotion and romance" (*Au,* 132). Later in the year he referred to Hyde's "perfect style" and expressed optimism that he might eventually produce a "monumental" Irish work.[142]

Hyde played an active role in the beginning of the National Literary Society, Dublin, and became its president. Late in 1892 he addressed to the Society his famous lecture on "The Necessity for De-Anglicising Ireland," a powerful exhortation to Irishmen to cease aping English customs and tastes and instead to cultivate native ones. As a strong enemy of West Britonism, Yeats was sympathetic with the message of the lecture, but he did not agree with Hyde's pessimism about the possibility of halting the denationalizing process, and in a letter to *United Ireland* he argued that the trend could be reversed even if the Gaelic language itself did die out. He suggested that the Irish works that were such excellent repositories of Celtic ideals could be salvaged by retelling them in "English, which shall have an indefinable Irish quality of rhythm and style." [143]

Yeats was hoping that Hyde himself would be a leader in such work, and for a while he must have thought that Hyde

140. *LNI,* p. 102 (May 17, 1890).
141. "Irish Folk Tales," *National Observer,* February 28, 1891, p. 383.
142. *LNI,* p. 131 (April 18, 1891).
143. "The De-Anglicising of Ireland," *United Ireland,* December 17, 1892.

was going to follow that road. In 1893 he published in collected form a series of *Love Songs of Connacht* which had previously appeared serially in *The Nation* and *The Weekly Freeman.* His original text had been entirely in Irish, but the exigencies of journalism had forced him to add translations (many of them in prose) of the poems and also of his prose running commentary. This book had a far greater impact than *Beside the Fire,* its eventual popularity being attested to by several reprintings and by the place given it in *Ulysses.* Yeats recognized its merit from the first. He praised and quoted extensively from the prose [144] and later related that "the prose parts of that book were to me, as they were to many others, the coming of a new power into literature." [145] He himself had by this time tried, and failed miserably, to give English prose a native flavor, and Hyde thus represented his central hope for the full development of such a vehicle.

All along, however, he had been seriously misjudging Hyde's own intentions. Hyde was really interested in the study and propagation of Irish literature *in Irish,* and had little desire to develop techniques for an Irish literature in English. It was for this reason that he was more pessimistic than Yeats about the future of Irish culture. The emphasis upon the language of his translations had been Yeats's, not his: in both *Beside the Fire* and the *Love Songs* his prefatory remarks definitely show that he was concerned with the medium solely as a necessary concession to those who had not sufficient Irish to read the works in the original. There is no evidence to indicate that he ever saw it as a potential national prose style. Consequently, for several years after the 1893 appearance of the *Love Songs* Yeats held the highest hopes of Hyde's contributing in a major way to the new movement and gradually saw those hopes disappointed.

During 1894, Yeats referred, in an article on the virtues of

144. "Old Gaelic Love Songs," *The Bookman,* October, 1893, pp. 19–20.

145. *Explor,* p. 93 (1902).

folklore, to Hyde's "incomparable skill as a translator from the Gaelic" [146] and printed a number of his translations in *A Book of Irish Verse.* In the following year he continued to place Hyde among the leading Irish literary figures and in his lists of best books included the early tale "Teig O'Kane," *Beside the Fire,* and the *Love Songs* (the prose of which he called "perfect after its kind" [147]), as well as his *The Story of Early Gaelic Literature,* a literary history published during 1895. This last volume helped spread awareness that Ireland had a past culture of which it could be genuinely proud, and a passage that detected in one of the songs attributed to the mythical bard Amergin a "curious pantheistic strain which reminds one of the East" [148] was read by AE just at the time he was turning his attention to the old Irish materials and provided support for his association of them with Oriental philosophies.[149] But Yeats had severe reservations; he lamented that Hyde had placed scholarship above imagination:

He is so anxious to convince his little group of enthusiasts of the historical importance of the early Irish writings, of the value to modern learning of the fragments of ancient customs which are mixed up with their romance, that he occasionally seems to forget the noble phantasy and passionate drama which is their crowning glory. He does not notice at all, for instance, "The Death of Cuchullin," which is among the greatest things of all legendary literature; and gives an entire chapter to "The Feast of Brian" [*sic* for "Bricriu"], which is among the least. . . . This defect is probably caused to some extent by the traditions of Irish learning which are hopelessly dry-as-dust, but if our own pro-

146. "The Evangel of Folk-lore," *The Bookman,* June, 1894, p. 86.

147. "Irish National Literature. Contemporary Prose Writers," *The Bookman,* August, 1895, p. 140.

148. *The Story of Early Gaelic Literature* (London: T. Fisher Unwin, Dublin: Sealy, Bryers and Walker, and New York: P. J. Kennedy, 1895), pp. 25–26.

149. See "The Legends of Ancient Eire. II.," *Irish Theosophist,* April 15, 1895, p. 119.

foundly imaginative Irish scholar cannot throw off the ancient chains we are lost indeed.[150]

Unfortunately, from Yeats's point of view, this little book became the nucleus for a much larger, comprehensive literary history of Ireland that Hyde finished in 1899.

It was also in 1895 that Yeats apparently stopped thinking of Hyde as potentially a poet in English. He had liked some of Hyde's early ballads,[151] and his review of the *Love Songs* praised Hyde's verse translations. But Hyde had not recently published any original English-language poetry, and it was perhaps significant that in the introduction to *A Book of Irish Verse*, while he was included in the passage dealing with the most prominent contemporary writers, Yeats categorized him as "before all else, a translator and scholar" (*BV,* xxiii). Then in 1895 a volume of his poetic renderings of the "Three Sorrows of Story Telling" appeared, almost simultaneously with *The Story of Early Gaelic Literature.* It was hardly a distinguished book. The poems were not new work but rather vestiges of his youth, when the "Deirdre" had won the Vice-Chancellor's Prize for 1887. The other two central poems were sent to the press by mistake in place of the manuscript of a volume for the New Irish Library, of which he was subeditor. All three were very undistinguished technically, and the style had none of the Gaelic flavor of his prose translations. In his review Yeats showed considerable dissatisfaction, though he feebly tried to make virtues of the work's defects. His first reaction had been "irritation," but reflection had persuaded him that perhaps Hyde had known what he was doing after all: if he had failed in a "high poetic attempt" or an effort to express more nearly the "native Celtic spirit" of the originals he might have fallen into obscurities or unfamiliarities that would have

150. "The Story of Early Gaelic Literature," *The Bookman,* June, 1895, p. 86.
151. *LNI,* pp. 79–80; *Letters,* pp. 46–48.

drawn only laughs or yawns from English readers. Quite possibly Hyde was wrong in anticipating such a failure: the *Love Songs* revealed him to be "a great deal more of a poet than anyone would guess," judging from the *Three Sorrows* volume. "But, at least," Yeats concluded, "the simplicity he has aimed at and achieved, the very want of ambition in his rendering—one might almost say, were it not gross ingratitude, the laziness that has left them as they are—have ended in their being models of clearness." [152] Despite the praise of his potential, Hyde did not try to fulfill it, and Yeats did not again include him among the poets of the movement.

At the century's end Hyde had also failed to contribute further to the development of a literary prose. He had done other relevant work, a series of "Religious Songs of Connacht," with the same format as its earlier counterpart. Yeats had referred to it in 1895, while it was appearing serially,[153] but its publication in volume form was delayed for a decade, and in the interim Yeats forgot about it. Meanwhile, Hyde was getting more and more involved in other activities. Yeats had had a high enough opinion of him to recommend him as editor of the book series if he himself could not get the position (*Letters,* 215); but when Hyde did become a participant the post he held proved from a literary point of view to be more time-consuming than fruitful and did not really help the movement. Furthermore, he was perennial president of the Gaelic League (which had been founded in 1893 as a result of his "de-Anglicising" speech), and his work for it helped sever his connections with "Yeats's" movement, for it took up much of his time and also of course emphasized literature in Irish. He did take a hand in the development of the theater, but with the exception of a bit of work on Yeats's *Where There Is Noth-*

152. "The Three Sorrows of Story Telling," *The Bookman,* July, 1895, pp. 116–117.
153. "Irish National Literature. IV.—A List of the Best Irish Books," *The Bookman,* October, 1895, p. 22.

ing,[154] his contributions generally used Irish as their medium.[155]

Yeats referred to his "beautiful prose" in an 1897 article and in 1900 recommended that dialect as a medium for folk stories be replaced by "that English, as full of Gaelic structions as the English of the countrypeople but without a special pronunciation, which Dr. Hyde has adopted in *Beside the Fire*, the one quite perfect book of Irish folklore." [156] He also enshrined the *Love Songs* in an early (1904) Dun Emer Press volume, in the introduction to which he noted that the verse was not as good as the prose, for even Hyde could not always "escape from the influence of his predecessors" when he rhymed in English.[157] But as early as 1902 he began to express in print his disappointment in the direction Hyde's career had taken. Reading Lady Gregory's translations of Hyde's plays had reminded him of his first discovery of the *Love Songs*, and the longer he thought about such a prose style the more virtues he could see in it:

I find myself now, as I found myself then, grudging to propaganda, to scholarship, to oratory, however necessary, a genius which might in modern Irish or in that idiom of the English-speaking countrypeople discover a new region for the mind to wander in. In Ireland, where we have so much to prove and to disprove, we are ready to forget that the creation of an emotion of beauty is the only kind of literature that justifies itself. Books of literary propaganda and literary history are merely preparations for the creation or understanding of such an emotion. . . . I wish . . . that he could put away from himself some of the interruptions of that ceaseless propaganda, and find time for the

154. See *Letters*, p. 503.

155. One of his plays was based on one of Yeats's Hanrahan stories, and Yeats did the scenario for it (*Au*, p. 266; *Letters*, p. 355).

156. *EI*, p. 184; "Irish Fairy Beliefs," *The Speaker*, July 14, 1900, p. 413.

157. *The Love Songs of Connacht* (Dundrum: Dun Emer Press, 1904), p. [xi].

making of translations, loving and leisurely, like those in *Beside the Fire* and the *Love Songs of Connacht*. He has begun to get a little careless lately. Above all I would have him keep to that English idiom of the Irish-thinking people of the West which he has begun to use less often. It is the only good English spoken by any large number of Irish people to-day, and we must found good literature on a living speech. . . . One can write well in that country idiom without much thought about one's words; the emotion will bring the right word itself, for there everything is old and everything alive and nothing common or threadbare.[158]

Hyde had in fact published in 1900 *Úbhla de'n Chraoibh*, which Yeats, though he could not read it, later praised for being "at once so romantic and so concrete" (*Au*, 132), but he had also become more involved than ever with other activities, such as editing the first volume of the new Irish Texts Society series and defending the study of Irish in a controversy with Professor Atkinson of his *alma mater*.

In the meantime, the character of the Gaelic League had been changing. It was conceived as a group in which Irishmen of all parties could work together oblivious of their political differences, but before long it was captured by the more extreme Nationalists, men like those who had opposed Yeats over the merits of Young Ireland, except that they were distrustful of *any* attempt to combine Irish literature and the English language. Hyde himself lamented and opposed this development, but Yeats came to feel that it had had a deleterious effect upon him nevertheless. He made the connection in *The Trembling of the Veil*:

I mourn for "the greatest folk-loreist who ever lived," and for the great poet who died in his youth. The Harps and Pepperpots got him, and the Harps and Pepperpots kept him till he wrote in our common English—"It must be either English or Irish," said some patriotic editor, Young Ireland practice in his head— that needs such sifting that he who would write it vigorously must

158. *Explor*, pp. 93–95; cf. *EI*, p. 335: "Those first translations he has not equalled since."

write it like a learned language, and took for his model the newspaper upon his breakfast table, and became for no base reason beloved by multitudes who should never have heard his name till their schoolmasters showed it upon his tomb [*Au*, 132–133].

He concluded this passage by quoting his own earlier poem "At the Abbey Theatre," which had similarly criticized Hyde for succumbing to popular influence. Yeats had been deeply impressed by the fact that even as a young man Hyde had been truly a popular poet, whose lyrics were sung by Irish peasants at work in the fields (*Au*, 131), but he very much disliked his more vulgar popularity (which took such forms as girls wearing hatbands bearing his pseudonym, *An Craoibhin Aoibhinn*) among his followers in the League, many of whom had agitated against *The Playboy* and other allegedly unpatriotic plays. While Yeats cannot, therefore, be said to have been impartial, his analysis of the causes of Hyde's later "apostasy" certainly did contain a measure of truth. But of course there really was no apostasy, for Hyde had never been as committed to Irish literature in English as Yeats himself had believed.

Hyde's prose style did, however, make an important contribution to the development of that literature. During the later nineties Yeats had become close with Lady Gregory, who could read and speak Irish, and he soon saw in her the ideal person to carry on the work that he could not, and Hyde would not, continue. She had already been familiar with Hyde's work,[159] but it was Yeats who provided the necessary stimulus to her efforts to develop a comparable prose. As early as 1898, when he was planning to collaborate with her on a book of fairy lore they had collected, he projected that she would do the "peasant talk" (*Letters*, 305). By 1901 he had already solicited her help in rewriting the Hanrahan stories in a language "closer to the thought of the people" and to the peasant side of his hero, and they successfully completed this

159. Elizabeth Coxhead, *Lady Gregory: A Literary Portrait* (New York: Harcourt, Brace and World, 1961), p. 44.

task by 1904.[160] She also helped him with the peasant dialogue in his plays.[161] Furthermore, using the same medium, she made a significant contribution to the development of another of Yeats's early ideals by translating the chief cycles of Irish legend (*Cuchulain of Muirthemne*, 1902, and *Gods and Fighting Men*, 1904),[162] and helped compensate for Hyde's abandonment of such a medium by using her own brand of it to translate the plays Hyde was writing in Irish. In 1903, Yeats termed the new prose "her discovery and Dr. Hyde's," [163] and Lady Gregory later wrote that she "was the first to use the Irish idiom as it is spoken, with intention and belief in it. Dr. Hyde indeed has used it with fine effect in his *Love Songs of Connacht*, but alas! gave it up afterwards, in deference to some Dublin editor." [164] The phrase "with intention and belief in it" was an excellent statement of the difference between Hyde's attitude and that of Yeats and Lady Gregory. John Synge, meanwhile, had read the works of both Hyde and Lady Gregory and combined the lessons he learned from them with personal experience in the West of Ireland to produce his own even more famous language.[165] The distance between "Teig

160. *Letters*, p. 361; see *Early Poems and Stories*, p. 528. The volume was finished in 1904, though not published until the following year (Wade, *Bibliography*, 3rd ed., p. 74). In *Early Poems and Stories*, p. 395, Yeats erroneously gave the date of the revision as 1907.

161. See *Letters*, p. 389 ("I find I manage the dialect pretty well, but will get you to go over it."); *VPlays*, p. 232; *Au*, p. 274.

162. Dowden praised the first of these except for its "needless affectations of Anglo-Irish peasant terms [turns?] of phrase" *(Letters of Edward Dowden*, p. 318). For even harsher strictures, see George Moore's attack in *Vale* (New York: Macmillan, 1914), pp. 187–193.

163. "A Canonical Book," *The Bookman*, May, 1903, p. 67.

164. *Our Irish Theatre* (New York: Capricorn Books, 1961), p. 124.

165. See Synge, *Collected Works* (London: Oxford University Press, 1961–1968), II, 47, 133, 366–368; David H. Greene and Edward M. Stephens, *J. M. Synge: 1871–1909* (New York: Collier Books, 1961), pp. 108, 135, 223; Lady Gregory, *Our Irish Theatre*, p. 124; and AE's letter to A. de Blacam of July 8, 1922 (Alan Denson manuscript).

O'Kane" and *The Playboy of the Western World* was great, but there was a link, and Yeats had helped to create it.

8. William Larminie: A Talent Overlooked

In his desire to further the growth of the movement, Yeats was always seeking out and encouraging literary talent. Generally he was quite discerning, but in the case of William Larminie (1849 or 1850–1900) he made a grievous oversight. Larminie shared almost all of his literary ideals and was both more promising and more capable as a writer than either Katharine Tynan or Nora Hopper; yet Yeats gave them all the attention and acclaim they deserved, even overpraised them, and took next to no interest in him. Larminie died prematurely in 1900; otherwise this neglect might have come to seem even more glaring.

Larminie was from the West of Ireland, having been born in Castlebar, County Mayo. Like Yeats and Hyde, he had developed during his life there an interest in the culture of the people.[166] He took a degree at T.C.D. and then spent some years in London in the India Office, but he did not fall prey to cosmopolitanism: as early as 1884 he had begun collecting folklore (he had at least some knowledge of Irish), and in 1887 he returned to Ireland to live, taking up residence in Bray, near Dublin, where he began a second career as a writer. Between that time and his death he published two volumes of poetry, a collection of folklore, and a number of articles (including a reply to Dowden during the *Express* controversy and a contribution to the Yeats-Eglinton debate [167]); he was also an active member of the National Literary Society.[168] Although a shy, retiring man, he knew at least slightly several

166. Biographical information on Larminie is very scarce; most of this is taken from John Eglinton's memoir "William Larminie," *Dublin Magazine*, New Series XIX (April–June, 1944), 12–16.

167. "Irish Literature," *Daily Express* (Dublin), January 25, 1895, p. 3; *Literary Ideals in Ireland*, pp. 57–68.

168. See Ryan, pp. 130, 142–144.

of the leading contemporary literary figures, including Eglinton, Rolleston, Hyde (who praised his folklore and called him "the most under-rated man in Ireland"),[169] AE, and Yeats himself.

He seems to have been very well read: his essays show a familiarity with ancient and modern philosophy, the Classics, the entire spectrum of English literature, and the major Continental traditions, including the Scandinavian. He had a considerable knowledge of early Irish literature and drew heavily upon it in his two books of poetry, *Glanlua and Other Poems* (1889) and *Fand and Other Poems* (1892). In addition to the title poem the latter included *Moytura,* a long and elaborate poetic rendering of the Battle of Magh Tuireadh. Furthermore, his interest in folklore and myth was combined with a concern for the spiritual. Presumably Protestant by birth, he seems to have shared the contemporary dissatisfaction with orthodox religion and to have turned to a personal vision that AE defined as a sort of mysticism.[170] He did a study of the ninth-century Irish Churchman Johannes Scotus Eriugena, but treated him as a philosopher, an "Irish Plato," rather than as a theologian.[171] He referred to the "pantheistic cast of his philosophy" and to the arguments of Arbois de Jubainville and Henri Martin that this supposed pantheism came to him through Irish tradition; and he linked this concept with the East by noting an "affinity of his ideas with those of India."

In his contribution to the 1898 symposium, one of the chief subjects of which was the spiritual, he indicated his belief in a realm "behind the veil" and expressed the opinion that "just

169. Eglinton, "William Larminie," p. 13.
170. *A Treasury of Irish Poetry,* pp. 476–477.
171. "Joannes Scotus Erigena," *Contemporary Review,* LXXI (April, 1897), 557–572. Larminie also made a translation of Eriugena that survives in manuscript in the National Library of Ireland (MSS 290–291). This translation, which was to have appeared in a Bohn Library edition, has been called by a later scholar a "superb work"; see Brien Stock, "The Philosophical Anthropology of Johannes Scotus Eriugena," *Studi Medievali,* serie terza, VII (1967), 1, note 2.

as the meaning and seriousness of life shrink to nothing in the absence of transcendentalism, so does the value of art shrink which deals with life from which transcendental belief has disappeared." [172] These concerns pervaded his poetry as well: he wrote one poem on "The Return of the Gods," and *Moytura* is a cosmic vision in which the battle between the Tuatha Dé Danann and the Fomorians is interpreted as an archetypal struggle between good and evil in the universe. According to Eglinton, he conceived his poetic mission as being the interpretation of the "Irish spiritual mystery." [173] In Nora Hopper and other writers of the later "Celtic Twilight" period this sort of vision was to become highly derivative, but in Larminie's case it was not only genuine but original as well: "The Return of the Gods" was published in 1889, and *Fand* and *Moytura* appeared before virtually all of the most prominent spiritual volumes of Yeats and AE.

Larminie's poetry was very different from that of Young Ireland. Interested in folklore, myth, and philosophy, he completely eschewed politics and current events as subject-matter and was, furthermore, a highly conscious stylist. In fact, he was as much concerned as Yeats with literary technique and made experiments that led to the introduction into modern Irish literature in English of the systematic use of assonance. He himself was not apparently concerned with it as a way of giving Irish writing a distinctively national character that would set it off from English literature, but it would have been very useful for satisfying this Yeatsian *desideratum,* for it had been one of the most common features of Celtic verse and when employed in English-language poetry (in combination with Irish subject-matter) could be seen as having an effect comparable to the use in English prose of Irish constructions and idiom.

The earliest Irish poetry was apparently rhymeless. By the seventh century, however, the country had felt the influence

172. *Literary Ideals in Ireland,* pp. 63–65.
173. "William Larminie," p. 13.

of medieval Latin rhymed verse, and a form of rhyme began appearing in the native literature. This was not the type of perfect rhyme characteristic of English verse, but rather what has been called "generic" rhyme, in which any member of a particular genus of phonetically similar consonants could rhyme either with itself or with any other member of that genus, so long as the preceding vowels were identical. Such rhyme was the backbone of an incredibly complex and demanding prosody, as may be seen from the following description of a goblet, written by an anonymous poet:

Eoin bas n-dearg 's a n-druim r' a thaoibh,
mar do chuim an ceard go cōir
lucht 'gar chasmhail cleasa ceoil—
eoin 's a sleasa d' asnaibh ōir.

(Birds red of claw stand backed against its border, just as the artist deftly shaped them as figures seeming really to sing—birds whose sides are ribbed with gold.)

The poetry of this period was syllabic, and this particular meter, *rannaigheacht mhōr* (the Great Versification), required stanzas of four lines, with each line containing seven syllables and ending with a stressed monosyllable. Other major requirements were that the last words in lines two and four show generic rhyme with each other; that the last words in one and three must consonate but not assonate with these; that all the stressed words in two other than the final rhyming word show generic rhyme with stressed words in one—*(ch)uim: (dr)uim, (c)eard: (d)earg*—and the same for lines three and four; and that every line must have at least one alliteration between adjacent stressed words, with the last line having the alliteration between the last two stressed words.

With the breaking up of the bardic schools during the seventeenth century, Irish prosody underwent a significant change. Accentual meters appeared, and the consonantal patterns of generic rhyme disappeared, leaving merely assonance. This too was used in highly complex patterns, both in terminal position and within the line, and sometimes in combination with the equivalent of English perfect rhyme. Even in its corrupted form Irish poetry was obviously very intricate and very different from English verse.[174] It is not surprising, therefore, that this tradition did not impress itself upon the Irish literature in English, which began to proliferate in the early nineteenth century: Mangan was perhaps the only writer of stature before Larminie to experiment with its use.

Larminie explained his interest in the use of assonance in his 1894 article "The Development of English Metres." [175] In the first place, he felt that English rhymes were not numerous, and that consequently many had been used so frequently as to be "worn out." Assonance could provide relief and variety. Secondly, whereas conventional English rhyme when used internally almost inevitably degenerates into a ludicrous jingle, even quite frequent internal assonance has no such effect, and consequently might be used to create complex series of harmonies, or to add music and sweetness to the verse. The third reason was a rather unusual one. In the main portion of the essay Larminie had argued that the basic principles of English versification were not yet properly understood: he challenged the popular theory of its entirely accentual nature and asserted that quantity plays an important though up to that time little recognized role in it. He wished to see the principle recognized and efforts made to extend the evolution of quantitative forms, especially ones involving trisyllabic feet. Rhyme, he felt, had distracted attention from "the qualities that are really essential to good verse" and retarded the development of such forms. He did not foresee the entire disappearance of

174. This summary is taken primarily from *The Encyclopedia of Poetry and Poetics*, ed. Alex Preminger (Princeton, N.J.: Princeton University Press, 1965), pp. 109–112; other sources consulted were Gerard Murphy, *Early Irish Metrics* (Dublin: Royal Irish Academy, 1961), pp. 1, 18–19, 30–34; Eleanor Knott, *Irish Classical Poetry* (Dublin: Colm O'Lochlainn, 1960), pp. 10–15; and Hyde, *A Literary History of Ireland*, pp. 539–551.

175. *Contemporary Review*, LXVI (November, 1894), 717–736.

rhyme, but he felt that "it is just possible that we might ultimately learn to do fairly well without it, or at least to restrict its use, finding both greater freedom and finer sound in quantity sweetened by assonance, in assonance strengthened by quantity." As proof that great poetry could be written relying thus heavily on assonance he pointed to Irish literature, and also to that of Spain. In urging writers to experiment with it, he theorized that while it might be presumed that Irish writers would be particularly receptive, too many of them would probably prefer to garb their works in the latest English fashion. He himself, however, had been exploring its possible uses for at least five years.

Three of the four poems in his first volume, *Glanlua and Other Poems* (1889), employ rhyme throughout. The fourth, *Glanlua*, nearly seventy pages in length, is written almost entirely in couplets, but there are a few relatively short passages in which final assonance is used sporadically, in combination with rhyme (for example, ". . . guarded / . . . spoil / . . . toil / . . . harm him"). The effect is unobtrusive, and if it were not for his later experiments, the assonance might be judged accidental. Three years later, in *Fand and Other Poems*, he employed it very extensively (in at least portions of eleven out of fifteen poems). In a prefatory note he called attention to the fact:

In this volume I have frequently, and in various forms, regular and irregular, employed assonance instead of rhyme. It ought hardly to be necessary, in these days of metrical experiment, to apologize for an attempt to introduce into English poetry a style of versification which, in the hands of Irish Gaelic bards, both ancient and modern, has shown itself to be in no way inferior to rhyme. But I must explain that only in one instance have I attempted to reproduce an actual Irish form; and that irregular forms both were and are unknown to Gaelic poetry.

His reference to "these days of metrical experiment" was a validation of Yeats's belief that it was necessary for Irish writers to study and learn from the writers of other countries. In 1892 there was very little metrical experiment going on in

Ireland, and Larminie was clearly thinking of English and probably of French literature: contact with those traditions as well as with the native literature had fostered his own experiments.

The prefatory note also underscored his efforts to solve the problem of adapting the complex Gaelic metrics to poetry in English. He wisely abandoned the idea of reproducing regular forms, trying instead to find the best way of working in the general features of assonance. He used it in a bewildering variety of patterns, sometimes by itself, more often in conjunction with rhyme. The opening lines of the title poem confronted the reader at once with many examples:

"Tell me the tale of Cuhoolin, Emer, reveal it to me,
As once was thy promise: 'tis thou that alone canst relate it aright:
How, from the wiles of the beautiful Fand, the immortal, the
    goddess, thou settest him free,
Leading him back, by the lure of thy love, to be chief of the heroes
    of Eirë forever."
Thus spake the bard of Cooalne, agèd and grey, to the lady,
The fair-browed Emer, agèd and grey.

This passage utilizes final assonance ("lady / . . . grey") mixed with rhyme, and internal assonance on long e and long a, the same sounds found in the rhyme and final assonance respectively. The assonantal pattern, frequent in Irish verse, in which the final vowel assonates with an internal vowel in the following line, is illustrated by ". . . me / . . . relate . . . aright / . . . wiles . . . free / . . . chief. . . ." Alliteration is employed profusely. And finally, the unusual stress-patterns and variations in line length show Larminie bringing into play his personal theories about the nature of English meter.

Less complicated, but considerably better poetry, was the "Epilogue" to *Fand:*

Is there one desires to hear
If, within the shores of Eirë,
Eyes may still behold the scene
Fair from Fand's enticements?

Let him seek the southern hills,
And those lakes of loveliest water,
Where the richest bloom of spring's
Burns to reddest autumn:
And the clearest echo sings
Notes a goddess taught her.

Ah! 'twas very long ago
And the words are now denied her:
But the purple hillsides know
Still the tones delightsome:
And their breasts impassioned glow
As were Fand beside them.

And though many an isle be fair,
Fairer still is Inisfallen,
Since the hour Cuhoolin lay,
In the bower enchanted:
See! the ash that waves to-day,
Fand its grandsire planted.

When from wave to mountain top
All delight thy sense bewilders,
Thou shalt own the wonder wrought
Once by her skill'd fingers,
Still, though many an age be gone,
Round Killarney lingers.

The "Epilogue" is probably Larminie's poetic high-water mark; the general level of metrical virtuosity in the book was closer to that of the first example quoted. In fact, Larminie's greatest strength as a poet was his imaginative vision, and while he was full of theories about improving metrics, he did not possess sufficient mastery of language to realize their full potential. The *Fand* volume contained no brilliant verbal effects, no subtle interplay of sound and sense, not even the sweetness and harmony that Larminie had hoped to obtain. In his hands, variations that might have been exciting were all too frequently simply annoying, and it was primarily this defect in his work that led to Yeats's failure to recognize how valuable he might be in developing the new literature.

In July, 1892, Yeats wrote to John O'Leary that he had George Armstrong's collected works to review for *The Bookman* and had given them a preliminary notice, "mainly hostile," in the current *United Ireland*, adding "also like treatment to Larminie" (*Letters*, 211). In the *United Ireland* piece Yeats played Larminie off against the cosmopolitan Armstrong: he admitted that Larminie's work, unlike that of Armstrong, was "Irish enough," but felt he did not "show at present the same innate poetic faculty as that which Mr. Armstrong has thrown away through a false philosophy of life." [176] Yeats was receptive to experiment not as an end in itself, but rather as a means to better literature, and Larminie had only failed nobly. Consequently Yeats was not enthusiastic, predicting, "Mr. Larminie may do much better when he has either abandoned or perfected the experimental rhythmic metres he has invented. He will probably find they are a mistake, for a metre is the slow growth of time and is evolved as blank verse was evolved in the last two or three centuries, to meet some practical need." He quoted a passage from the poetry and asserted that while the thought it contained was "poetical," it lost rather than gained from the meter employed. He ended the very short notice with the statement that the two major poems in the volume, *Fand* and *Moytura,* contained many passages "of equal or greater interest." He made no mention of the use of assonance, in spite of the prefatory note and the fact that it was used in the very passage he quoted. Apparently his dislike of the roughness of Larminie's writing had been so strong that he had not carefully considered the other aspects of the volume. Both the potential national technique and the subject-matter and world-view would otherwise have made a greater impression upon him. The appeal of the visionary *Moytura* is obvious, and the focus Larminie gave to the Fand story anticipated Yeats's *The Only Jealousy of Emer:* Cú

176. "Some New Irish Books," *United Ireland,* July 23, 1892, p. 5.

Chulainn was depicted as torn between the divine realm (represented by Fand) and the mortal world (Emer), with the former urging him "Return not to that pale imperfect world, / Where all things seem to be, but nothing is." Here was the "choice" pattern central to so much of Yeats's work. The prediction that Larminie might do better, and the reference to passages of "interest," suggest that Yeats must have responded in spite of himself to the positive features of the book; but the impact was highly ephemeral, for he never afterwards referred to Larminie as a *poet*.

Larminie's *West Irish Folk-Tales* appeared the following year, and Yeats reviewed it very warmly, but his emphasis was on the virtues of folklore, not on Larminie, and he did not mention the volumes of poetry.[177] It was from this book that he got the image in "O'Sullivan Rua to the Secret Rose" (first published in 1896) of

> . . . him who sold tillage, and house and goods,
> And sought through lands and islands numberless years,
> Until he found, with laughter and with tears,
> A woman of so shining loveliness
> That men threshed corn at midnight by a tress,
> A little stolen tress.[178]

During 1895 he included Larminie with Hyde, Johnson, Ashe King, and George Sigerson as having been busy denouncing rhetoric and "interpreting Gaelic history or modern romance in lectures and speeches," but he was clearly thinking primarily of the folklore book, which he had referred to earlier in the same article and which he put in the second of his lists of best Irish books.[179] In neither list, however, did he recommend Larminie's poems, and he had also excluded him from *A Book of Irish Verse*.

177. "The Evangel of Folk-lore," *The Bookman,* June, 1894, p. 86.

178. See *VP,* p. 813; and *West Irish Folk-Tales* (London: Elliot Stock, 1893), p. 211ff.

179. "Irish National Literature. Contemporary Prose Writers," *The Bookman,* August, 1895, p. 140; "Irish National Literature. IV.—A List of the Best Irish Books," *The Bookman,* October, 1895, p. 22.

Despite this neglect, Larminie remained at least on the fringe of the movement. In 1898, in his contribution to the Eglinton controversy, he showed that while he liked Yeats's work, agreed that the Irish legends could be used in modern literature, and desired spiritual content in literature, he could not share Yeats's enthusiasm for Symbolism (which to him smacked of decadence) and warned that in its concern with the spiritual, literature must not, as Yeats's more recent work probably seemed to Larminie in danger of doing, lose *all* contact with the "physical plane." [180] He still had enough respect for Yeats to be present early the next year at a meeting of the National Literary Society during which Yeats spoke about the impending first performance of the Literary Theatre,[181] and if he had not died soon afterwards might have become involved in that phase of the movement. On the other hand, he had published no further collections of poetry and at the time of his death was engaged primarily in a scholarly project, a translation of Eriugena.[182] It is therefore not impossible that he was rather discouraged with his prospects as an Irish writer.

What Yeats *might* have done for him is suggested by the case of Standish O'Grady. He was the "distinguished elder" of the movement, and his devotion to Irish literature had antedated Yeats's own. Yeats borrowed much from him (including not only legendary subject-matter but also even something of his attitude towards the Irish heroic past), but O'Grady was too highly individualistic in his beliefs to be influenced very greatly by anyone, and Yeats's attempts to affect him in return were limited to providing him with opportunities to write and creating an audience for him. His *History of Ireland,* though it had had a tremendous impact upon a few sensitive minds, had been a failure commercially, and his other books did not sell well either. Yeats frequently sought to improve this situa-

180. *Literary Ideals in Ireland,* pp. 63–65.
181. "Irish Literary Theatre. Lecture by Mr W B Yeats," *Daily Express,* Dublin, 1899 (press clipping, Houghton Library, Harvard University; datable by internal evidence).
182. Eglinton, "William Larminie," p. 12.

tion. When he was first conceiving the book-scheme, he thought of O'Grady as a possible contributor and noted as an advantage of the series not being sponsored by a clearly Nationalistic publisher that the Unionist O'Grady would write for it "without fear of the *Express* in his heart" (*Letters,* 201, 217). While Yeats's version of the scheme fell through, O'Grady's book of historical stories, *The Bog of Stars,* did appear in the New Irish Library and proved in fact to be the only book in the series that had any *literary* merit. Yeats reviewed O'Grady's new productions with lavish praise [183] and included practically all of his work in his book lists; when attacked for having done so, he firmly defended his position:

I could do no more than give Mr. O'Grady the lion's share, because his books have affected one more powerfully than those of any other writer. . . . I believe them to be ideal books of their kind, books of genius, but even if they were not, they would still contain more of ancient legend and circumstance than any other.[184]

When AE planned a negative criticism of O'Grady's *All Ireland* (a politicoeconomic work), Yeats successfully dissuaded him: "All right, I won't attack O'Grady's book. I never intended to—only to separate ideal from method, but as you say it is best to leave him alone." [185] And as Yeats became occupied with plans for an Irish theater he tried to get O'Grady to contribute a play (*Letters,* 279). Of course Yeats's enthusiasm did not have enough power to make O'Grady a popular writer, but it must have encouraged him and helped keep him working: O'Grady himself later acknowledged that the enthusiasm of Yeats and some of his associates for the *History* caused London publishers to offer to take some of his subsequent books.[186]

183. See, for example, "Battles Long Ago," *The Bookman,* February, 1895, p. 153.
184. "Irish Literature," *Daily Express* (Dublin), March 8, 1895.
185. *Letters from AE,* p. 29.
186. *Standish O'Grady: Selected Essays and Passages,* ed. E. A. Boyd (Dublin: Talbot Press, n.d.), p. 5. For further information about

Despite the fact that Yeats made no such efforts on Larminie's behalf, his poetry was fortunately not completely neglected. AE had read it, and as might be expected he found the world-view in it very attractive. In one 1899 article he included Larminie in the spiritual group of contemporary Irish writers and added that his "striking imaginative work is too little known." [187] He introduced the selections from Larminie's work in *A Treasury of Irish Poetry*, and the high praise he bestowed upon *Moytura* was striking when compared with Yeats's silence:

He is a mystic, but his mysticism is never incoherent and always profoundly philosophical. . . . [In *Moytura*] the battle fought between the De Danann gods and the Fohmors becomes the eternal war between light and darkness, and the Celtic legend is interwoven with wonderful skill into more universal hopes and traditions. For sustained imaginative power this poem is not surpassed by anything in modern Irish poetry, and I cannot read it without an excitement of the spirit.[188]

Nor was his response limited purely to the vision embodied in the works. He admitted that the metrical experiments made the poetry rugged and often disagreeable; but unlike Yeats he not only noticed but was even impressed by the use of assonance, found in it a "novel charm," and theorized that "used by a more skilled artist in words, the assonance might very well replace rhyme."

Fittingly, it was AE himself who was largely responsible for Larminie's experiments ultimately affecting the course of Irish literature. His prodigious memory absorbed the "Epilogue"

O'Grady's place in the Renaissance and his relationship with Yeats, see Phillip L. Marcus, *Standish O'Grady* (Lewisburg, Pennsylvania: Bucknell University Press, 1970).

187. "The Irish Literary Drama," *Daily Express* (Dublin), January 28, 1899, p. 3. Larminie in turn found AE's work very attractive: see *Literary Ideals in Ireland*, p. 58.

188. *A Treasury of Irish Poetry*, pp. 476–477.

to *Fand* and also apparently the gist of the essay on meter.[189] His enthusiasm had no immediate effect: Hyde was using assonance in some of his translations, but only to convey more fully the effect of the original texts. Many years later AE found an interested listener in Austin Clarke, who had produced a very promising book of poetry (*The Vengeance of Fionn,* 1917) but then entered a period of psychological stress that interrupted the development of his style. AE "was continually quoting the 'Epilogue' to *Fand"* and drew Clarke's attention to Larminie's work, suggesting that Larminie's failure was not conclusive and his experiments might be improved upon.[190] Clarke's knowledge of Irish enabled him to study assonance in the language's poetry, and because he had the poetic gift that Larminie lacked, he made of it a viable technique. By making possible the free use of polysyllabic words at the end of a line it opened up for him a wide variety of new rhythmic patterns and thus helped give his style toughness and energy, as did the effect created by assonance between a final vowel and an internal vowel in the succeeding line. Furthermore, his perception of the virtues of assonance led him to experiment with other replacements for conventional English rhyme, especially stopped rhyme and punning *rime riche,* and in combination these devices became central in his later work, where they were particularly effective in creating currents of satire. Thus, in "Irish-American Dignitary" his critical attitude toward the subject is expressed more through the style than by direct commentary:

> Glanced down at Shannon from the sky-way
> With his attendant clergy, stayed night
> In Dublin, but whole day with us
> To find his father's cot, now dust

189. Robert Farren, *The Course of Irish Verse in English* (London: Sheed and Ward, 1948), p. 57.

190. Letter to me from Mr. Clarke, September 5, 1966, quoted with his permission; and Clarke, *Poetry in Modern Ireland* (Dublin: Colm O'Lochlainn, 1951), pp. 42–46.

And rubble, bless new church, school buildings
At Glantworth, drive to Spangle Hill
And cut first sod, hear, answer, fine speeches,
Accept a learned gown, freedom
Of ancient city, so many kissing
His ring—God love him!—almost missed
The waiting liner: that day in Cork
Had scarcely time for knife and fork.

There is no question that the revolution in Clarke's style was central in his development into the greatest Irish poet since Yeats, and Clarke's friend F. R. Higgins was also induced by AE to work with assonance.[191] Eventually, therefore, Larminie's pioneer efforts achieved at least indirect realization.

In 1899, Yeats had an opportunity to prepare a second edition of *A Book of Irish Verse*. He was unable, probably because so much of his time was currently being devoted to the drama, to revise it as completely as he would have liked to do;[192] but such revisions as there were, in introduction and contents, have a particular interest because they make the anthology in its new form represent his final contemporary judgment of the movement to that time.

In his 1894 discussion of it he listed as its writers Hyde, Johnson, Rolleston, and Katharine Tynan; in a separate paragraph he discussed AE and Charles Weekes, the separation probably representing a scruple similar to that which led him to leave *Homeward* out of his first list of national books. By the end of the century Hyde and Rolleston had shown more clearly than before that their creative work was to be far less important than their translations and scholarship, and Yeats's scruple had vanished as he became increasingly conscious of a spiritual element in Irish literature. Consequently, he com-

191. AE, letter to Yeats of "late April, 1932" (Alan Denson manuscript); Farren, pp. 145–146; Clarke, *Poetry in Modern Ireland*, pp. 44–46.

192. *A Book of Irish Verse*, revised ed., p. xiii.

bined the two paragraphs: he deleted Rolleston's name and shifted the reference to Hyde to a later passage dealing with the Gaelic movement; he brought in AE to fill one of their places, added Nora Hopper to take the other, and introduced also John Eglinton. Furthermore he rephrased the passage in question to make clearer the suggestion that one of the distinguishing characteristics of the group was their "deliberate art," and introduced the new characteristic of "preoccupation with spiritual passions and memories." In sum, he made the movement sound more cohesive and gave more emphasis to its devotion to some of his own chief ideals.

The actual contents of the volume were changed slightly but significantly. (A comparative chart of the contents is given in Appendix B.) The selections of Rolleston and Hyde remained static. Katharine Tynan, who had similarly disappointed him, lost one poem, "In Iona"; it is possible that this deletion was caused by Nora Hopper's "imitation" of the poem in question, but the fact that her representation was not *increased* may have been a sign of Yeats's slackening enthusiasm. Larminie and Savage-Armstrong continued to be unrepresented. On the other hand, Yeats included for the first time Nora Hopper and John Eglinton, greatly increased the number of pieces by AE, and added two poems to the selection of Johnson's work. Thus, its new form rendered the volume more suitable for attracting an intelligent audience for the new Irish writers.

5. Old Irish Myth and Modern Irish Literature

1. The Tradition before Yeats

One of the major contributions to the development of modern Irish literature in English was the rediscovery of the old Irish legends. References to them had begun to appear in English-language works in the late 1500's,[1] and during the ensuing centuries they attracted increasing scholarly attention, so that by the second half of the nineteenth century a substantial body of fairly accurate translations was available. By that time there were also many Irish writers who had to use English as their medium but were interested in Irish subject-matter, and they saw the early stories as perfect material for a creative literature. Not only were they fresh and unexplored, but they also seemed virtually inexhaustible—"the most plentiful treasure of legends in Europe."[2] There was much discussion of how many hundreds of octavo volumes it would take to publish all the surviving texts. In fact, there proved to be far more than were necessary, as most of the writers stuck to a few particularly appealing characters and tales.

1. See Russell K. Alspach, *Irish Poetry from the English Invasion to 1798* (Philadelphia: University of Pennsylvania Press, 1964), pp. 61ff.

2. *Letters*, p. 308; see also *LNI*, p. 158; and Standish O'Grady, *History of Ireland: Critical and Philosophical* (London: Sampson Low and Co., and Dublin: E. Ponsonby and Co., 1881), p. 61.

Furthermore, these legends, although of course in origin connected with those of other countries, had taken on distinctively Irish features, and being national they offered Irish authors a way of breaking with the custom of merely echoing at a distance the writers of other countries. On the other hand, they represented a subject that, while intensely national, was uncolored by modern politics or sectarian religious controversy and thus might appeal to writers of differing persuasions and to a wider, more heterogeneous audience. Stopford Brooke epitomized this virtue in his address at the inaugural meeting of the Irish Literary Society, London:

The earliest and noblest part of the [ancient Irish] literature was national, but not nationalist. It was fully Irish; written out of the heart of her own people, it was but little influenced by other literatures; and in it, at least, we can forget our quarrels of party, and quarrels of religion. It is not so easy to forget these quarrels when we read the literature which followed the invasion of Ireland by the English. . . . That literature may be said to be nationalist as well as national. It was forced to conceive Ireland as a whole and as set over against England.[3]

These theoretical advantages had already been abundantly exemplified in practice, for Ferguson and de Vere, both non-Nationalists politically, had been early users of the legendary materials; another example, their contemporary T. Caulfield Irwin, seeking to avoid political themes in his *Irish Poems and Legends* (1869) in order that it might "be acceptable to *all* classes who read Irish or English verses," had included several poems based on Irish myths.[4] Finally, contrasted with an often sordid present, the Ireland depicted in the old texts, full of beauty and epic heroism, appeared extremely attractive; the contrast in fact made that earlier period seem far more noble and idealistic than it really was.

As soon as the Irish writers began turning their attention to the old stories they were faced with determining precisely

3. *The Need and Use of Getting Irish Literature into the English Tongue* (London: T. Fisher Unwin, 1893), pp. 11–12.
4. "Preface," *Irish Poems and Legends* (Glasgow, 1869), n.p.

how they were to be used. No one answer seemed obvious, and consequently extremely diverse solutions were adopted.

The most rudimentary literary approach can be seen in Gerald Griffin's "The Swans of Lir" (1842). In this rendering of *Aided Chlainne Lir* (The Fate of the Children of Lir) Griffin stayed so close to his original that the eminent Irish scholar Eugene O'Curry, in a note to his own edition of the Irish text with literal translation, gave special praise to his fidelity.[5] Griffin took what was virtually a piece of scholarship and used it in a collection of stories linked by a frame tale. Obviously he hoped the novelty of the story, not anything unique in his handling of it, would appeal to his readers.

A similar approach was used by Denis Florence MacCarthy in his *Ferdiah* (1882), a retelling of the most famous of Cú Chulainn's battles, except that while Griffin had reproduced the prose with interspersed lyrics of his source, MacCarthy tried to give his work more literary appeal by using a poetic medium throughout. The structure and content of the source were preserved intact: he neither rearranged his material nor omitted any incident. And his fidelity to the language was equally great; the following passages reveal how rigidly he adhered to the literal translation from which he was working:

Source

They rested there that night. They arose early the next morning, and they came forward to the ford of battle. Cuchulaind perceived an ill visaged and a greatly lowering cloud on Ferdiah that day. "Badly dost thou appear this day, O Ferdiah," said Cuchulaind. "Thy hair has become dark this day, and thy eye has become drowsy, and thine own form and features and appearance have departed from thee." [6]

MacCarthy

They rested there that night. Next morn they rose,
And to the Ford of battle forward came.

5. "The Fate of the Children of Lir," *Atlantis*, IV (1863), 113–157.
6. Eugene O'Curry, *On the Manners and Customs of the Ancient Irish,* ed. W. K. Sullivan (London: Williams and Norgate, Dublin: W. B. Kelly, and New York: Scribner, Welford and Co., 1873), III, 443.

That day a great, ill-favoured, lowering cloud
Upon Ferdiah's face Cuchullin saw,
"Badly," said he, "dost thou appear this day,
Ferdiah, for thy hair has duskier grown
This day, and a dull stupour dims thine eyes,
And thine own face and form, and what thou wert
In outward seeming have deserted thee." [7]

MacCarthy maintained this textual fidelity even when the source offered serious difficulties: thus the redundancy of "And it was then he put on his battle suit of battle and combat and fight" [8] was only partially eliminated in his "Then was it for the first time he put on / His battle suit of battle and of fight." [9]

For most of the early myth-users, however, such scrupulous faithfulness to the old texts was impossible. Sometimes the reason was artistic: many of the texts survived in corrupt form, aesthetic virtues they may once have had blurred through centuries of oral transmission and manual copying. Often elements in the stories were judged repugnant on moral grounds or conflicted with idealized visions of the heroic age.

Both artistic and moral or idealistic objections can be seen in the work of P. W. Joyce, whose *Old Celtic Romances* (1879), a pioneer book in the field, was used by many more significant figures. Joyce was a scholar, but, as he indicates in his preface, his renderings were not done "for linguistic purposes":

A translation may either follow the very words, or reproduce the life and spirit, of the original, but no translation can do both. If you render word for word, you lose the spirit; if you wish to give the spirit and the manner, you must depart from the exact words and frame your own phrases. I have chosen this latter course. My translation follows the original closely enough in narrative and incident; but so far as mere phraseology is concerned I have used the English language freely, not allowing myself to

7. *Ferdiah* (Dublin: M. H. Gill and Son, 1882), p. 66.
8. O'Curry, *Manners and Customs*, III, 445.
9. *Ferdiah,* p. 69.

be trammelled by too close an adherence to the very words of the text. The originals are in general simple in style; and I have done my best to render them into simple, plain, homely English.[10]

This suggests that Joyce, like MacCarthy, deviated from his sources only in not always using their very words. And yet, as other passages in the same preface reveal, Joyce did occasionally tidy up the "narrative and incident" of certain tales. For example, in "The Pursuit of the Gilla Dacker and his Horse" he "omitted altogether a long episode towards the end, which travels away from the main story," and in the Diarmaid and Gráinne story he made several changes:

I cannot help believing that this fine story originally ended with the death of Dermat, though in all the current versions . . . there is an additional part recounting the further proceedings of Grania and her sons, after the death of the hero. But this part is in every respect inferior to the rest—in language, in feeling, and in play of imagination. It seems to me very clear that it was patched on to the original story by some unskilful hand; and I have accordingly omitted it, and ended the story with the death of Dermat. I have also omitted two short episodes—that of the *cnumh* or reptile of Corca Divna, as a mere excrescence; and Finn's expedition to Scotland for aid against Dermat. And, for the sake of clearness, I have slightly changed the place of that part of the tale which recounts the origin of the Fairy Quicken Tree of Dooros. There are one or two other trifling but very necessary modifications, which need not be mentioned here.[11]

Some of the changes, such as the elimination of the expedition to Scotland, were certainly aimed at structural improvement; but prudishness may have prompted the omission of the conclusion, in which Gráinne, instead of remaining faithful to Diarmaid, gives herself to Fionn. Recent scholarly opinion supports Joyce's assertion that the episode is not of the same origin as the rest of the tale;[12] nevertheless, it is clear from

10. *Old Celtic Romances* (London: Kegan Paul and Co., 1879), p. vii.
11. Joyce, *Old Celtic Romances*, pp. xiv–xv.
12. See *Tóruigheacht Dhiarmada agus Ghráinne*, ed. Nessa Ní Sheaghdha (Dublin: Irish Texts Society, 1967), pp. xvii–xviii.

Joyce's comments that he *wanted* it not to be canonical. And one of those "trifling but very necessary modifications" involved the bowdlerization of a passage which relates that "Diarmuid kept himself from Grainne, and . . . he left a spit of flesh uncooked in Doire dha bhoth as a token to Fionn and to the Fenians that he had not sinned with Grainne." [13]

Thus, Joyce did take considerable liberties with his sources in regard to rearrangement and omission, but he did not take the far greater liberty of *adding* to the original texts. Other, less scholarly minded writers of the time, in trying to make the old legends into "good stories," resorted to modifying plot through invention as well as deletion, expanding the characterizations and making them consistent and convincing, and combining elements from different versions.

A good example of a formal justification of this approach is found in de Vere's preface to *The Foray of Queen Maeve* (1882), where he asserted,

It is not in the form of translation that an ancient Irish tale of any considerable length admits of being rendered in poetry. What is needed is to select from the original such portions as are at once the most essential to the story, and the most characteristic, reproducing them in condensed form, and taking care that the necessary additions bring out the idea and contain nothing that is not in the spirit of the original.[14]

Joyce had been rather apologetic about his structural alterations; but in de Vere's case modification of the plot structure of the original was taken for granted, even elevated into an ideal in its own right. Such alterations were to preserve "the spirit of the original," but that was quite another thing than merely diverging from the letter of the *language,* for it involved a diminished concern with adherence to the *content* of

13. The omitted passage is quoted from the version of Standish Hayes O'Grady, *The Pursuit of Diarmuid and Grainne* (Dublin: M. H. Gill and Son, 1880–1881), I, 28.

14. *The Foray of Queen Maeve/And Other Legends of Ireland's Heroic Age* (London: Kegan Paul, Trench and Co., 1882), p. vii.

the original texts: additions as well as omissions would be necessary.

De Vere's own modifications of his sources were numerous but fairly restrained. He toned down certain elements and omitted others, such as the passage in the Fight at the Ford in which the combatants' wounds are said to be big enough for birds to have flown through. Elsewhere he expanded the scope or significance of incidents present in the source: the banquet at which Medb bribes Fer Diad to fight Cú Chulainn was developed into a little dramatic scene, and the encounter of Findabair and Reochaid became a romantic tragedy.[15] Sometimes elements were introduced that had *no* basis in the source: he brought in a banshee howling on the night of Deirdre's birth and, to heighten the pathos of Fer Diad's feelings toward Cú Chulainn, fabricated the idea that the former had been in love with Aoife and had lost her to his friend.[16] He frequently added "poetic" descriptive passages such as the following, again from the Fight at the Ford:

> . . . the vernal day
> Panted with summer arduous, while aloft
> Noontide, a fire-tressed Fury, waved her torch,
> Kindling the lit grove and its youngling green
> From the azure-blazing zenith.

Here the spirit of the originals has vanished.

Unlike de Vere, John Todhunter did not in practice always exemplify his theory. His statement, in regard to his versions of the "Three Sorrows," that "in telling again these old stories, I have freely rehandled my materials—not following precisely any one of the many versions of each legend, but appropriating and adopting whatever best suited my purpose in each," [17] was misleading in its suggestion of radical modification of his sources. In fact he stayed rather close to the original stories in

15. De Vere, *Foray*, pp. 162–168, 194–200.
16. *Ibid.*, pp. 3, 166–167.
17. *Three Irish Bardic Tales* (London: J. M. Dent and Co., 1896), p. v. The three poems in this volume had all been written by 1888.

structure and incident, modifying them mainly by adding copious quantities of often trivial detail.

Katharine Tynan, in her *The Pursuit of Diarmaid and Grainne* (1887), was another writer who used the "good story" approach. Like P. W. Joyce, she omitted the serpent, Fionn's expedition to Scotland, and most of the events following the death of Diarmaid. But she went even further than he had: she dropped also the rather dull opening of the tale, in which Fionn sends emissaries to propose to Gráinne, and began her poem with the more dramatic marriage banquet. Furthermore, in the received tradition, the years in which the lovers lived together in peace are only referred to briefly; Miss Tynan picked up the hint and created a highly sentimental domestic scene:

> And lovely was the wedded life,
> For sixteen years unclouded over
> Of noble husband, tender wife,
> Each still the constant lover;
>
> They loved as in the hour's surprise,
> When, with a sudden flush and quiver,
> Each looked to meet the other's eyes
> And knew they loved for ever.[18]

This sort of treatment certainly was not faithful to the emotional tenor of the legend; nor could it be harmonized with Gráinne's final apostasy, and thus she found that episode as unacceptable as Joyce had.

The story as she presented it was still not sufficiently modified to suit Rolleston, who felt very strongly that "these old Celtic tales do not bear retelling in the form in which they have reached us." [19] He was disturbed by her retention of the incidents in which Diarmaid slew a giant, singlehandedly dispatched two thousand warriors, and leaped unseen over an encircling army:

18. *Shamrocks* (London: Kegan Paul, Trench and Co., 1887), p. 43.
19. "Shamrocks," *The Academy*, July 9, 1887, p. 19.

This turgidity is a blot in the ancient Irish mythic poetry, and it is neither wise nor patriotic to reproduce it. We want the Irish spirit, certainly, in Irish literature; but we want its gold, not its dross; its spirituality, not its superstition; its daring fancy, not its too frequent recourse to mechanical exaggeration.

Joyce had tended to excuse the imperfections he found as not being genuine parts of the legends, though this was only partially true. Rolleston readily admitted the undeniable fact that the early Gael *was* capable of grossness and other faults, and thus he had to advocate a highly selective form of rehandling.

An exponent of the "good story" method who exploited its possibilities much more fully was Robert Dwyer Joyce. An Irishman by birth, he emigrated to America, where he wrote two long poems on heroic subjects, *Deirdre* (1876) and *Blanid* (1879). These works, immensely successful when they first appeared, soon fell into virtual oblivion; but they were read by a number of other Irish writers who were working with similar materials, and Yeats wrote one of his earliest "Irish" articles about them.[20]

The brother of P. W. Joyce, he shared none of the latter's reverence for the original texts; both of his poems contain such extensive elaboration and addition of invented material (sometimes even long episodes) that the sources are often altered almost beyond recognition. For example, in *Deirdre* thirty pages are devoted to a manufactured episode in which Naisi's forces seize a fleet of Fomorian galleys in which to sail to Scotland. *Blanid*, a poem several thousand lines in length, is elaborated from a few pages in Keating: the incidents are greatly expanded, long descriptive passages abound, and there is an attempt at fuller characterization. The alterations were not only extensive but also violated the spirit of the old texts. This is particularly true of *Blanid*, in which the source is transformed into a satiny medieval romance: Cú Chulainn and the other warriors are called "knights," Blanid is the maiden in distress,

20. "The Poetry of Robert Dwyer Joyce," *Irish Fireside*, December 4, 1886, p. 348.

and there are castles, dungeons, and even some Spenserian dragons.

In Samuel Ferguson's first treatment of a heroic subject, an 1834 prose retelling of the Deirdre story, he anticipated Griffin by using an almost literal translation as one of a series of stories set in a frame tale.[21] Generally, however, he disliked too much in the legends to reproduce them virtually intact. His books are full of references to "vulgarity" and "turgid extravagances and exaggerations" in the old stories.[22] *Congal* was originally to have been a translation, until he found his source's "inherent repugnancies too obstinate for reconcilement."[23] He remedied the problem partly by omitting or changing offensive elements, as in the case of the following vivid battle detail:

He . . . made a drag and mighty pull to draw back the spear, but he failed; he made a second effort, and failed; but in the third effort he dragged out his viscera and bowels between his skin and his warlike attire.[24]

In *Congal* this passage became

> And with both hands essayed to drag the weapon from its seat
> But failed: a second time he tugged with painful sick essay,
> And failed: but at the third attempt the javelin came away.[25]

Although a scholar and antiquarian, he felt free also to make numerous and extensive additions. Many of these have an obviously artistic motive: in *Congal*, for instance, he developed the defiant old warrior Kellach, one of the most vivid and

21. *The Hibernian Nights' Entertainments*, published serially in the *Dublin University Magazine*, 1834–1836. The Deirdre story appeared in December, 1834.

22. *Lays of the Western Gael* (London: Bell and Daldy, 1865), pp. 5, 153.

23. *Congal*, p. vii.

24. *The Banquet of Dun Na N-Gedh and the Battle of Magh Rath*, ed. and trans. John O'Donovan (Dublin: Irish Archaeological Society, 1842), p. 287.

25. *Congal*, pp. 125–126.

successful characters in the poem, from a mere sketch in the source, and entirely invented the maiden Lafinda and betrothed her to Congal in order to provide a love interest.

But Ferguson was an earnest Victorian, not an aesthete, and his conception of good literature included edification. Consequently he praised de Vere for giving "the dignity of a high religious philosophy to his subjects" [26] and sought to do the same. Many of his works illustrate a variation upon the "good story" method in which the author chooses from among the old texts subjects conducive to edifying moral or religious interpretation and even fabricates suitable vehicles when he cannot find them to hand. Lady Ferguson thus approvingly quoted T. W. Lyster's observation that in nearly all the poems based on Irish heroic myth her husband had been "attracted by some moral, or religious, or humane idea, either inherent in the myth or read into it in his imaginative scrutiny." [27] One of Ferguson's favorite devices was to conclude poems with one of the characters having a prescient vision of Christianity. *Conary,* "Mesgedra," "The Healing of Conall Carnach," "The Burial of King Cormac," and "The Death of Dermid" all fit this pattern. In *Congal,* Ferguson attributed to the title character (who is definitely pagan throughout the original text) an apparent death-bed religious illumination. His Naisi is given a long invented speech, unlike anything the Naisi of the original texts would say and reminiscent of Ulysses on "degree" in *Troilus and Cressida,* the burden of which is

> Man lives by mutual trust. The commonwealth
> Falls into chaos if man trust not man.
> For then all joint endeavours come to naught,
> And each pursues his separate intent
> Backed by no other labour than his own.[28]

26. *Congal,* p. 208.
27. *Lays of the Red Branch* (London: T. Fisher Unwin, and Dublin: Sealy, Bryers and Walker, 1897), p. xxiv.
28. *Poems* (Dublin and London: W. McGee, 1880), p. 129.

In these and other instances Ferguson, too, clearly deviated from the spirit of his originals.

Like all other fresh sources of subject-matter, the legendary materials had sometimes been appropriated for less elevated purposes, a practice lamented by P. W. Joyce:

Scraps and fragments of some of these tales have been given to the world in popular publications, by writers who, not being able to read the originals, took their information from printed books in the English language. But I am forced to say that many of these specimens have been presented in a very unfavourable and unjust light—distorted to make them look *funny*, and their characters debased to the mere modern conventional stage Irishman.[29]

Surely one of the main reasons for the tremendous impact produced upon reader after reader by Standish O'Grady's work was the greatly idealized image it embodied of the Irish heroic age. In contrast to the debased visions described by Joyce, O'Grady depicted it as a culture of which any nation could be proud:

I cannot help regarding this age and the great personages moving therein as incomparably higher in intrinsic worth than the corresponding ages of Greece. In Homer, Hesiod, and the Attic poets, there is a polish and artistic form, absent in the existing monuments of Irish heroic thought, but the gold, the ore itself, is here massier and more pure, the sentiment deeper and more tender, the audacity and freedom more exhilarating, the reach of imagination more sublime, the depth and power of the human soul more fully exhibit themselves.[30]

He stressed the tradition's nobility and excitement:

Out of the ground start forth the armies of her demigods and champions—an age bright with heroic forms, loud with the trampling of armies and war-steeds, with the roar of chariot-wheels, and the shouting of warriors.[31]

Cú Chulainn's combat with Fer Diad was "the most profoundly

29. *Old Celtic Romances,* pp. vi–vii.
30. *History: Critical and Philosophical,* p. 201.
31. *Ibid.*

tragic scene in all literature," and Cú himself "the noblest character." [32]

AE's description of his own feelings upon first reading O'Grady reveals that it was this heroic grandeur that moved him: he felt like a man "who suddenly feels ancient memories rushing at him, and knows he was born in a royal house, that he had mixed with the mighty of heaven and earth and had the very noblest for his companions." [33] Rolleston's reaction was similar:

The shadowy gods and warriors ceased to be mere names; they took heroic shape and form. They were filled with passions, terrific and superhuman sometimes, but profoundly moving. Anger was there, and vengeance, malice and craft, honour and loyalty, self-sacrifice and devotions, and at times a pathos and tenderness which, in their poignant keenness, matched the gigantic scale on which all the passions of this early legendary age were conceived.

This [the *History*] was the first book I ever read which convinced me that there was such a thing as a spiritual Ireland.[34]

O'Grady consciously fostered this idealized image of the period. As he later admitted, he found in the early texts things that he "simply could not write down and print and publish," such as the "very loose morality" of Queen Medb.[35] An even greater problem was presented by the central figure of the Red Branch cycle of legends, Cú Chulainn himself: at times he appeared extremely noble and heroic, but other features of the story tended to undercut this image. O'Grady could not accept Cú's three-colored hair, the seven pupils in each of his eyes, the seven digits on each of his hands and feet,[36] let alone his grotesque "distortions":

32. *Ibid.*, pp. 207–208.

33. "A Tribute by AE," *Standish O'Grady: the Man and the Writer*, p. 64.

34. C. H. Rolleston, *Portrait of an Irishman*, p. 18.

35. Untitled editorial comment, *All-Ireland Review*, August 9, 1902, p. 357.

36. *Táin Bó Cúalnge*, ed. Cecile O'Rahilly (Dublin: Dublin Institute for Advanced Studies, 1967), p. 204.

Then his first distortion came upon Cú Chulainn so that he became horrible, many-shaped, strange and unrecognisable. His haunches shook about him like a tree in a current or a bulrush against a stream, every limb and every joint, every end and every member of him from head to foot. He performed a wild feat of contortion with his body inside his skin. His feet and his shins and his knees came to the back; his heels and his calves and his hams came to the front. The sinews of his calves came on the front of his shins and each huge, round knot of them was as big as a warrior's fist. The sinews of his head were stretched to the nape of his neck and every huge, immeasurable, vast, incalculable round ball of them was as big as the head of a month-old child.

Then his face became a red hollow (?). He sucked one of his eyes into his head so that a wild crane could hardly have reached it to pluck it out from the back of his skull on to the middle of his cheek. The other eye sprang out on to his cheek. His mouth was twisted back fearsomely. He drew the cheek back from the jawbone until his inner gullet was seen. His lungs and his liver fluttered in his mouth and his throat. . . . The hero's light rose from his forehead so that it was as long and as thick as a hero's whetstone. As high, as thick, as strong, as powerful and as long as the mast of a great ship was the straight stream of dark blood which rose up from the very top of his head and became a dark magical mist like the smoke of a palace when a king comes to be attended to in the evening of a wintry day.[37]

Only MacCarthy faithfully reproduced such descriptions: all the other early writers, and Yeats and Lady Gregory after them, followed O'Grady's example and omitted them. Nor did O'Grady find congenial the idea of Cú Chulainn having an invincible weapon; consequently he made the fearful *ga bulga* into a "rude spear," thrown in the ordinary manner.[38] And if he knew the Stowe version of the *Táin* he must have found elements even harder to reconcile with his own vision of his hero, for in that manuscript there is a passage in which Cú and two

37. *Táin,* ed. O'Rahilly, pp. 201–202.
38. *History of Ireland* (London: Sampson Low, Searle, Marston, and Rivington, and Dublin: E. Ponsonby, 1878–1880), I, 236.

invisible fairy helpers gang up on Fer Diad and attack him from all sides simultaneously.[39] O'Grady's general practice was to make Cú Chulainn seem more heroic by depriving him of all his superhuman features and advantages.

Despite the title of his most famous work, he did not really pretend he was dealing with the past in a scholarly manner. His *History* was almost immediately reprinted, with a few introductory chapters omitted, under the title *Cuculain: An Epic*, and in a new preface he declared, "The style which partly as a substitute for metre I have adopted, and partly in imitation of the bards, would seem rather to relegate [the book] to that species of composition which is termed epic, than to any of the other known kinds of literary workmanship." [40] He was quite concerned with the aesthetic values of the legendary tales and sought to enhance them. In his method, as he himself described it, "actual historical fact" was "seen through an imaginative medium" and the whole of the original account reduced to its "artistic elements." [41] This was essentially the "good story" approach, and he used it fully, adding as well as omitting. He introduced not only descriptive passages and details for creating atmosphere, but also elements of characterization and even, on occasion, whole incidents. The degree of freedom he allowed himself is indicated by the episode in which he depicted Cú Chulainn and Láeg visiting Dublin on Christmas and seeing there in a shop window a shiny toy chariot, which they buy for Cú's small son.[42]

This incident was certainly a gross breach of both the fact and the spirit of the heroic period, but O'Grady's motive in fabricating it was probably "literary." In at least one case, however, he altered his sources in a way comparable to Ferguson's interjection of religious pieties. In the chapter of the

39. *The Ancient Irish Epic Tale Táin Bó Cúalnge,* trans. Joseph Dunn (London: David Nutt, 1914), p. 255.
40. *Cuculain: An Epic* (London: Sampson Low, Searle, Marston, and Rivington, and Dublin: E. Ponsonby, 1882), p. 1.
41. *History of Ireland,* I, iv–v; II, 32.   42. *Ibid.,* II, 290–291.

History entitled "A Pioneer," Láeg, rushing to rejoin his master, seeks lodging for the night at the house of a former slave who has attained his freedom and purchased some land of his own, but the niggardly, base-minded owner refuses to offer any hospitality without recompense.[43] In creating this episode O'Grady set up a contrast with the heroic magnanimity of the great warriors and provided a change of tempo from the scenes of combat, but his main purpose was almost certainly the introduction of a commentary upon the Ireland of his own day. His political preoccupation with the Irish aristocracy is well known.[44] Elsewhere in the *History* there is what seems to be a direct reference to them and to what O'Grady considered their fallings-off: "In the days of Maeve, the great knights and champions of Eire concerned themselves more with knightly deeds and thoughts, and relinquished to the base born excessive zeal concerning wealth and its distribution."[45] "A Pioneer" offered that aristocracy he both loved for their virtues and hated for their weakness a picture of what would come if they did not assert themselves: the land passing into the hands of men with no trace of the old heroic qualities, "a hungry, greedy, and anarchic *canaille*."[46] It was, in other words, a moral parable in which the primitive events had a modern application.

O'Grady himself soon became a source for another myth-user, William C. Upton, whose *Cuchulain: The Story of his*

43. *Ibid.,* I, 243–258.

44. Thus E. A. Boyd, *Standish O'Grady: Selected Essays and Passages* (Dublin: The Talbot Press, and London: T. Fisher Unwin, n.d.), p. 16, says: "Through all his political writings runs one motive, a lament for the downfall of the Irish aristocracy."

45. *History of Ireland,* II, 171.

46. *Selected Essays and Passages,* p. 166. On the following page O'Grady refers to "the isolated, crafty farmer," another phrase pertinent to "A Pioneer." For a full account of O'Grady's mythic writings, his political beliefs, and the relationships between them, see my *Standish O'Grady.*

Combats at the Ford appeared in 1887.[47] The Irish myths had already been recast in a wide variety of forms, from short lyrics to prose epic; Upton added yet another, the "dramatic poem." He accepted the image of Cú Chulainn and the *Táin* as O'Grady presented it, but instead of relating it in a leisurely narrative he tried to compress it into a drama: his work was divided into scenes, observed the unities, had a list of *dramatis personae,* and even stage directions. It was, however, neither a satisfactory rendering of the story nor a performable work. The limitations of time and place and of dramatic probability ruled out direct representation of almost all the more exciting parts of the tale, and Upton had to compensate by using the very awkward and inadequate device of having Cú Chulainn simply *tell* Láeg at great length about his exploits. The form, certain elements in his vocabulary, and the presence of spirits singing short lyrics, all suggest that Upton's model was Shelley's *Prometheus Unbound.* The combination of Shelley and O'Grady was a strange one, but no stranger than that in the Noh-patterned Cú Chulainn plays Yeats would later write.

Upton's use of O'Grady was indicative of the fact that literary renderings of the early legends were beginning to attract attention. During the seventies and eighties there were many other examples of one laborer in the field being aware of his fellows. De Vere and Todhunter, for instance, both referred to O'Grady in their own works; de Vere also praised Ferguson and MacCarthy and was in return recommended by them. P. W. Joyce presented a copy of *Old Celtic Romances* to Katharine Tynan, and Ferguson was even familiar with the work of R. D. Joyce.[48] There was by this time a substantial quantity

47. See Upton, *Cuchulain: The Story of his Combats at the Ford* (Dublin: M. H. Gill and Son, 1887), pp. 90ff, a virtual paraphrase of O'Grady's *History of Ireland,* I, 264ff.
48. See de Vere, *Foray,* pp. xxiv, 231, and the dedication to "The Children of Lir"; Todhunter, dedication to *The Banshee;* Ferguson, *Congal,* p. 208, and *Poems,* p. 97; MacCarthy, *Ferdiah,* p. 53; the in-

of literature in the new mode, and nearly all of what would become the most frequently used legends were available in at least one version.

2. Yeats and the Tradition

It is hardly surprising that Yeats's own attention was soon drawn to the old myths and their modern advocates. He read what scholarly translations he could find, and Ferguson, R. D. Joyce, de Vere, Katharine Tynan, and O'Grady. His earliest published articles were almost all on writers who had used legendary material, and he absorbed what they had to teach him in regard to method. But when, as could be expected, he began to draw upon that material for his own work, he went beyond them and introduced an important new approach.

So rich a body of traditional stories offered the poet abundant potential means for self-expression. They could serve him as allegorical vehicles, sources of symbols, "objective correlatives" for his own feelings and ideas. A story in its received form might prove suitable for such interpretation, might fit perfectly the elements he wished to express; or some modifications of the original myth might be required, either rearrangement of existing features or addition of entirely new elements. The subjectivity of the personal content would be balanced and controlled by the public, traditional nature of the myth. This approach was at least as old as Classical Greek drama: in *The Trojan Women,* for example, Euripides "used heroic legend for the expression of his feelings about the horrors of aggressive war in his own time." [49] It was of course common in English literature: Keats, turning the Endymion story into an allegory concerning the human imagination; Shelley, imprinting the Prometheus legend with his own idiosyncratic world vision; and Tennyson, embodying aspects of his feelings about

---

formation about *Old Celtic Romances* is listed in Catalogue 300 of Carraig Books, Dublin, Ireland, p. 29.

49. *Greek Tragedies,* ed. David Greene and Richard Lattimore (Chicago: University of Chicago Press, 1965), II, 245.

the death of Hallam in the myths of Ulysses, Tithonus, and King Arthur, are only a few of the writers who might be mentioned. But as the preceding survey illustrated, it was not found in Irish literary tradition before Yeats. Ferguson and O'Grady approached it in some of their modifications of the early texts, but neither of them was egoistic enough to actually cultivate it; it was one thing for Ferguson to add a conventional love affair or religious sentiment, but quite another to distort the texts for *personal* ends; and O'Grady, in the preface to his *History*, expressed his *regret* that he could not efface from the work all traces of his own personality.[50]

The first two legendary poems Yeats wrote were "The Madness of King Goll" and *The Wanderings of Oisin*. It is probable that Yeats began *Oisin* before writing "King Goll"; Richard Ellmann says the former was begun in 1886,[51] and on June 25, 1887, Yeats indicated that the first two sections of it had been composed (*Letters*, 41–42), while "King Goll" was first mentioned on July 1, 1887.[52] However, that letter speaks of "King Goll" as ready to be sent out, and it was therefore his earliest complete poem based on Irish myth. In it his new approach to such material seems already to be present.

His source was a passage in O'Curry's *Manuscript Materials* dealing with the Battle of Ventry (*Cath Finntrága*):

50. *History of Ireland*, I, v–vi. Cf. also John V. Kelleher, "Yeats's Use of Irish Materials," *Triquarterly*, No. 4 (Fall, 1965), pp. 122–123.

51. *Yeats: The Man and the Masks*, p. 50. See Katharine Tynan, "The Literary Revival in Ireland," *The Outlook*, June 30, 1894, p. 1190: "I think it was in 1886 that Mr. Alfred Percival Graves . . . suggested to Mr. Yeats and myself that we should join him in writing a volume of poetical tales from the Irish, to be called 'Tales from Tara.'" Yeats did *The Wanderings of Oisin*, Miss Tynan did *The Pursuit of Diarmuid and Grainne;* Graves apparently did not write such a poem.

52. *Letters*, p. 42. Ellmann, *The Identity of Yeats*, p. 287, dates "King Goll" 1884, but this seems doubtful in view of its Irish subject-matter and of Yeats's statement that it was O'Leary, whom he did not meet until 1885, who set him to reading O'Curry (*EI*, p. 511).

Tidings of the invasion were soon carried into Ulster also; and Gall, the son of *Fiacha Foltleathan,* king of that province, a youth of fifteen, obtained leave from his father to come to Finn's assistance, at the head of a fine band of young volunteers from Ulster. Young Gall's ardour, however, cost him rather dear; for having entered the battle with extreme eagerness, his excitement soon increased to absolute frenzy, and after having performed astounding deeds of valour, he fled in a state of derangement from the scene of slaughter, and never stopped until he plunged into the wild seclusion of a deep glen far up the country. This glen has ever since been called *Glenn-na-n-Gealt,* or the Glen of the Lunatics, and it is even to this day believed in the south, that all the lunatics of Erinn would resort to this spot if they were allowed to be at large.[53]

This legend (which may be a confusion of the story of Goll the boy-king of Ulster in *Cath Finntrága* with that of Suibhne Geilt) was not well known, nor did O'Curry present it as particularly interesting or important. A mere summary of a minor event, with no aesthetic form, it must have attracted Yeats for other reasons.

To suggest that he found in this story a vehicle for personal feelings is not to insinuate that he ever had fears of madness. His father did a picture of him as King Goll to accompany the poem, and Yeats's humorous later recollection of the incident gives a clue to the nature of his empathy with the figure:

I write for boys and girls of twenty but I am always thinking of myself at that age—the age I was when my father painted me as King Goll, tearing the strings out [of] a harp, being insane with youth, but looking very desirable—alas no woman noticed it at the time—with dreamy eyes and a great mass of black hair. It hangs in our drawing room now—a pathetic memory of a really dreadful time [*Letters,* 705].

53. *Lectures on the Manuscript Materials of Ancient Irish History,* 2nd ed. (Dublin: Hinch and Traynor, 1878), p. 316. See *VP,* p. 796, where Yeats paraphrases part of this passage; and VP, 1966 ed., p. 857.

In the pathetic boy-king Yeats found an image of his own youthful unhappiness.[54]

In *The Wanderings of Oisin,* Yeats used his approach with much greater complexity. His principal source for the story of Oisin's adventures was an eighteenth-century Irish poem attributed to Michael Comyn, which he found translated in the fourth volume of the *Transactions of the Ossianic Society.*[55] In reshaping this material he made a very significant structural alteration. In Comyn's poem, Oisin visited only two places, a Land of Virtues and a Land of Youth, stopping at the former on the way to the latter. Yeats brought him to three: the Island of the Living (corresponding to Comyn's Land of Youth), the Island of Victories (the equivalent of Comyn's Land of Virtues), and the Island of Forgetfulness. Furthermore, he altered the order and relationship as found in Comyn, making Oisin go to the Island of Victories after he has lost his desire to stay on the Island of the Living, and to the Island of Forgetfulness when he is no longer content on the Island of Victories. In a contemporary letter Yeats himself confessed that his intention in modifying his sources was the creation of an allegory: in 1889 he wrote to Katharine Tynan, "There are three incompatible things man is always seeking— infinite feeling, infinite battle, infinite repose—hence the three islands" (*Letters,* 111). At the end of his life, in "The Circus Animals' Desertion," he still saw the poem this way, as indicated by the reference to "three enchanted islands, allegorical dreams, / Vain gaiety, vain battle, vain repose."

Two other allegorical interpretations have been suggested by Professor Ellmann, who argues that "on a personal level

54. Grossman, *Poetic Knowledge,* pp. 27–29 offers an additional "personal" reading of the poem; he sees it as an allegory concerned with the impact upon the artist of the pursuit of Wisdom.

55. See *Letters,* p. 132; and Russell K. Alspach, "Some Sources of Yeats's *The Wanderings of Oisin," PMLA,* LVIII (September, 1943), 849–866.

[the three islands] represent Yeats's idyllic boyhood at Sligo, his subsequent fights with the English boys in West Kensington because he was Irish, and his daydreaming adolescence on Howth," as well as paralleling "the periods of childhood, of aggressive maturity, and of senility in the lives of all men." [56] Yet another reading of the pattern was offered by Yeats in a retrospective account:

When I was a boy everybody talked about progress, and rebellion against my elders took the form of aversion to that myth. I took satisfaction in certain public disasters, felt a sort of ecstasy at the contemplation of ruin, and then I came upon the story of Oisin in Tir nà nOg and reshaped it into my *Wanderings of Oisin*. He rides across the sea with a spirit, he passes phantoms, a boy following a girl, a hound chasing a hare, emblematical of eternal pursuit, he comes to an island of choral dancing, leaves that after many years, passes the phantoms once again, comes to an island of endless battle for an object never achieved, leaves that after many years, passes the phantoms once again, comes to an island of sleep, leaves that and comes to Ireland, to Saint Patrick and old age. I did not pick these images because of any theory, but because I found them impressive, yet all the while abstractions haunted me [*Explor*, 392].

In another passage written during the same period he put it more tersely: "The choral song, a life lived in common, a futile battle, then thought for its own sake, the last island, Vico's circle and mine, and then the circle joined" (*Explor*, 401). Of course Yeats did not know Vico's theories at the time he wrote the poem, but as Thomas Whitaker has shown, he had already found similar ideas in Theosophy, Balzac, and Blake. From this perspective Oisin's travels represent a cyclical theory of history.[57]

In connection with the introduction of the three-island pat-

56. *The Identity of Yeats*, p. 18. See also *Yeats: The Man and the Masks*, pp. 51–53.

57. *Swan and Shadow: Yeats's Dialogue with History* (Chapel Hill: University of North Carolina Press, 1964), pp. 22–26.

tern, Yeats greatly expanded the nostalgia felt by Oisin for his Fenian companions in Comyn's poem: in *The Wanderings*, Oisin's departure from each of the immortal realms is precipitated by contact with some item that calls to mind his former life. In making this modification Yeats made central to the poem a theme that runs throughout all his work: the "choice" dichotomy, a tension between the claims of this world and the one beyond. Oisin, like Yeats himself, was continually drawn back to the former.

This theme was reinforced in the poem by the conflict between Oisin and Saint Patrick. In Comyn's poem this conflict was very muted: Patrick is mainly interested in hearing the tale, and when their differences of opinion at one point threaten to get out of control, he says, "Let us leave off our controversy on each side / And continue thy story, O valiant Oisin!" [58] Yeats strengthened the tension by drawing upon other dialogues between them in the same volume of the *Ossianic Society* series, in which the opposition is virulent and unremitting. In this form the two figures represented perfectly the attractions of the antithetical realms. Yeats was eventually to make the parallel overt, and in the process to relate it to one of his most famous "choice" poems, "Vacillation," and to the development of his entire literary corpus: "The swordsman throughout repudiates the saint, but not without vacillation. Is that perhaps the sole theme—Usheen and Patrick—'so get you gone Von Hügel though with blessings on your head'?" [59] Read from this point of view, *The Wanderings of Oisin* can be seen as a personal *psychomachia*.

The Oisin-Patrick controversy also helped develop the theme of historical cycles. As Whitaker points out, Yeats was already familiar with theories of the alternation of "pagan" and "religious" eras, and his poem focuses upon a man caught in the transition. Patrick seemed victorious, but in one popu-

58. "The Land of Youth," *Transactions of the Ossianic Society*, IV (1859), 277.
59. *Letters*, p. 798.

lar Fenian legend the heroes were said to be still alive and only awaiting the proper time to return; Yeats, seeing himself at the end of the Christian period, would suggest a similar hope in his last poem, "The Black Tower."

In 1888, while preparing a corrected fair copy of *The Wanderings*, Yeats made an important comment on his technique in the poem:

In the second part of "Oisin" under the disguise of symbolism I have said several things to which I only have the key. The romance is for my readers. They must not even know there is a symbol anywhere. They will not find out. If they did it would spoil the art. Yet the whole poem is full of symbols—if it be full of aught but clouds [*Letters*, 88].

There is something here of the mystery and secretiveness with which the French *Symbolistes* approached their art, and also perhaps an element of personal reticence; but Yeats did want at least some of his many meanings discerned, for when the early reviews of the poem proved uncomprehending, he wrote to Katharine Tynan, " 'Oisin' needs an interpreter" and then—possibly hoping that she herself would review it—dropped the hint about the "three incompatible things" (*Letters*, 111).

In addition to the larger "structural" symbolism already discussed, the poem is full of specific symbols. In several instances vehicles already present in the sources were merely endowed with the desired significances. This was particularly true in the case of the dear-hound-lady-youth procession. It appears only once in Comyn, and its meaning is never explained. Yeats brought it in three times, always in relation to the love of Oisin and Niamh and always during the crucial periods in which the lure of the mortal world is being evaded by flight to one of the islands: thus he set up a pattern emblematical of eternal desire and pursuit.[60] The lines written long after in "The Circus Animals' Desertion" about Yeats's having been "starved for the bosom of [Oisin's] faery bride"

60. See *VP*, pp. 806–807.

suggest also a personal level to Niamh, though this may be only an anachronistic reference to Maud Gonne, whom he had not even met by the time he finished the poem. And the burden of old age that descends upon Oisin may have reflected Yeats's feelings about having lost the gift of spontaneous composition [61] or a facet of the sense of *fin de siècle* and premature decrepitude that pervades his early volumes.

In other cases Yeats modified his sources more radically or even introduced new elements with symbolic value. For example, in Comyn's poem Oisin fights a battle with a Fomorian giant. Yeats turned the giant into a demon of vague origins and unspecified nationality and thus paved the way for widely varying interpretations of him as representing England (with the maiden he holds captive corresponding to Ireland), Yeats's own father, and "orgasm incarnate." [62] Furthermore, whereas in the earlier poem Oisin dispatched his opponent permanently after a fight of only three days and nights, Yeats supported some of his main themes by making the combat recur every few days for a hundred years and "end" only when Oisin departs. In greatly elaborating upon Comyn's description of the palace in which the fight took place, Yeats added the detail of two statues, one associated with the heavens and the other with the seas, which have been identified as "spiritual and physical man." [63] He also brought into the poem two of his favorite symbols, the dance and the rose. Dancing constitutes the main activity of the immortal inhabitants of his first island; and in the course of their dancing he had them come to a grove of "damask roses" which, because they never decay, represent the eternality of life there. The poem also contained many other, less precise hints of hidden meaning, such as the reference in one of The Immortals' songs to "Asian trees" (*VP*, 27).

61. Suggested by Ellmann, *Yeats: The Man and the Masks*, p. 53.

62. See Ellmann, *The Identity of Yeats*, pp. 18–19; and John Unterecker, *A Reader's Guide to William Butler Yeats* (New York: Noonday Press, 1959), p. 49.

63. Ellmann, *Yeats: The Man and the Masks*, p. 53.

It should be clear by now that Yeats's response to the myth materials was far more involved than those of writers who were concerned merely with improving them aesthetically or morally: it was an act of personal interpretation and personal expression. Yeats's one contemporary account of the process of composition of *The Wanderings* is illuminating in this respect:

I have corrected the first two parts of "Oisin." The second part is much more coherent than I had hoped. . . . It is the most inspired but the least artistic of the three. The last has most art. Because I was in complete solitude—no one near me but old and reticent people—when I wrote it. It was the greatest effort of all my things. When I had finished it I brought it round to read to my Uncle George Pollexfen and could hardly read, so collapsed I was. My voice quite broken. It really was a kind of vision. It beset me day and night. Not that I ever wrote more than a few lines in a day. But those few lines took me hours. All the rest of the time I walked about the roads thinking of it. I wait impatiently the proofs of it. With the other parts I am disappointed— they seem only shadows of what I saw. But the third must have got itself expressed—it kept me from my sleep too long. Yet the second part is more deep and poetic. . . . The first parts I felt. I saw the second [the third?]. Yet there too, perhaps, only shadows have got themselves on to paper [*Letters*, 87].

The shadowiness is certainly present, but Yeats's vision did get expressed; the content seems almost over-rich. He was so deeply engaged with the problem that both the approach of *The Wanderings* and some of its key themes also pervaded the story "Dhoya," which he was writing at about the same time. Yeats himself created the character of Dhoya, the giant abandoned in Sligo by the Fomorians who had held him captive, but the basic situation of the story, the man who marries a fairy bride and then loses her to her fairy husband in a chess game, was borrowed from the Irish legend of King Eochaid, Edain, and Midhir.[64] Yeats used it to express the tension be-

64. See Phillip L. Marcus, "Possible Sources of Yeats's 'Dhoya,' " *NQ*, XIV (October, 1967), 383–384.

tween the immutable realm and the world of change: the woman of the *sidhe* cries,

"Dhoya, I have left my world far off. My people—on the floor of the lake they are dancing and singing, and on the islands of the lake; always happy, always young, always without change. I have left them for thee, Dhoya, for they cannot love. . . . I left the places where they dance for thee!" [65]

Here was a variant of Niamh's love for Oisin, the chief difference being that in "Dhoya" the lovers do not try to escape the mortal world—and consequently their relationship becomes the victim of the inevitable change. [66] Yeats set the story long before Fenian times, but twice in the story drew parallels with Diarmaid and Gráinne.

At the time he wrote these early works Yeats was deeply caught up in philosophical speculations and occult studies and naturally tended to see the early legends in their light. But even before *The Wanderings of Oisin* was actually published, Yeats had found scholarly "support" for his interpretations. In a letter of October 8, 1888, he spoke of a desire to review John Rhys's "book on ancient Celtic religion," *Lectures on the Origin and Growth of Religion as Illustrated by Celtic Heathendom (Letters, 92)*. His interest in this book is easy to explain: Rhys treated all the heroic stories as religious myths, Cú Chulainn, Fionn and the rest as euhemerized deities; and he constantly drew parallels between his Irish examples and Welsh, Continental, Classical, and Eastern legends. At this time or shortly afterwards Yeats was also impressed by the French scholar Henri D'Arbois de Jubainville's *Le Cycle Mythologique Irlandais*, which had been published in 1884. This book was not translated until 1903, and the apparent feebleness of Yeats's French may have made reading it difficult: possibly Hyde, O'Leary, or Maud Gonne (who knew de Jubainville personally) helped him or outlined its main con-

65. *John Sherman and Dhoya*, p. 183.
66. Cf. also the 1892 story "The Devil's Book," in which Owen Roe O'Sullivan is loved by a women of the *sidhe* and rejects her.

cerns. It interpreted the early texts in a manner similar to that of Rhys, but with much more emphasis upon the Tuatha Dé Danann and the other pre-Milesian groups, and discussed Celtic conceptions of reincarnation and the other world.

By 1890, Yeats had absorbed these lessons and was preaching them to others. In a review of Mrs. Sophie Bryant's *Celtic Ireland* he criticized her for treating the early legendary races as historical:

Rhys, Joubainville, and others have made it certain that they were merely bardic myths. Their present was not their ancient shape. The monks amused themselves by humanizing these old gods, turning them into pious early colonisers, and tracing their descent to Noah. It has been found possible, however, to pick out something of their old significance, and discern in them the gods of light warring on the spirits of darkness—on the Fomorians who had but one leg under them and one arm in the middle of their breasts, and lived under the sea: creatures who turned under the monkish touch into common two-armed and two-legged pirates. Some few of the divine races, indeed—the Tuath dé Danann chiefly—preserved a parcel of their ancient dignity, and, becoming the fairies, dwell happily near their deserted altars.[67]

During the same year he brought these points to bear upon the development of the study of folklore:

To the old folk-lorists, fables and fairy tales were a haystack of dead follies, wherein the virtuous might find one little needle of historical truth. Since then Joubainville and Rhys and many more have made us see in all these things old beautiful mythologies wherein ancient man said symbolically all he knew about God and man's soul, once famous religions fallen into ruin and turned into old wives' tales, but still luminous from the rosy dawn of human reverie [*LNI*, 101].

During the following decade Yeats found further support in Alfred Nutt's long study of Irish tales dealing with the other world. Yeats reviewed this study, which was written to accom-

67. "Bardic Ireland," *Scots Observer*, January 4, 1890, p. 183.

pany Kuno Meyer's edition of *The Voyage of Bran,* and asserted, "D'Arbois De Jouvainville's 'Mythologie Irlandaise [*sic*],' Professor Rhys' 'Celtic Heathendom,' and it are the three books without which there is no understanding of Celtic legends." [68] By the end of the century this triumvirate seemed so important to him that he saw it as virtually the main force behind the literary renaissance:

Most of us who are writing in Ireland now are dreaming of a literature at once romantic and religious, and . . . we search for the religious life of other times among old Irish monuments and legends. The work of Mr. Nutt and Professor Rhys and M. De Joubainville has made known something of the religious life in the Pagan legends, and the greater part of contemporary Irish and Highland literature has come of the discovery.[69]

This was certainly too great a claim for such studies, but they had indeed been important in the development of his work from the time he read them, increasing his confidence in the approach he had already taken in using the old legends and providing him with further interpretations along the same lines.

In the nineties Yeats continued to use the myth materials as vehicles for expressing himself and his world vision. His two "Fergus" poems provide an interesting example. Fergus Mac Róich, as Yeats knew from O'Grady's *History* and other sources, was a warrior of tremendous prowess who was tricked into giving up his throne. Yeats disregarded this image in favor of the dreamy and most unwarlike monarch of Ferguson's "The Abdication of Fergus Mac Roy." In this form he was a suitable vehicle for expressing Yeats's "flight into fairyland" motif ("Who Goes With Fergus") and the pursuit of occult knowledge in which he himself was engaged ("Fergus and the Druid"). The "dreaming wisdom" Fergus obtained

68. "Celtic Beliefs about the Soul," *The Bookman,* September, 1898, p. 159.

69. "High Crosses of Ireland," *Daily Express* (Dublin), January 28, 1899, p. 3.

included the doctrine of reincarnation, which Yeats knew to be found in a poem attributed to the Welsh bard Taliesin and paralleled by de Jubainville with the "pantheistic" "Song of Amergin": [70]

> I have been many things:
> A green drop in the surge, a gleam of light
> Upon a sword, a fir tree on a hill,
> An old slave grinding at a heavy quern,
> A king sitting upon a chair of gold.

In the same passage Yeats also drew upon Rhys's and de Jubainville's interpretations of the battle between the Tuatha Dé Danann and the Fomorians at Magh Tuireadh as a mythic version of the opposition of light and darkness, heat and cold, good and evil:

> . . . in my heart the daemons and the gods
> Wage an eternal battle, and I feel
> The pain of wounds, the labour of the spear,
> But have no share in loss or victory.[71]

The unfortunate end of Fergus's quest showed Yeats's awareness of the potential limitations of such a life. A related perspective appears in the story "The Wisdom of the King." In writing it he made use of the legend of Fergus Mac Leide, a king with a facial deformity the presence of which his retainers tried, and ultimately failed, to keep secret from him. Yeats would have known Ferguson's version of the story, "Fergus Wry-Mouth," but his immediate source was probably Katharine Tynan's "The Fate of King Feargus," for his plot is much closer to hers. While Ferguson had depicted him as a bluff warrior, she makes the king a sensitive, poetic man, thus opening the way for Yeats to blend him with his other Fergus. His character's philosophy had a familiarly Yeatsian ring: in

70. *Le Cycle Mythologique Irlandais* (Paris: Ernest Thorin, 1884), pp. 243–246.

71. *VP*, p. 104. These lines were eliminated in revised versions of the poem.

order to woo his beloved, "he poured his wisdom at her feet, and told her how the heroes, when they die, return to the world and begin their labour anew; . . . and of the great Moods, which are alone immortal, and the creators of mortal things." [72] But he loses her to a virile boxer and horse-trainer (who is not in either Ferguson's version or Miss Tynan's), probably reflecting Yeats's realization that he must be a man of action to win Maud Gonne.[73]

The Countess Cathleen was an attempt to do with Christian Irish legend what he had already done with pagan sources: "to mingle personal thought and feeling with the beliefs and customs of Christian Ireland." [74] (Yeats had included the story of Countess Kathleen O'Shea in *Fairy and Folk Tales,* believing it to be a traditional Irish tale.) But in the play, as in the narrative poem, Yeats brought one era to bear upon the other. In the first version he included, along with the "Who Goes with Fergus" lyric, references to the ride of Oisin and Niamh and to Edain (*VPlays*, 44, 62). In revising the text for *Poems* (1895), he drew upon the *Magh Tuireadh* legend as a parallel to the struggle of Christian angels and devils for the soul of Cathleen:

> Angels and devils clash in the middle air,
> And brazen swords clang upon brazen helms.
> [*A flash of lightning followed immediately by thunder.*]
> Yonder a bright spear, cast out of a sling,
> Has torn through Balor's eye, and the dark clans
> Fly screaming as they fled Moytura of old.[75]

The "spear" was hurled by Lugh, the sun god, whose killing of Balor precipitated the rout of the Fomorians.

72. "Wisdom," *New Review,* September, 1895, p. 288. In *The Secret Rose* this story was retitled "The Wisdom of the King."

73. Ellmann, *Yeats: The Man and the Masks,* p. 80.

74. *VP,* p. 845; see also "The Circus Animals' Desertion," and Peter Ure, *Yeats the Playwright* (New York: Barnes and Noble, 1963), pp. 17–20.

75. *VPlays,* p. 165; see also p. 155, and Yeats's note on "Balor," p. 1285.

The Shadowy Waters, which Yeats apparently conceived even before his dedication to national concerns, and upon which he continued to work after the emergence of the theater movement, contained at various stages a considerable quantity of mythological material. The work itself was not a retelling of any traditional Irish story, though Forgael's voyage with a woman towards an unchanging realm can be seen as simply another version of the personal concern expressed in *The Wanderings* by the ride of Oisin and Niamh. Because his central plot, being self-fabricated, was highly subjective, Yeats sought to surround and ballast it with as much traditional legend as possible. During the early nineties his main source was again the stories of the Tuatha Dé Danann and Fomorians and their conflict. At the beginning of the work Forgael is in league with the forces of evil, and the index of the psychological change he undergoes is his eventual resolution to love "none but the children of Danu." [76] Yeats also worked in a reference to the youth and lady of *The Wanderings* (another indication of the connection between Forgael and Oisin) and an allusion to the birds of Óengus. [77]

There was one disadvantage to this method, as Yeats revealed in an 1894 letter: "In my struggle to keep it concrete I fear I shall so overload it with legendary detail that it will be unfit for any theatrical purposes" (*Letters,* 236). However, he still believed in the truth of the principle, for he recommended it two years later in an article on "Fiona Macleod": "Emotions which seem vague or extravagant when expressed under the influence of modern literature, cease to be vague or extravagant when associated with ancient legend and mythology." [78] And when at the end of the century he took up the

76. David R. Clark, "W. B. Yeats: *The Shadowy Waters* (Ms. Version)," in *Irish Renaissance,* ed. Robin Skelton and David R. Clark (Dublin: The Dolmen Press, 1965), p. 55. I am indebted to Mr. Clark's excellent article throughout my discussion of *The Shadowy Waters.*

77. Clark, "Ms. Version," pp. 39, 41.

78. "Miss Fiona Macleod as a Poet," *The Bookman,* December, 1896, p. 92.

[254]

Shadowy Waters manuscript again he indicated—in phrasing that perfectly epitomizes the highly personal nature of his approach to the old stories—that such materials still played a key part in his plans:

I am working at my *Shadowy Waters* and it is getting on far better than when I left it aside a couple of years ago. Since then I have worked at Irish mythology and filled a great many pages of notes with a certain arrangement of it for my own purposes; and now I find I have a rich background for whatever I want to do and endless symbols to my hands.[79]

Yeats was, with considerable reluctance, persuaded to eliminate the Fomorians,[80] but he compensated for the loss by expanding the role of Óengus. He now brought in the story of Óengus' relations with Edain before she become the wife of King Eochaid, interpreting it "in my own way" (*VP*, 188). On the basis of dreams and visions experienced by himself and AE, he endowed Forgael with a harp supposedly sent by Óengus and having strings woven by Edain from Óengus' hair. The procession from *The Wanderings of Oisin* also reappeared; Yeats made it a more integral part of the new version by having the hound and deer function as signs to Forgael and Dectora, as they had before to Oisin and Niamh:

> The pale hound and the deer wander for ever
> Among the winds and waters; and when they pass
> The mountain of the gods, the unappeasable gods
> Cover their faces with their hair and weep.
> They lure us to the streams where the world ends
> $$[VP, 764].$$

Further proof of Yeats's later remark that "for a long time symbols of this kind had for me a very intense, a very personal importance" (*VPlays*, 1283) was the contemporary lyric "The Desire of Man and of Woman," in which the deer and hound

79. *Letters,* p. 322 (June 21, 1899).
80. See *Letters,* p. 327; and Clark, "Ms. Version," pp. 30–31.

were depicted as being in reality human lovers whose shapes had been transformed by Óengus.[81]

After the turn of the century, Yeats occasionally directly revealed the personal element in works based on Irish myth. Thus, in *Baile and Ailinn* the parallel between the title characters and Yeats and Maud Gonne, implicit in such lines as "Being forbid to marry on earth / They blossomed to immortal mirth," is made explicit at the end of the poem:

> Let rush and bird cry out their fill
> Of the harper's daughter if they will,
> Beloved, I am not afraid of her,
> She is not wiser nor lovelier,
> And you are more high of heart than she
> For all her wanderings over-sea;
> But I would have bird and rush forget
> Those other two, for never yet
> Has lover lived, but longed to wive
> Like them that are no more alive.

Similarly in *The Old Age of Queen Maeve* he interrupted his description of the legendary character with the question

> O, unquiet heart,
> Why do you praise another, praising her,
> As if there were no tale but your own tale
> Worth knitting to a measure of sweet sound?

But during the inaugural period of the Renaissance, and generally even thereafter, he avoided such definite internal evidence. Consequently, awareness of his particular concerns in the rehandling of a given legend depends upon a combination of knowledge of the received form of the legend (so that variations will be apparent and their significance pondered) and of Yeats's personal vision and sometimes even his personal affairs. Nor can one always be sure even then. The early poem "The Death of Cuchulain" (later retitled "Cuchulain's Fight with

81. For additional "personal" associations for these symbols, see Grossman, *Poetic Knowledge*, pp. 175–179.

the Sea") is a case in point. In a contemporary note, Yeats himself pointed out his source as Jeremiah Curtin's *Myths and Folk-lore of Ireland*, adding, "The bardic tale of the death of Cuchullin is very different." [82] As Curtin gives it, the folk tale is far less noble and heroic than O'Grady's rendering of the "bardic" version in the *History*. Yeats's choice of the former suggests that it fit a need which the "better" story did not, and Richard Ellmann has suggested that he found in it a vehicle for expressing his own often antagonistic relations with his father.[83] There is, however, nothing specific in Yeats's handling of the story to support this reading: he makes the young man Cú Chulainn's son by Emer rather than by Aoife (Curtin has simply "a son whose mother was called the Virago of Alba") and changes his name from "Conlán" to "Finmole," but neither of these changes point to a personal motivation. Yeats also added a scene in which Emer is told by a swineherd named Aleel of Cú's arrival with another woman. "Aleel" was obviously a name of personal importance to him at this period, for he used it in the first revised version of *The Countess Cathleen* as the name of the bard, and in one early draft of *The Shadowy Waters*, again for a poet, Dectora's lover when she is captured by Forgael. However, while the poet in *The Countess Cathleen* can easily be seen as representing Yeats, and while the same is true of the corresponding figure in *The Shadowy Waters* (Forgael's having him put to death reflecting the rejection of the more purely subjective, dreamy aspect of Yeats's personality by a more powerful, active side), any attempt to identify Aleel with Yeats in "The Death of Cuchulain" produces only confusion. The best arguments in support of a personal reading of the poem are therefore the choice of the subject, Yeats's contemporary practice in other myth-based works, and his repeated later use of various portions of the Cú Chulainn legend. Beginning with *On Baile's Strand* he drew upon it repeatedly

82. *VP,* p. 799; see Curtin, *Myths and Folk-lore of Ireland* (Boston: Little, Brown and Co., 1890), pp. 324–326.
83. *Yeats: The Man and the Masks,* p. 22.

to express himself and his world-view (*The Only Jealousy of Emer* and "Cuchulain Comforted," for example, both being full of *Vision*-type doctrine) and at the end of his life reverted to the "bardic" version of the death of Cú, which now fit his own situation better than the folk tale.

Throughout the early years of the movement Yeats propagandized for study and literary recreation of the legends, and even in the first article he published praised their potential for "healing our nation" and helping Irishmen "to live the larger life of the spirit." [84] It was not until 1892, however, that he made any public reference to the approach towards such materials that he personally favored, and even then he did so briefly and obliquely: "If we can but take that history and those legends and turn them into dramas, poems and stories full of the living soul of the present, and make them massive with conviction and profound with reverie, we may deliver that new great utterance for which the world is waiting." [85]

He became more explicit as the years passed. In 1895, having predicted the replacement of the current "age of criticism" with an "age of revelation," he went on to suggest, "This revolution may be the opportunity for the Irish Celt, for he has an unexhausted and inexhaustible mythology to give him symbols and personages." [86] Two years later, in an article on "Fiona Macleod," he referred to contemporary Irish writers taking "a peasant legend" and making it "the symbol of some personal phantasy." [87] The influential essay "The Celtic Movement in Literature," which dates from the same period, placed the approach in an international perspective:

A new fountain of legends, . . . a more abundant fountain than any in Europe, is being opened, the fountain of Gaelic legends.

84. "The Poetry of Sir Samuel Ferguson," *Irish Fireside,* October 9, 1886, p. 220.

85. "Hopes and Fears for Irish Literature," *United Ireland,* October 15, 1892, p. 5.

86. "Irish National Literature. III.—Contemporary Irish Poets," *The Bookman,* September, 1895, p. 168.

87. "Miss Fiona Macleod," *The Sketch,* April 28, 1897, p. 20.

. . . "The Celtic Movement," as I understand it, is principally the opening of this fountain. . . . It comes at a time when the imagination of the world is as ready as it was at the coming of the tales of Arthur and of the Grail for a new intoxication. The reaction against the rationalism of the eighteenth century has mingled with a reaction against the materialism of the nineteenth century, and the symbolical movement, which has come to perfection in Germany in Wagner, in England in the Pre-Raphaelites, in France in Villiers de l'Isle-Adam, and Mallarmé, and in Belgium in Maeterlinck, and has stirred the imagination of Ibsen and D'Annunzio, is certainly the only movement that is saying new things. The arts by brooding upon their own intensity have become religious, and are seeking, as I think Verhaeren has said, to create a sacred book. They must, as religious thought has always done, utter themselves through legends. . . . [The] Irish legends . . . have so much of a new beauty that they may well give the opening century its most memorable symbols [*EI,* 186–187].

And in one of the introductions he wrote for *A Treasury of Irish Poetry* he referred to the Irish poets seeking "to express indirectly, through myths and symbols, or directly in little lyrics full of prayers and lamentations, the desire of the soul for spiritual beauty and happiness." [88]

Even these passages do not refer to specific instances in Yeats's own work; it was only in private letters that he became so personal. As a result, the readers most likely to have been aware of his approach towards the myth materials were those who knew him well or had a substantial knowledge of the traditional forms of the legends so that they could distinguish the idiosyncrasies in his treatment of them. When these circumstances are understood, it will not seem surprising that Yeats's example did not at once attract numerous emulators. Legendary works employing the "good story" approach continued to appear. [89] Even the debased, stage Irish treatment calumniated years before by P. W. Joyce remained alive: in 1893, *United Ireland* printed (next to an article by Yeats) a

88. *A Treasury of Irish Poetry,* p. 475.
89. See, for example, T. D. Sullivan, *Blanid and Other Irish Historical and Legendary Poems* (Dublin, 1891).

story by P. J. M'Call entitled "Cuchullin and Emir," which reduced O'Grady's "noblest character" in all literature to a ludicrous clown:

Long, long ago, there lived a great prence in Ulsther, be the name of Cucullin. Be all accounts he was a great lepper in his day, an' signs on it, it stood him upon . . . of'en and of'en, when he'd be circumvented by some vagabone or other, to be able to show his inimies a clane pair of heels, be the fair dent of soopleness.

Well, it so happened, that a purty little prencess, be the name of Emir, tuk his taste, an', as she didn't mislike him, up he goes to her father, Conor, the king ov Ulsther, . . . to see about bringin' matters to a close. Egonneys, who does he see there but another lad come on the same tack, an' . . . this same fella was dhressed out in all the colours ov the rainbow, an' his hair all perfumery an' marra', an' his mustache curlin' around his lugs like a hairy leech around a stone in a river. An', what was worse than all, he'd afther got at the soft side of King Conor an' was makin' his own ov him, deludherin' him with larnin' an' tall talk—makin' a fine hand of him altogether.

"Is that yourself, Cucullin?" sez King Conor, wavin' his hand at him stoopin', comin' in at the doore.

"Ay, is it," sez Cucullin, stoppin' short, half way in an' half way out, like he was to houldin' a horse.[90]

A few writers, however, did begin to treat the early literature in the Yeatsian manner.

One such writer was Larminie. His first volume, *Glanlua and Other Poems*, appeared in the same year as *The Wanderings of Oisin*. It contained, in addition to "The Return of the Gods," a short poem on Óengus and Edain, and the long title-poem itself. There is nothing about the lyric to suggest a personal reading, and *Glanlua* seems a most unlikely vehicle. The plot tells the story of one Dohnal, a Firbolg monarch whose mother Morna, one of the Tuatha Dé Danann, has given him

90. *United Ireland*, December 23, 1892.

invincibility in battle. He is married to Glanlua, whom he loves but who despises him; they are said to be the parents of Cú Chulainn's future friend and adversary Fer Diad. Fergus Mac Róich and a war-party come and attack Dohnal, but all are slain except Fergus, who is taken prisoner. Glanlua develops a passion for him and, obtaining from Dohnal's mother the secret of his strength, reveals it to Fergus. He kills Dohnal and flees with Glanlua, but Morna arouses the elements and the birds against them, and finally forces Fergus to cast Glanlua into the sea, from which she rises incarnate as a crane. On Fergus, Morna places the curse that he shall lose his throne and be unhappy through love. The poem is laced with ghosts, skulls, and other bizarre manifestations of the supernatural and seems to represent an example of the "good story" approach used to create a gothic romance. A personal interpretation here would be almost out of the question.

Moytura, in Larminie's *Fand* volume of 1892, does reveal a treatment comparable to Yeats's approach. He not only equated the Tuatha Dé Danann with good and the Fomorians with evil, but also placed their conflict within a larger scheme of cosmic origins. His account begins with the creation of the world by the Tribes of Danu, brings in the evolution of lower forms of life, including dinosaurs, and culminates with the good gods, having routed evil, willingly turning over the earth to men and endowing them with various gifts. Larminie had read de Jubainville's *Cycle Mythologique,* for he quoted from it in his first book, and consequently could have derived the religious interpretation of the myth independently of Yeats, who had referred to it in articles but not yet used it in his own work. On the other hand, Larminie did know the old legends well, and if he had read *The Wanderings of Oisin* he may have sensed something of what Yeats was doing.

AE was a second writer in this category. In March, 1895, he published an article on "The Legends of Ancient Eire," and in September of the same year Yeats noted, "A.E. has begun to dig for new symbols in the stories of Finn and Oisin, and in the song of Amergin." [91] AE himself formally stated his position a few years later, during the Eglinton controversy:

These dreams, antiquities, traditions, once actual, living, and historical, have passed from the world of sense into the world of memory and thought; and time . . . has not taken away from their power nor made them remote from sympathy, but has rather purified them by removing them from earth unto heaven: from things which the eye can see and the ear can hear; they have become what the heart ponders over, and are so much nearer, more familiar, more suitable for literary use, than the day they were begotten. They have now the character of symbol, and, as symbol, are more potent than history. They have crept through veil after veil of the manifold nature of man, and now each dream, heroism, or beauty, has laid itself nigh the divine power it represents the suggestion of which made it first beloved; and they are ready for the use of the spirit, a speech of which every word has a significance beyond itself.[92]

The world-vision that AE was to employ those symbols to express was epitomized in his first article on the legendary materials:

Life is one; . . . nature is not dead but living; the surface but a veil tremulous with light—lifting that veil hero and sage of old time went outwards into the vast and looked on the original. All that they beheld they once were, and it was again their heritage, for in essence they were one with it—children of Deity. The One gave birth to the many, imagining within itself the heaven of heavens, and the heavens, and spheres more shadowy and dim, growing distant from the light. Through these the Rays ran outward, falling down through many a starry dynasty to dwell in clay. Yet—once God or Angel—that past remains, and the Ray, returning on itself, may reassume its old vesture, entering as a God into the Ancestral Self.[93]

91. "Irish National Literature. III.—Contemporary Irish Poets," *The Bookman,* September, 1895, p. 169.
92. *Literary Ideals in Ireland,* pp. 50–51.
93. "The Legends of Ancient Eire," *Irish Theosophist,* March 15, 1895, pp. 101–103.

In that article he showed how this vision could be discerned in the legend of Oisin in Tir-na-nOg, and his interpretation makes an interesting contrast with Yeats's poem:

We . . . are met on the threshold of diviner spheres by terrible forms embodying the sins of a living past when we misused our spiritual powers in old Atlantean days. These forms must be conquered and so Oisin battles with the Fomor and releases the power—a princess in the story. This fight with the demon must be fought by everyone who would enter the land of the Gods. . . . Tir-na-noge, the land of Niam, is that region the soul lives in when its grosser energies and desires have been subdued, dominated, and brought under the control of light; when the Ray of Beauty kindles and illuminates every form which the imagination conceives, and where every form tends to its archetype.

In the second installment he used in a similar manner Fionn, Diarmaid and Gráinne, and Cú Chulainn.[94]

Soon, however, he began drawing most of his symbols not from the Ulster and Fenian cycles, but rather from the "mythological" cycle, that of the old Irish deities. This was quite natural: his vision, though unorthodox, was essentially religious, and a key element in it was his belief that man is incarnate divinity. The early Celtic mythology offered a ready-made pantheon, including some figures potentially equatable with the One and many gods in human form. Furthermore, AE seems to have had at about this time an actual visionary experience in which his world-view was represented by various members of the Tuatha Dé Danann.[95] His efforts to embody that experience in a long poem lasted far into the next century and finally culminated successfully in *The House of the Titans,* of which AE wrote to a friend that it "does not follow legend. It is a symbolic treatment of the tale." [96] Among the earlier poems using figures from the mythological cycle was

94. *Irish Theosophist,* April 15, 1895, pp. 119–122.
95. See *Letters from AE,* pp. 17–18, 20, 34–35.
96. Letter to Osborn Bergin, tentatively dated October 19, 1934 (Alan Denson manuscript).

"Twilight by the Cabin." This lyric began with a description of a peasant girl staring into the twilight from her cabin door. AE then equated her with Edain while the latter was in human form:

> This is Edain's land and line,
> And the homespun cannot hide
> Kinship with a race divine,
> Thrill of rapture, light of pride.
>
> There her golden kinsmen are:
> And her heart a moment knew
> Angus like the evening star
> Fleeting through the dusk and dew.
>
> Throw the woman's mask away:
> Wear the opal glimmering dress;
> Let the feathered starlight ray
> Over every gleaming tress.[97]

He also used Óengus in an 1897 story, "A Dream of Angus Oge," the god summoning a boy to come away with him to the realm of the immortals.

Perhaps the most imaginative and successful of all AE's interpretations of Irish myth is "The Children of Lir," a short lyric probably written at about the turn of the century:

> We woke from our sleep in the bosom where cradled together we lay:
> The love of the Dark Hidden Father went with us upon our way.
> And gay was the breath in our being, and never a sorrow or fear
> Was on us, as singing together, we flew from the infinite Lir.
>
> Through nights linked with diamond and sapphire, we raced with the Children of Dawn,
> A chain that was silver and golden linked spirit to spirit, my swan.
> Till day in the heavens passed over, and still grew the beat of our wings,
> And the Breath of the Darkness enfolded to teach us unspeakable things.

97. *The Divine Vision and Other Poems*, pp. 50–51.

Yet lower we fell and for comfort our pinionless spirits had now
The leaning of bosom to bosom, the lifting of lip unto brow.
Though chained to the earth yet we mourned not the loss of our
heaven above,
But passed from the vision of Beauty to the fathomless being of
Love.

Still gay is the breath of our being, we wait for the Bell Branch
to ring
To call us away to the Father, and then we will rise on the wing,
And fly through the twilights of time till the home lights of
heaven appear;
And our spirits through love and through longing made one with
the infinite Lir.[98]

In the original legend (*Aided Chlainne Lir*) the Lir is a
deity of ordinary, finite proportions and has none of the shadowy, mysterious grandeur of Lir as the "Great Deep" (to borrow a phrase from AE's note to the poem). AE substituted this
image for the swan-children's father, so that Lir could represent the One and they the many springing from the One.
Their sojourns upon increasingly more harsh waters then become, in AE's system, the stages of the divine soul's descent
towards mortal existence. Once on earth the soul loses memory
of its former nobility and finds satisfaction in human love,
represented by the close bond among the swan-children. And
the ultimate baptism and salvation of the children of Lir becomes the return after long ages of the many—conscious once
more of their own divinity—to the One.

Certainly AE came as naturally as did Yeats to this way of
treating the old legends, and it may well be that he began
using it independently. The evidence for Yeatsian influence is
primarily indirect: AE's intimate knowledge of his friend's
work, and the fact that he showed himself to be conscious of
Yeats's approach—and of its essential agreement with his
own—in the exchange with Eglinton.[99] Something must also

98. *Ibid.,* pp. 47–48.

99. For additional evidence that AE was conscious of Yeats's way of
interpreting the old legends, see "The Legends of Ancient Eire," pp.

be said of the possibility that Larminie's example affected him. Exactly when AE read the *Fand* volume is not known, but it is perhaps significant that his first full-length literary recreation of an Irish myth, a prose "Enchantment of Cuchulain," was based on the story of Fand. By 1898, in any case, he had not only read Larminie, but also found very sympathetic the vision and approach of *Moytura:*

The genius of our modern writers has caught the last tales told in the cabins, and the dying fall of the songs: they have given them new meaning. They retell the old stories with a hitherto unknown splendour, and find in them a universal significance and fitting symbols for moods which never die. The battle fought in the tumultuous dawn-light of legend, between gods and demons at Moytura on the shores of the west, has been retold with profound spiritual significance by Larminie, and in his mystical drama it becomes the eternal battle between good and evil. . . . The battle is over in the heavens perchance, but it has yet to be fought out on earth, and the interest we feel in the antique story is that it is the fittest symbol for the conflict today.[100]

This passage was followed immediately by a poem on the subject by AE himself, "The Everlasting Battle":

When in my shadowy hours I pierce the hidden heart of hopes
    and fears
They change into immortal joys or end in immemorial tears:
Moytura's battle still endures, and in this human heart of mine
The Golden sun-powers with the might of demon darkness inter-
    twine.

I think that every teardrop shed still flows from Balor's eye of
    doom,
And gazing on his ageless grief my heart is filled with ageless
    gloom.

102–103, where AE quotes from *The Wanderings of Oisin* a passage which he says shows Yeats's awareness of the "true significance" (i.e., the occult meaning) of the hound-deer procession.

100. "In the Shadow of the Gods," *The Internationalist,* March 15, 1898, p. 105.

I close my ever weary eyes and in my bitter spirit brood
And am at one in vast despair with all the demon multitude.

But in the lightning flash of hope I feel the Sun-god's fiery sling
Has smote the horror in the heart where clouds of demon shades
    take wing.
I lay my heavy grief aside and seize the flaming sword of will.
I am of Dana's race divine and know I am immortal still.

The proximity of the poem to the comment on Larminie certainly suggests a direct connection, though in form AE's lyric is much different from the long, semidramatic *Moytura*. The periodical version of Yeats's "Fergus and the Druid" provides a closer parallel in that it uses the myth to express a psychological state and is similar verbally as well, with "the demons and the gods" waging "an eternal battle" in the speaker's "heart." Even if AE's turn to the old stories was spontaneous, his awareness of their literary potential may well have been reinforced by the twin examples of Yeats and Larminie, the two contemporary Irish poets he ranked highest.

Nora Hopper borrowed so much from Yeats that he must surely have influenced her also in her use of and method of treating the Irish legends. It is difficult to credit her with a genuine personal vision, but her myth-based works do have a distinctive characteristic, which might be termed "extreme deconcretization." This is well illustrated in her treatment of the Diarmaid and Gráinne tale, the prose story "Boholaun and I." The story is set at some unspecified but apparently modern period, and the author provides almost no information about the narrator of the story, one Maurice Cahill. Cahill tells how Boholaun, an ordinary ragweed by day, was transformed by the twilight into a fairy steed with "a shining silken coat of elfin grey, and a flowing mane and tail of hair fine as woven glass, and moonshine coloured." In a dream vision Cahill mounted the horse, and

lough and valley flashed by us, a medley of green and grey, and next, sharp spears of mountain glorious with sunset: after that a blinding mist, and then a flash of pearl and rose that may have been a gate, and then—Ah! *then!* Asleep or awake, I slid from the saddle, and sank at the feet of a great and gracious figure, robed with mist. And as I lay at her feet, other figures came and closed about me, grave and splendid and stately, looking at me with eyes that probed my soul.

Maurice Cahill is really Diarmaid reincarnate, and one of those spirits is Gráinne: "The body of Maurice Cahill holds the soul of Diarmuid, and Grainne is weary till the twain come to her." The story ends with the narrator, who has returned to consciousness, yearning for the same reunion.

It should be clear from this sketch that very little of the original myth remains: Miss Hopper took up the strength of passion between the two lovers and used it to suggest the imperishability of the things of the soul. Her interest lay there, and not with the present, the fleshly, not with Maurice Cahill. Yeats felt that she had gone too far, that by using the legends in this manner she had stripped them of their power to counterbalance the subjective elements added by the author. Her uncertainty about specific settings seemed to him particularly unfortunate: "Our legends are always associated with places, and not merely every mountain and valley, but every strange stone and little coppice has its legend, preserved in written or unwritten tradition. Our Irish romantic movement has arisen out of this tradition, and should always, even when it makes new legends about traditional people and things, be haunted by places." [101] The two other stories based on mythological materials, "The Sorrow of Manannan" (which stays fairly close to the original legend) and "Cuchullin's Belt" (which does not), are open in varying degrees to the same criticism. Yeats could not fully accept her legendary works, but he did recognize her as following the path that he had been the first to mark out.

By the end of the century, then, at least four writers had

101. "The Poems and Stories of Miss Nora Hopper," *Daily Express* (Dublin), September 24, 1898.

made use of the personal approach; and Yeats repeatedly, and AE more sporadically, continued to do so.

Meanwhile, some authors did continue to rely upon the "good story" method. "Ethna Carbery," for example, retold a number of tales in her *In the Celtic Past* (1902), using prose as her medium and modifying minor elements freely but adhering quite closely to the major outlines of her sources; though with obvious reluctance, she even brought in Gráinne's apostasy:

And happy were it for me if I could tell of Grainne's faithfulness to her dead lord and lover, and how the long years of her widow-hood passed in tender, regretful memories of him, his valour, and his devotion, who gave up all for love; but alas, it was not so, nor shall her name be surrounded with a halo of praise, as Deirdre's will be until the ages shall end in Erinn. For though she drew her children about her after their dead father had been borne to the Palace of Angus, and exhorted them, . . . [yet] she was the first in after days to revoke the vengeful tenor of her speech.[102]

Rolleston's *The High Deeds of Finn* (1910) began with a theoretical statement of method recalling the comments years before of P. W. Joyce, Todhunter, and de Vere:

My aim, however I may have fulfilled it, has been artistic, not scientific. I have tried, while carefully preserving the outline of each story, to treat it exactly as the ancient bard treated his own material, or as Tennyson treated the stories of the *Mort d'Arthur,* that is to say, to present it as a fresh work of the imagination. In some cases . . . I have done little more than retell the bardic legend with merely a little compression; but in others a certain amount of reshaping has seemed desirable. The object in all cases has been the same, to bring out as clearly as possible for modern readers the beauty and interest which are either manifest or implicit in the Gaelic original.[103]

102. *In the Celtic Past* (New York: Funk and Wagnalls, 1902), p. 74.
103. *The High Deeds of Finn* (London: George G. Harrap, 1934), pp. v–vi.

He knew P. W. Joyce's work and was aware of how he had changed the ending of the Diarmaid and Gráinne story from a "tough" to a "romantic and sentimental" one.[104] In his own book he went even further, omitting the story entirely, "partly because it presents the character of Finn in a light inconsistent with what is said of him elsewhere, and partly because it has in it a certain sinister and depressing element [i.e., sexual passion] which renders it unsuitable for a collection intended largely for the young." A third writer, James Stephens, rehandled his sources freely, telescoping events to increase dramatic effect, filling in gaps in tales that have survived only in fragmentary form, and imbuing them with his own brand of delicate humor and whimsy, but apparently never used them as vehicles for self-expression.[105]

Nevertheless, many of the more important Irish writers who turned their attention to the myth materials did treat them in what was essentially the personal manner. Thus, an already much retold story like that of Diarmaid and Gráinne continued to prove viable in the hands of such diverse figures as Lady Gregory, Austin Clarke, and James Joyce.

In *Gods and Fighting Men* (1902) Lady Gregory had simply given the traditional version of the ending, and it is strongly hinted at in Yeats and Moore's *Diarmuid and Grania,* for the writing of which she prepared a synopsis of the legend (*VPlays,* 1169). But her own play *Grania* (1912) showed her taking a different course, retaining the apostasy but inventing a rationale for it. In the last act Diarmaid is brought in, dying. His last thoughts are all of Fionn—for whom his old affection returns strongly—and the world of men and battle. He has com-

104. *Myths and Legends of the Celtic Race* (New York: Thomas Y. Crowell Company, n.d.), p. 304.

105. See Hilary Pyle, *James Stephens* (London: Routledge and Kegan Paul, 1965), pp. 97–98 and *passim.* Two other writers who fit this category are Mary Hutton and Thomas Kinsella; the former in 1907 and the latter over sixty years later produced "good-story" versions of the *Táin.* See Mary Hutton, *The Táin* (Dublin: Maunsel, 1907) and Thomas Kinsella, *The Táin* (Dublin: Dolmen Press, 1969).

pletely forgotten Gráinne, who finds herself ranked as nothing in comparison with the heroic life. After this she is of course very bitter, and her return to Fionn, whom she practically has to force to take her, becomes intelligible, even natural. Why did Lady Gregory make this change? The unusual modification calls attention to itself, and her biographer, Elizabeth Coxhead, has argued cogently that she was sublimating in the feelings of Gráinne her own frustration at the masculine society in which her closest friends moved but "from which a woman, through her talent as much a part of the movement as any of them, would be forever excluded." [106]

Clarke's first treatment of the legend, *The Vengeance of Fionn* (1917), was a long poem full of hazy romanticism. Such modifications as he made do not suggest a strong personal element, but it may be that in the "flight" episode he found a correlative for some of the anxieties that later culminated in his breakdown. Fear and flight are also central in his second work employing the Diarmaid-Gráinne story, the novel *The Bright Temptation* (1932). But here he gave the legend a new interpretation or at least a fresh emphasis. The book is about the initiation into love of a youth and a girl in medieval Christian Ireland, and Clarke treated their innocent delight in each other as something beautiful and good. Throughout the book he repeatedly paralleled their love and flight together with the love of Diarmaid and Gráinne, which he suggests was equally innocent and beautiful. Furthermore, both levels are meant to function together as an oblique comment upon the repressive sexual morality in Ireland of the Free-State period.

The approach Joyce adopted in *Finnegans Wake* clearly falls into the personal category. He selected from among the many available stories those most adaptable to the highly idiosyncratic vision expressed in the book. In the interest of inclusiveness he referred in one place or another to most of the famous incidents in the life of Fionn, but the two most important elements from his point of view were the tradition

106. *Lady Gregory,* p. 145.

that Fionn still lived and would return, and the Fionn-Diarmaid-Gráinne triangle. The former naturally appealed to him because it could be harmonized with the cyclical theories of history that dictated the structure of the *Wake*. He interpreted Fionn's fate in the light of Vico, as Yeats did retrospectively in regard to Oisin. Furthermore, Joyce's identification of Fionn as "the dreamer," while it has not been widely accepted, can in any case be seen as an improvisation upon the same tradition. And if he was familiar with Lady Gregory's reference to this part of the legend in *Gods and Fighting Men,* he must have found the version she gave attractive, for it included the suggestion that Fionn had already "been on the earth now and again since the old times, in the shape of one of the heroes of Ireland." [107]

Not, of course, that Joyce felt himself in any way bound by received versions of the figure and his actions. His pleasure at finding a scholarly theory that Fionn was of Scandinavian origin came from having "discovered" the connection himself (in the same way he was delighted by the resurgence of Finland), and not from any scholarly reverence for the integrity of his sources. In Clarke's *Bright Temptation* the images and behavior of the more modern characters are reflected back upon their mythological counterparts, and something similar happens in the *Wake* with Fionn. His modern avatar HCE is a tremendously comic figure, and references like that to "the exploits of Fjorgn Camhelsson when he was in the Kvinnes country with Soldru's men," [108] an obvious permutation of HCE's crime in the park, transfer much of that comedy to the "heroic" level in a way that makes Joyce's Fionn contrast strikingly with the idealized heroes which other writers had sought in the early stories. Joyce's closest kinsman in this respect was probably James Stephens.

Fionn's relationship with Diarmaid and Gráinne fit without modification one of the basic patterns of *Finnegans Wake,* the

107. *Gods and Fighting Men,* p. 436.
108. *Finnegans Wake* (New York, 1960), p. 124, lines 29–30.

old man loving a young girl and losing her to someone of her own generation. Joyce gave this episode particular emphasis by including a great many references to even small details: thus "Clanruckard for ever!" (376.32), Clann Riocaird being the first place Diarmaid and Gráinne stopped in their flight, and "Three climbs threequickenthrees in the garb of nine" (377.11–.12), the nine Garbhs being henchmen of Fionn who lose their lives trying to dislodge Diarmaid from a quicken tree. He also exploited the comic potential of such details, so that the hound Bran's aid of the lovers emerges as "buy bran biscuits and you'll never say dog" and Diarmaid's "feats" become attractions in a circus sideshow—"Kniferope Walker and Rowley the Barrel" (376.29–.31); but he readily modified the order in which they traditionally occurred. Moreover, free of the prudishness which had characterized many of his predecessors, he quite openly emphasized the element of sexual passion in the incident, Gráinne's physical desire for Diarmaid ("The eitch is in her blood, arrah! For a frecklesome freshcheeky sweetworded lupsqueezer"—376.19–.20) and the calculating nature of her treatment of Fionn ("that . . . hot coney *a la Zingara* which our own little Graunya of the chilired cheeks dished up to the greatsire of Oscar, that son of a Coole."—68.9–.11). Both points, of course, coincided with the general "triangle" pattern in the book. Most important of all, he found a new value in Gráinne's final apostasy. Gráinne as a young girl corresponds to Issy, but the older Gráinne who survives the death of Diarmaid becomes an ALP role, and "E'en Tho I Granny a-be He would Fain Me Cuddle" (105.3) includes a reference to Fionn's continuing desire for her. Thus ALP's "Finn, again!" on the final page proclaims not only his "resurrection" but also her eventual return to him, and ties together the two major Fionn motifs.

In the middle of a section of the "Night Lessons" chapter dealing mainly with Tristan and Isolde, Joyce planted a few references to Diarmaid and Gráinne (291.24 and .28) to indicate his awareness of the parallel nature of the two stories.

(See also 232.19–.20.) The following passage adds another level to the parallel:

Wait till they send you to sleep. . . . Then old Hunphydunphyville'll be blasted to bumboards by the youthful herald who would once you were. He'd be our chosen one in the matter of Brittas more than anarthur [375.4–.8].

The primary allusion here is to the drugging of Fionn at the marriage banquet, but the final sentence brings in the adulterous Arthur-Lancelot-Guinevere triangle. It might seem surprising that Joyce did not connect this complex with the even more famous Irish story of Conchobor, Deirdre and Naisi, especially since Naisi and his two brothers provided a perfect embodiment for the "three soldiers" motif. Possibly the idea never occurred to him, though this seems unlikely. The passage quoted above from "Ethna Carbery," with its contrast between the morals of Gráinne and Deirdre, suggests another reason: the long-standing associations of the latter figure with purity and virtue make her much less suitable to his purpose.

In many ways *Finnegans Wake* was a literary dead end, but it did not have this effect on the Diarmaid and Gráinne tale: as recently as 1964, Eugene R. Watters drew upon its structure for a modern poem, *The Week-End of Dermot and Grace*.[109] In that poem the flight of the legendary lovers underlies a romantic interlude in the lives of a post-World War Two Irish couple, with Fionn apparently represented by all the troubles from which they are trying to escape.

Even John Synge, who is more often thought of in connection with folk subjects and who spoke scornfully of the mythological figures and their literary use in "The Passing of the Shee"—

> Adieu, sweet Angus, Maeve and Fand,
> Ye plumed yet skinny Shee,
> That poets played with hand in hand
> To learn their ecstasy.

109. *The Week-End of Dermot and Grace* (Dublin: Allen Figgis and Co., 1964).

[274]

> We'll search in Red Dan Sally's ditch,
> And drink in Tubber fair,
> Or poach with Red Dan Philly's bitch
> The badger and the hare.

—turned to legend in his last play, *Deirdre of the Sorrows.* AE and Yeats had both written plays on Deirdre in the years immediately preceding Synge's decision to do so, yet when he was asked if he would not be accused of copying them he replied "There isn't any danger of that. People are entitled to use those old stories in any way they wish. My treatment of the story of Deirdre wouldn't be like either of theirs." [110] His estimate was correct, for AE had given prominence to the druid Cathbad and Yeats had embodied in his version aspects of his response to Maud Gonne's marriage to John MacBride, while in Synge's hands the legend became a vehicle for personal feelings about imminent death and the ephemerality of mortal happiness.

This survey should illustrate that Yeats's early myth-based works occupy a pivotal position in the development of this literary mode during the modern Irish literary movement: before he began to write, variations upon the "good story" method predominated; in the mature years of the Renaissance the personal approach came to the fore. This change was certainly not due entirely to Yeats, but it must have received a powerful stimulus from his own repeated practice.

110. Greene and Stephens, *J. M. Synge,* pp. 277–278.

6. Conclusion: The Theater Movement and Beyond

Yeats's role in the beginning of the literary renaissance was indeed decisive. Some of his ideals had been entertained by others, and there was considerable latent talent; but it was primarily he who, by giving those ideals form and life and propagandizing vigorously for them, as well as by the compelling example of his own outstanding creative work and his interaction with contemporary Irish writers, initiated the actual movement. The extent of his influence was certainly even greater than that delineated in preceding chapters, for beyond the area of immediate contacts there was a periphery in which connections appear without any evidence of direct communication. The case of Edith Somerville and Violet Martin is illustrative in this regard. Their literary collaboration began in 1889 with *An Irish Cousin* and soon produced two of the finest Irish novels of the nineteenth century, *Naboth's Vineyard* (1891) and *The Real Charlotte* (1894). Both of these books were penetrating, realistic studies of the seamier side of Irish life, the first dealing with a "gombeen man" (a usurer who lends money at ruinous interest to peasants and small farmers) and the second with ruthless economic and social behavior among the middle class. The authors were isolated both geographically and by their ties

[276]

with the Anglo-Irish upper class from the current center of Irish literary activity; at this period Yeats and his associates knew little or nothing about them, and there is no specific proof of greater awareness in the opposite direction. (After the turn of the century Somerville and Ross did come into direct contact with Yeats and many of his colleagues.) Nevertheless, the treatment of Ireland in their next novel, *The Silver Fox* (1897), differs in an important way from anything in their previous works. The silver fox of the title is believed by the Irish peasants to be a witch, and they predict bad luck to anyone who harms it. While the authors clearly feel that the peasants are dirty, ignorant and superstitious, the fact that misfortune does pursue the various hunters and other people involved suggests that some credence is to be given to the validity of the preternatural in the book. One of the characters even sees a vision of a dead man, easily enough explicable as a hallucination, but the decision is left up to the reader. Furthermore, the main spokesman for reason and common sense is the villain of the story, the railway contractor Mr. Glasgow. That this novel appeared during the very period at which Yeats was proclaiming the wisdom of the peasants, the closeness in Ireland of the spiritual world, and contrasting this situation with English materialism probably does not represent a direct influence, but it may be that the climate of opinion he was creating touched even the two fox-hunting cousins.

Nor was Yeats content with merely initiating: he worked diligently to insure that Irish literature would continue to develop along the lines he had conceived for it. In the years immediately following the period upon which this study has focused, his main vehicle was the Irish Theatre. A passage from the preliminary manifesto sent to various people who the founders hoped would guarantee the project financially very plainly reveals his designs:

We propose to have performed in Dublin in the spring of every year certain Celtic and Irish plays, which whatever be their degree of excellence will be written with a high ambition, and so to build up a Celtic and Irish school of dramatic literature. We hope to find in Ireland an uncorrupted and imaginative audience trained to listen by its passion for oratory, and believe that our desire to bring upon the stage the deeper thoughts and emotions of Ireland will insure for us a tolerant welcome, and that freedom to experiment which is not found in theatres of England, and without which no new movement in art or literature can succeed. We will show that Ireland is not the home of buffoonery and of easy sentiment, as it has been represented, but the home of an ancient idealism. We are confident of the support of all Irish people, who are weary of misrepresentation, in carrying out a work that is outside all the political questions that divide us.[1]

The provision that the work of the theater movement would be "outside all the political questions that divide us" is obviously intended to deal with the problem of national literature. At the time this manifesto was written there was, in addition to the old opposition of Nationalist and Unionist, the new bitterness left by the split within the Nationalist Party following the fall of Parnell. Consequently, the position that political relevance was not an essential requirement for national literature was particularly useful in providing a sufficiently broad basis of appeal for what was intended to be a national theater. Of course political plays—ranging from the transparent Nationalist allegory of *Cathleen Ni Houlihan* to the satire of *The Bending of the Bough,* which contained hits at all factions —were produced, but they were put on for their artistic, not their political, merits, and not to the exclusion of apolitical works.

The call for "freedom to experiment" as a necessary condition for the future success of Irish literature perpetuated another of Yeats's early concerns. The theater project itself, in a country with no viable dramatic tradition, was an experiment; and once in existence the theater became the trying ground for many specific dramatic experiments, in subject-matter, style, staging, and acting.

1. Quoted in Lady Gregory, *Our Irish Theatre,* pp. 8–9.

Also significant was the promise to "show that Ireland is not the home of buffoonery and of easy sentiment, as it has been represented, but the home of an ancient idealism." Until the beginning of the theater movement, Ireland had been depicted in drama primarily by the stage Irishman. While that figure did have a basis in fact in relation to one segment of the population, he was nevertheless an exaggeration; furthermore, his "buffoonery and easy sentiment" greatly impeded recognition of higher qualities of Irish life, the "ancient idealism" and the "deeper thoughts and emotions." Consequently, Yeats and his associates substituted subjects drawn from Irish folklore and mythology. Admittedly, much of the idealism attributed at this time to the ancient Irish was a misinterpretation arising from romanticized texts like those of O'Grady; and folk and mythological themes were before long somewhat displaced by realistic studies of contemporary life. But the later work would not have had a hearing if the earlier had not made serious Irish drama respectable.

Yeats's desire to spread a sense of group effort is discernible in this passage, and his rhetorical intimations were in fact valid, for the theater movement, despite serious internal dissensions, *was* a group effort and was conceived within the context of a living movement. Consequently it became for a period so much the center of Irish literary activity that even the young Joyce, who found it hard to curb his pride enough to associate with any group, is believed to have planned to submit a play for consideration.[2]

Finally, the manifesto exudes ambition and confidence. The attempt to inaugurate a theater movement was in itself most ambitious, and the response of the Irish people to the literary activities of the 1890's had been far from enthusiastic. Yeats had been discouraged about the possibility of a popular audience after the book-scheme fiasco, but now he hoped that if the people could not be made to read good literature, they

2. *The Critical Writings of James Joyce,* ed. Ellsworth Mason and Richard Ellmann (New York: The Viking Press, 1959), p. 68.

might at least be persuaded to see and hear it. In this hope he was not entirely wrong: people did come to the theater. The audiences were not, needless to say, uniformly "uncorrupted and imaginative": the heirs of Yeats's opponents in the controversy over national literature made their presence felt from the beginning of the actual performances, and disturbances like those over *The Countess Cathleen* were repeated periodically, *The Playboy of the Western World* and *The Plough and the Stars* being notable examples. But there was enough support so that the idea of a theater in Dublin became a permanent reality.

Similarly, Yeats's confidence that the movement could write, cast, and stage plays was based upon the general confidence he had developed during the nineties about the solid literary beginnings made at that period rather than upon any specific evidence of dramatic talent among the early workers in the field. He himself had already written *The Countess Cathleen* and *The Land of Heart's Desire,* and Edward Martyn had some work in hand, but they were virtually alone as playwrights, and neither had any substantial practical knowledge of the theater. The addition of George Moore was a help, because he had not only written plays, but also had had experience with the stage in London. And the very existence of confidence helped produce the event that justified it. It led to the establishment of the theater; the theater offered a chance to write for performance; and given that chance Yeats became a master of the craft; Synge, Padraic Colum, and the Fay brothers were able to reveal their great talent; and Lady Gregory, who would otherwise probably never even have written a play, soon learned to produce very competent work. Other, lesser names were drawn into the movement in the same way, and the result was that "Irish school of dramatic literature," rich and diverse, which the preliminary manifesto had promised. And the drama movement in turn served to perpetuate its inheritance from the years surveyed in this study.

Yeats's anticosmopolitan stance, implicit in the reference to "Celtic and Irish plays," emerged explicitly in other pieces of theater propaganda, in which he declared that at first only plays specifically Irish in content would be put on, with the range of subjects gradually being expanded once the national character of the drama movement was firmly established. So too he envisioned that the Irish writers upon whom the theater would principally depend would be those "who wrote as men should write who have never doubted that all things are shadows of spiritual things." [3]

During the post-1900 years of the literary renaissance Yeats remained faithful to all of his early literary ideals, though the emphasis upon the spiritual did undergo an important modification. Soon after the turn of the century Yeats felt that a change had taken place in the world: "The close of the last century was full of a strange desire to get out of form, to get to some kind of disembodied beauty, and now it seems to me the contrary impulse has come. I feel about me and in me an impulse to create form, to carry the realization of beauty as far as possible" (*Letters*, 402). Hereafter, while the spiritual world remained one of his primary concerns, he no longer consistently felt that he must completely devalue the concrete, and thus gave full expression in his work to mundane as well as supernatural life.

The mature phase of the movement also saw his ideals become firmly established among virtually all the better writers. For example, while there were quarters in which Nationalistic work continued to be written and championed, verse in the manner of Young Ireland scarcely represented a temptation to young poets who had in Yeats the example he himself had lacked: a great national poet who did not feel compelled to write political propaganda. The dominance of Yeats's principle was of particular importance when between 1916 and 1922 Nationalist politics became the central fact of Irish life. Yeats

3. "The Irish Literary Theatre," *Daily Express* (Dublin), January 14, 1899.

and AE both praised the Uprising in their poetry but preserved certain reservations about it and did not celebrate it to aid the cause, while O'Casey was severely critical. After the Civil War the problem took on a new dimension as the internal concessions required to establish the Free State added to the already great power of the Church, which in turn produced pervasive, often tasteless shows of piety, a repressive sexual code, literary censorship, and a tremendous loss of "life" and vitality. Irish society became antipathetic to many Irish writers, and their works often reveal extreme antagonism towards it. Yeats placed more and more positive emphasis on the vanishing Anglo-Irish tradition, and AE compared the country to "a lout I knew in boyhood who had become a hero and then subsided into a lout again." [4] O'Casey attacked the current situation in his later plays, offering in its place a natural and exuberant sensuality; and Austin Clarke emerged as an excellent poetic satirist, sharpening his wits upon the latest examples of folly and narrow-mindedness. Frank O'Connor and Liam O'Flaherty were others who found themselves violently opposed to much of contemporary Irish life. All of these writers accepted the position that an Irish artist has the right to include in his art criticism of his country's faults.

Yeats's *dictum* that "a writer is not the less national because he shows the influence of other countries and of the great writers of the world" also found wide acceptance. James Stephens followed the lead of Yeats and AE in turning to Eastern thought. Joyce decided early that there was virtually nothing in past Irish literature that could be of use to the supreme artist and turned abroad for inspiration, yet was careful to anchor all his major works from *Dubliners* through *Finnegans Wake* in the life of his nation. Even writers such as O'Casey, O'Connor, O'Flaherty and Sean O'Faolain, who *had* found good local models when they began to write, would not cut themselves off from the best foreign traditions: O'Casey drew upon the Expressionist playwrights, and the fiction

4. Letter to Yeats of March 6, 1932 (Alan Denson manuscript).

writers were attracted to the works of such figures as Dostoevski, Chekhov, Turgenev, and Maupassant.

The particular sources of subject-matter that Yeats had stressed continued to arouse interest, and gradually Irish literature expanded to embrace *all* aspects of Irish life, temptation-ridden priests and the brothels of Nighttown as well as the fairy mounds and the hovels of the peasants. Virtually every possible theme and technique found exploiters, and craftsmanship, so widely suspect during the eighties and nineties, became a matter for pride among many Irish writers. (Concerned with this problem till the very end of his life, Yeats in "Under Ben Bulben" had exhorted: "Irish poets, learn your trade.")

In sum, while during the twentieth century Ireland itself actually became *less* receptive to the burgeoning of a native artistic movement, that burgeoning did take place, largely as a result of a liberation of the minds of the Irish writers from restricting conceptions of literature, and it was Yeats who through means direct and indirect had been the primary liberator.

Appendix A. Yeats's Best Book Lists

I. The list given in Yeats's "The Best Thirty Irish Books," *Daily Express* (Dublin), February 27, 1895 was as follows:

NOVELS AND ROMANCES

1. *Castle Rackrent* by Miss Edgeworth.*
2. "Father Tom and the Pope" by Sir Samuel Ferguson (in *Tales from Blackwood*).*
3. *Fardorougha the Miser* by William Carleton (out of print).*
4. *The Black Prophet* by William Carleton (out of print).*
5. *Traits and Stories of the Irish Peasantry* by William Carleton.*
6. *The Nolans* by John Banim (out of print).*
7. *John Doe* by John Banim (bound up with *Crohore*).*
8. *The Collegians* by Gerald Griffin.*
9. "Barney O'Reirdan" by Samuel Lover (in *Legends and Stories of the Irish Peasantry*).*
10. *Essex in Ireland* by Miss Lawless.
11. *Charles O'Malley* by Charles Lever.*
12. *The Bog of Stars* by Standish O'Grady (New Irish Library).*
13. *Ballads in Prose* by Miss Hopper.*

FOLK LORE AND BARDIC TALES

14. *History of Ireland—Heroic Period* by Standish O'Grady (out of print).*
15. *The Coming of Cuchullin* by Standish O'Grady.*

[285]

16. *Finn and his Companions* by Standish O'Grady.*
17. *Old Celtic Romances* by P. W. Joyce.*
18. *Silva Gadelica* by Standish Hayes O'Grady.*
19. *Beside the Fire* by Douglas Hyde.*
20. "Teig O'Kane" by Douglas Hyde (in *Fairy and Folk Tales of the Irish Peasantry*).*
21. *History of Early Gaelic Literature* by Douglas Hyde (New Irish Library).*
22. *Mythologie Irlandaise* [*sic* for *Le Cycle Mythologique Irlandais*] by D'Arbois Joubainville.

HISTORY

23. *The Story of Ireland* by Standish O'Grady.*
24. *Red Hugh's Captivity* by Standish O'Grady (out of print).*
25. *A Short History of Ireland* by P. W. Joyce.*

POETRY

26. *Irish Poems* by William Allingham.*
27. "Conary" by Sir Samuel Ferguson (in *Poems*).*
28. *Lays of the Western Gael* by Sir Samuel Ferguson.*
29. *Love Songs of Connacht* by Douglas Hyde (second edition in the press).
30. *Ballads and Lyrics* by Miss Tynan.*

II. The list of books given by Yeats in "Irish National Literature. IV.—A List of the Best Irish Books," in *The Bookman*, October, 1895, pages 21–22, included those items starred in the preceding list, plus the following:

Father Connell by Michael Banim (out of print).
Flitters, Tatters, and the Councillor by Miss Laffan (out of print).
Maelcho by Miss Lawless.
Irish Idylls by Miss Barlow.
Ancient Legends by Lady Wilde.
West Irish Folk Tales by William Larminie.
Hero Tales of Ireland by Jeremiah Curtin.
Myths and Folklore of Ireland by Jeremiah Curtin.
Tales of the Irish Fairies by Jeremiah Curtin.

Fairy Legends of the South of Ireland by Crofton Croker.

Manuscript Materials by Eugene O'Curry.

The Jail Journal by John Mitchell.

The Autobiography of Wolfe Tone (in Mr. Barry O'Brien's edition).

Selections from the Poems of Aubrey De Vere edited by G. E. Woodberry.

Homeward: Songs by the Way by A.E.

The Love Songs of Connaught by Dr. Douglas Hyde (and to this should be added his "The Religious Songs of Connaught," as soon as it is reprinted from the Irish magazine in which it is now appearing).

The Irish Song Book by A. P. Graves (New Irish Library).

Irish Love Songs edited by Mrs. Hinkson.

A Book of Irish Verse.

Appendix B. Revisions of A Book of Irish Verse

1894/1895	1899/1900
Rolleston	
The Lament of Queen Maev	
The Dead at Clonmacnois	repeated
The Spell-struck	
Hyde	
"Were you on the Mountain?"	
"My Grief on the Sea"	
My Love, O, She is my Love	repeated
I shall not die for thee	
Riddles	
Katharine Tynan	
The Children of Lir	
St. Francis to the Birds	repeated
Sheep and Lambs	
In Iona	omitted
The Gardener Sage	repeated
Nora Hopper	
none	The Dark Man
	The Fairy Fiddler

AE
    Our Thrones Decay   repeated
    The Place of Rest   (substitution) Immortality
                                        The Great Breath
                                        Sung on a By-way
                                        Dream Love
                                        Illusion
                                        Janus
                                        Connla's Well

John Eglinton
    none   Names

Charles Weekes
    That
    Think   } repeated

Lionel Johnson
    Ways of War
    The Red Wind
    Celtic Speech   } repeated
    To Morfydd

                                        Te Martyrum Candidatus
                                        The Church of a Dream

Index

Hone, Joseph, 35n, 36n, 91n, 121n
Hopkins, G. M., 142
Hopper, Nora, 62–63, 75, 78, 118, 123, 147–157, 179, 207, 222, 267–268, 285, 288
Hutton, Mary, 270n
Hyde, Douglas, 15, 17, 22, 50n, 55, 74, 77, 87, 89, 91, 93, 94, 95, 98, 101–102, 110–111, 116, 118, 127, 130n, 131, 132, 145, 151, 161, 171–172, 175, 179, 195–207, 208, 211n, 216, 221–222, 249, 286, 287, 288

Ibsen, Henrik, 123, 259
Ideals in Ireland, 11, 29, 68n, 69
Ingram, John Kells, 99, 176
Irish Literary Society, London, 67–68, 80, 83, 84, 85–86, 91, 92, 93, 158, 159, 162, 168, 224
Irish Republican Brotherhood, 12
Irwin, T. Caulfield, 224

Jeffares, A. N., 110n, 112n, 181n
Johnson, Lionel, 2, 74, 76, 80, 95, 102, 110–111, 127, 167–181, 185, 216, 221–222, 289
Johnston, Charles, 21, 161
Joyce, James, 26, 33n, 35, 58, 199, 270, 271–274, 279, 282
Joyce, P. W., 226–228, 230, 231, 234, 239–240, 259, 269–270, 286
Joyce, Robert Dwyer, 231–232, 239, 240
Jubainville, Henri D'Arbois de, 120, 208, 249–252, 261, 286

Kavanagh, Rose, 130–131, 132
Keating, Geoffrey, 231
Keats, John, 20, 240
Keeling, Elsa d'Esterre, 73
Kelleher, John V., ix, 2, 241n
Kickham, Charles, 41, 83–84
King, Richard Ashe, 74, 87, 101–102, 110–111, 163, 175, 216
Kinsella, Thomas, 270n
Knott, Eleanor, 211n

Laffan, Mae, 286
Larminie, William, 20, 110, 127, 207–221, 222, 260–261, 266–267, 286

Lawless, Emily, 62–63, 98, 114, 118, 285, 286
Lecky, W. E. H., 167
Lever, Charles, 114, 285
Literary Ideals in Ireland, 20, 29n, 122–129, 183n, 185n, 194, 207, 208, 217, 219n, 262
Loftus, Richard J., ix
Lover, Samuel, 181n, 285
Lynch, Arthur, 26
Lynch, Miss E., 94–95

Macaulay, T. B., 12, 19, 102, 172
MacCarthy, Denis Florence, 11, 99, 172, 225–226, 236, 239
MacDermott, Martin, 12
MacDonagh, Michael, 94
Mac Manus, Anna, see Carbery, Ethna
Magee, W. K., see Eglinton, John
Magrath, John, 87, 94
Mahony, Francis Sylvester ("Father Prout"), 100
Mangan, James Clarence, 9–10, 11–12, 21–22, 23, 32, 72, 97, 98, 99, 100, 111, 118, 133, 145, 174, 176, 181n, 186, 189, 195, 211
Martin, Henri, 208
Martyn, Edward, 184, 280
Mary of The Nation (Ellen Mary Downing), 83–84, 99, 103
Mason, Ellsworth, 279n
M'Call, P. J., 20, 260
McCarthy, Justin, 15, 171n
McConnell, Frank, ix
McGee, Thomas D'Arcy, 99
Meagher, Thomas, 84
Meredith, George, 117
Meyer, Kuno, 49n, 251
Mill, John Stuart, 125
Milligan, Alice, 175
Mitchel, John, 19, 90, 101, 120, 197, 287
Moore, George, 35, 76n, 163, 175, 206n, 278, 280
Moore, Thomas, 18–19, 32, 75, 188
Moran, D. P., 74n
Morris, William, 16, 117
Murphy, Gerard, 211n
Myth, Irish, 4, 18, 27, 33, 41, 44–45, 54–55, 62, 63, 64, 75, 77, 80, 83, 98, 104–105, 108, 116, 118, 120,

[294]

Yeats, W. B., works by (*cont.*)
"The Irish Literary Theatre," 281
"Irish Literature," 116–117, 218
"Irish Literature: A Poet We Have Neglected," 6n, 16
"Irish National Literature: Contemporary Prose Writers," 30, 78, 118, 152–154, 175, 200, 216
"Irish National Literature. III.— Contemporary Irish Poets," 29n, 34, 118–119, 141, 145–146, 154–155, 160, 178–179, 182, 183, 186, 258, 261–262
"Irish National Literature. IV.— A List of the Best Irish Books," 7n, 10n, 15, 106n, 109n, 117n, 119–120, 144, 202, 216, 286–287
"Irish National Literature: From Callanan to Carleton," 10n, 12n, 14, 19, 117–118
"An Irish Patriot," 9n, 10
"An Irish Visionary," 29n, 181
"Irish Wonders," 55, 197
"John Eglinton," 78, 128
"John Eglinton and Spiritual Art," 124
John Sherman, 36–41, 50, 54, 58, 105, 137
"The Lake Isle of Innisfree," 151
The Land of Heart's Desire, 34, 280
Letters of W. B. Yeats, 10n, 19, 20, 21, 22, 24n, 27, 34, 35n, 36, 37, 38, 40, 42, 43, 48, 54, 56, 58, 59, 60, 61, 62, 63, 64, 65, 67, 69, 71, 72–73, 75, 76, 77, 79, 80, 82, 83n, 85n, 88, 89–90, 91, 92, 93, 94, 95, 96, 100, 103n, 105, 109, 113, 115–116, 117, 120, 121, 122, 127–128, 130, 135, 136, 137, 139, 140, 141, 142, 143n, 144, 152, 156, 158, 161, 162, 163, 166–167, 168, 172n, 175n, 178, 179n, 181, 183, 184, 187, 189n, 190, 191, 192, 193, 197, 198, 201, 202, 203, 205, 206, 215, 218, 223, 241, 242, 243, 245, 246, 248, 249, 254, 255, 281
Letters to the New Island, 1, 6n, 14, 15, 16, 25, 32n, 34, 42n,
47n, 69, 73, 130n, 158, 159, 160, 161, 197, 198, 201, 223n, 250
"The Life of Patrick Sarsfield," 101
"Love Song," 132
"The Madness of King Goll," 132, 241–243
"The Man Who Dreamed of Faeryland," 148, 152, 155
"The Message of the Folk-lorist," 47n
"Michael Clancy, the Great Dhoul, and Death," 35, 43n, 57–58
"Miss Fiona Macleod," 34n, 258
"Miss Fiona Macleod as a Poet," 27n, 254
"Miss Tynan's New Book," 135–136
"Mourn—and Then Onward," 176
Mosada, 134
"Mr. John O'Leary," 9n
"Mr. Lionel Johnson and Certain Irish Poets," 147, 155, 179–180, 182
"Mr. Lionel Johnson's Poems," 180
"Mr. Rhys' Welsh Ballads," 29n
"Mr. W. B. Yeats," 17n, 74, 174n, 186
Mythologies, 61n
"Nationality and Literature," 16, 18, 32, 109, 189
"The National Publishing Company," 87
"The National Publishing Company. Should the Books be Edited?" 86n
"The New Irish Library," 34n, 101–102
"A New Poet," 30, 46n, 77n, 182, 190
"Noetry and Poetry," 164
"Of Costello the Proud, of Oona the Daughter of Dermott, and of the Bitter Tongue," 49, 54, 55
The Old Age of Queen Maeve, 256
"Old Gaelic Love Songs," 199
"The Old Men of the Twilight," 46, 49, 50
The Only Jealousy of Emer, 215–216

[297]